Democracy Without Journalism?

Democracy Without Journalism?

Confronting the Misinformation Society

VICTOR PICKARD

OXFORD
UNIVERSITY PRESS

OXFORD
UNIVERSITY PRESS

Oxford University Press is a department of the University of Oxford. It furthers
the University's objective of excellence in research, scholarship, and education
by publishing worldwide. Oxford is a registered trade mark of Oxford University
Press in the UK and certain other countries.

Published in the United States of America by Oxford University Press
198 Madison Avenue, New York, NY 10016, United States of America.

© Victor Pickard 2020

CIP data is on file at the Library of Congress
ISBN 978-0-19-094676-0 (pbk.)
ISBN 978-0-19-094675-3 (hbk.)

Contents

Introduction

When Commercialism Trumps Democracy

This book is about the journalism crisis and the policies we need to confront it. Challenges to our news and information systems have taken on greater urgency in recent years, with concern growing about misinformation and the unaccountable power of platform monopolies. As public attention turns to these media failures, now is an opportune moment to address core weaknesses in US communication infrastructures and push for alternatives. Recent criticism has understandably focused on problems with television news, print journalism, and social media platforms, but too little of this scrutiny recognizes that these are mere symptoms of deeper maladies. To understand what ails our news media and what reforms are needed, we must penetrate to the roots of systemic problems. Toward this aim, *Democracy Without Journalism?* underscores the *structural* nature of commercial journalism's collapse while exploring entirely new models. Ultimately, the goal should be to *reinvent* journalism. Although my analysis focuses on the United States, where the journalism crisis is most pronounced, similar problems afflict democratic societies to varying degrees around the world.

US News Media Pathologies

Systemic problems typically remain overlooked until shocks to the status quo render them more visible. Donald Trump's ascendance and the 2016 US presidential election revealed a number of structural pathologies in the US news and information systems, especially toxic commercialism that prioritizes profit over democratic imperatives. From imbalanced, low-quality coverage in traditional news media to the proliferation of misinformation on social media, commercial imperatives drove news organizations to popularize a dangerous politics.

Democracy Without Journalism?. Victor Pickard, Oxford University Press (2020). © Victor Pickard
DOI: 10.1093/oso/9780190946753.001.0001

Television coverage exhibited some of the worst of these media malpractices. TV news outlets lavished far more attention on Trump than all other presidential candidates. During a critical period in the primary season, he received nearly three times more coverage than Hillary Clinton and sixteen times more than Bernie Sanders.[1] Various estimates show that news outlets gifted Trump billions of dollars' worth of free advertising in the run-up to the election, often allowing him to simply phone in to their popular news shows.[2] Despite constant campaign coverage, content analyses show that our leading news media—including major print outlets such as the *New York Times*—barely covered candidates' policy positions prior to the election.[3] These informational deficits in mainstream news media coincided with torrents of misinformation circulating through social media. However, simplistic explanations that blame Trump's rise on "fake news" amplified on Facebook are clearly insufficient. While these platforms are now the subject of well-deserved scrutiny for facilitating various kinds of dis/misinformation, traditional news media contributed as much if not more to the lack of high-quality information leading up to the elections.[4]

These data points paint a depressing portrait of the entire US news media apparatus. Yet they are merely surface-level symptoms of a deeper structural rot in our news and information systems. What is it about the US media system that encourages such socially irresponsible coverage? What are the historical conditions that produced such a system in the United States? What are the policies and ideologies that keep it intact? This book highlights specific media failures and recommends new models.[5]

"Damn Good for CBS"

Three core media failures helped enable Trump's election.[6] First, the news media's excessive commercialism—driven by profit imperatives, especially the need to sell advertising—resulted in facile coverage of the election that emphasized entertainment over information. For ratings-driven news outlets, the always-controversial Trump was the ultimate boon. CNN's CEO Jeff Zucker, ever seeking to "maximize the emotional impact of the moment" (as a *New York Times* article put it), approvingly compared CNN's election coverage to that of ESPN's sports commentary. He casually professed, "The idea that politics is sport is undeniable, and we understood that and approached it that way."[7] The now-disgraced CEO of CBS Leslie Moonves admitted that "[Trump's candidacy] may not be good for America, but it's damn good for CBS." He continued: "The money's rolling in and this is fun . . . this is going to be a very good year for us . . . bring it on, Donald. Keep going."[8]

These comments reveal how US news media privilege profits over public service. Although many prominent news outlets have since become more adversarial toward Trump—and more likely to call out his brazen lies and resist his attacks—their coverage continues to focus on his impolitic behavior while giving short shrift to growing income inequality, institutional racism, environmental collapse, and other severe problems exacerbated by his policies. Constantly reporting on the reality-television-like "Trump Show" spikes ratings and ad revenue. Prime-time ratings have more than doubled at CNN and nearly tripled at MSNBC since Trump took office.[9] Part of this financial windfall comes from the fact that Trump coverage is cheap to produce: pundits and panels of experts can simply discuss the President's latest tweets and outrageous comments. This kind of superficial coverage is irresistible for profit-driven commercial news media but detrimental to democratic discourse.

A second failure in the US media system is the tremendous amount of misinformation circulating on social media platforms, especially Facebook. Although many analysts attribute the problems with misinformation to political polarization and foreign interference, commercial incentives facilitate its dissemination. Facebook's reckless behavior stems from maximizing advertising revenues, and more generally from its unregulated monopoly power. Some observers have downplayed concerns about "fake news" (a deeply problematic term) as little more than moral panic and social hysteria. And skepticism is certainly warranted, especially since much of the criticism is ahistorical, often stemming from a desire for simplistic, mono-causal explanations of Trump's unexpected election.

Nonetheless, concerns about widespread misinformation deserve serious attention. Some reports suggest that fabricated stories circulated more often than fact-based news during the weeks leading up to the election.[10] With Americans—as well as people around the world—increasingly accessing their news through Facebook, concerns about the company's central position within the entire media system is entirely warranted.[11] However, much scrutiny continues to overlook the structural roots of misinformation, especially the commercial motives that accelerate it. Because its business model depends on user engagement, Facebook is not incentivized to address the problem, opting instead to rely on outside parties, crowdsourcing, and algorithmic tweaks to stem the flow of misinformation.

The rise of misinformation is one more manifestation of the asymmetric relationships stemming from Facebook's status as a gigantic social media monopoly with profound political-economic power and little independent oversight—all while dodging responsibilities that normally belong to media companies.[12] As a global internet platform and an algorithm-driven publisher, Facebook has tremendous gatekeeping power over much of the world's information system. Yet, unlike "natural monopolies" or public utilities of old, Facebook has avoided close regulatory oversight and shirked any obligation to uphold a social contract with meaningful public interest requirements in exchange for the many benefits that society grants it. As I will discuss in chapter 4, growing media monopoly power—from Facebook and Google to Sinclair and AT&T—is a major threat to the integrity of news and information systems.[13]

A third systemic failure is the slow-but-sure structural collapse of professional journalism. As market support for news production erodes, the number of working journalists has continued to decline. Print newsrooms have lost more than half of their employees since 2000.[14] Yet newspapers still provide the bulk of original reporting, serving as the information feeder for the entire US news media system. Even casual observers will note that television news coverage is typically pegged to issues covered in that day's newspapers. On leading cable news shows, the host's routine often consists of essentially reading the headlines of the latest breaking newspaper stories to their viewers. Similarly, news content from social media—where Americans increasingly consume their information—derives largely from professional news organizations.

While it is difficult to see how, exactly, the collapse of professional journalism has affected what is or is not being covered—or how issues are being covered differently—some trends are obvious. In particular, the rise of "news deserts"—entire regions bereft of news media coverage and access to reliable information—is undeniable.[15] Furthermore, information scarcity and news deficits are disproportionately harming specific groups and areas, especially communities of color, rural districts, and lower socioeconomic neighborhoods. This phenomenon represents a major failure in US media policy.

Taken together, these structural flaws in the US news media system create the ideal conditions for what I call the "misinformation society"[16]—an electorate that is increasingly served sensationalistic news coverage, clickbait, and degraded journalism instead of informative, fact-based, policy-related news. While many demand-side challenges have emerged, including a growing lack of trust and polarization, these and other audience-related problems are intertwined with an increasingly diminishing supply of reliable news and information and proliferating misinformation and low-quality news media. Unless we first address the supply-side problems—especially the commercialism that lies at the center of the system's maladies—we cannot overcome the other harms plaguing American news media.

Competing Narratives about Journalism

To highlight the structural nature of the journalism crisis, this book will scrutinize the ways that we talk about journalism. Several meta-narratives about journalism emerged after Trump's election. The first narrative was that news media enabled Trump's ascendance—especially television news coverage, but the critique also applies to print news. In addition to giving him an inordinate amount of attention, news organizations often overlooked Trump's troubling history or falsely equated his actions with other candidates' imperfections. Typical news media coverage also sensationalized and trivialized the elections via "horse-race" coverage that fetishized polling data and personal insults hurled by candidates instead of offering critical analysis of their policy positions.

The second narrative, in tension with the first, is a newfound appreciation for the Fourth Estate. Many people increasingly see news institutions as the last bulwark of civil society, protecting them against everything from fake news to fascism. As Trump attacked the press, public sympathies naturally redounded to news organizations (although the opposite appears true for Trump partisans). One direct result was a "Trump bump," in which many publishers saw a sudden and dramatic spike in subscriptions shortly after the 2016 election. However, this desperately needed boost in financial support did not solve media organizations' economic problems and moreover turned out to be short-lived for most outlets.

This leads us to a third narrative that predates the election: Despite an increasing need for public service journalism (local, policy-related, and investigative news), it is precisely this kind of reporting that is failing economically. As consumers and advertisers have migrated to the web, where digital ads pay pennies to the dollar of traditional print ads (with most of that revenue going to Facebook and Google), the 150-year-old advertising revenue model for commercial newspapers is now beyond repair. In many ways, advertising previously served as a subsidy for media organizations, with news and information a kind of byproduct or positive externality resulting from the primary exchange between advertisers and newspapers. Because this advertising revenue model has been around for so long, it appears to be part of the natural order, with alternative models falling beyond our policy discourse and political imagination.

And yet, alternative models are exactly what we should be discussing. With the exception of a brief period in 2008 and 2009, there has been little public discussion, and virtually no policy response; meanwhile, the crisis in US journalism keeps getting worse. Already in 2016 the Pew Research Center—the gold standard for assessing the health of US news industries—warned that "this accelerating decline suggests the industry may be past its point of no return."[17] For Pew to make such a statement speaks volumes about the severity of journalism's collapse. Such a serious social problem deserves a public conversation proportionate to the scale of what should be seen as a national crisis.

The American Journalism Crisis

How we talk about the demise of journalism matters. Some narrations of the journalism crisis naturalize it as a kind of evolutionary metamorphosis of the "media ecosystem."[18] Others see it as a shift into a "post-industrial" era for the US press system.[19] Taking for granted the internet's role in journalism's "creative destruction," many observers typically downplay the commercial news model's endemic structural vulnerabilities, especially its overreliance on advertising support. Metaphors and phrases such as "perfect storms" and "disruptive innovation" implicitly construct the crisis as something beyond our control and outside the realm of public policy.

While some scholars and pundits view this structural transformation as a tragic loss for democracy and a once-noble profession, for others it has been a source of great excitement. These optimists—albeit a decreasing lot in recent years—argue that new digital start-ups herald a potentially better future for journalism. Such analyses overlook these models' questionable sustainability and the low number of journalists they employ relative to the tens of thousands of jobs lost from traditional newsrooms. These more utopian views tend to emphasize digital journalism's potential for innovation and enabling greater citizen participation, while often neglecting negative externalities such as the proliferation of clickbait and misinformation.

Vexing questions remain about new digital technologies: What is the normative role of journalism in today's digital age? Should we be concerned about the growing prominence of invasive and deceptive forms of advertising within digital journalism's business model? What are the social implications as news work becomes increasingly precarious, reliant on free or low-paid labor? What happens as local journalism disappears? What should society do when a functioning press system no longer exists? If this loss amounts to a crisis, what accounts for the absence of any public policy response? /

In what follows, I argue that policy discourses about the future of news in the United States are constrained by libertarian assumptions. If we are to break free of this discourse, we must first understand where it comes from. To that end, this book situates the journalism crisis within specific political and historical contexts. Such an analysis can begin to flesh out under-examined assumptions about the normative relationship between the press and the polity. This framework positions the journalism crisis as a social problem that requires a social democratic alternative—namely, a public media option.

Focus of the Book

Democracy Without Journalism? focuses on the structural transformations in US journalism while emphasizing their implications for democracy. Thus far, our social imaginary about the ramifications of journalism's deinstitutionalization—and what should be done about it—has been outpaced by its material collapse. It is perhaps symptomatic of our neoliberal age that many have looked to charitable and entrepreneurial individuals— and mostly wealthy, white men such as Jeff Bezos—to save journalism. But the crisis requires a deeper conversation about the considerable stakes for local communities, democratic culture, and society writ large. This book intervenes in this debate by pushing normative questions about journalism's democratic imperatives back to the fore. In doing so, it historicizes seemingly new developments and proposes structural alternatives to today's failing commercial models. The book also addresses many of the issues facing today's digital news media, from the loss of net neutrality to concerns about monopoly power—from Fox News to Facebook.

Given that the ongoing crisis is inextricably bound up with how we think and talk about journalism, this approach requires a critical analysis of contemporary policy discourses. To give one example: First Amendment assumptions that privilege negative-freedom interpretations (concerns about "freedom from" government interference) ultimately protect corporate power, delegitimate government regulation, and impoverish the US regulatory imagination. These factors all contribute to the ongoing policy failures in addressing the journalism crisis. *Democracy Without Journalism?* interrogates these often-invisible discursive parameters within policy debates, particularly regarding the legitimacy of government intervention into media markets.

Throughout the book, I examine contemporary discourses about what journalism's public service mission should be in a democratic society—and government's role in protecting that relationship. I draw from historical materials, policy documents, and industry data to contextualize the journalism crisis. My analysis also incorporates a decade's worth of participant observations of hearings and meetings about the journalism crisis and numerous conversations with journalists, media analysts, and scholars who are actively engaged in the ongoing debate about journalism's future.

Over the years, many analysts have tried to make sense of journalism's structural transformations by focusing on technological and cultural changes among audiences or the practices and routines of journalists themselves. Increasingly, scholars and commentators discern new categories of newsgathering, with much discussion centering on data journalism, hacker journalism, networked journalism, and many other variants. In heralding these purportedly new forms of journalism, many optimists assume that new technological affordances enable journalists and entrepreneurs to produce better journalism with less time and money and in ways that are inherently participatory and democratic. Yet, it remains doubtful that legacy media institutions can innovate themselves out of this crisis, that new digital start-ups can fill the journalism vacuum, or that technology and the market will combine to produce sustainable forms of journalism. Many advocates still hope that some new profit-seeking model will emerge triumphant, despite little evidence that digital models have long-term commercial viability. Others feel that we can rely on media billionaires and foundation-supported news institutions with varying motives to support news outlets. None of these models is sufficient. By critically examining how they fall short, this book sheds new light on the perilous future of the US press and shows that a public media system is journalism's last, best hope.

Toward this objective, I underscore the historical and ideological contingency of US press freedoms, the structural contradictions of contemporary news institutions, and potential policy interventions aimed at changing these arrangements. I draw attention to the US media system's normative foundations, especially as they are historically situated—and often contested—within ongoing policy debates.[20] This book operates from the assumption that most democratic theories presuppose the existence of healthy information and communication systems. Without a viable news media system, democracy is reduced to an unattainable ideal.

My theoretical approach to misinformation and the journalism crisis falls within the communication research tradition of political economy. This subfield focuses on how media institutions are organized, owned, and controlled, and how media figure within larger power relationships. For example, political economists look at how concentrated markets perpetuate power hierarchies and foreclose on media's democratic potentials. In general, this framework scrutinizes how power operates through communication systems, asking questions like: What ideologies are implicitly embedded in a media system's design? Whose interests are being served? What is the basis for ownership and control, terms of access, production, and dissemination of media? In addressing these structural questions, political economy traditionally has been committed to anti-fascism and progressive social movements.[21] With a clear normative vision, it interrogates power structures in the hopes of changing them.[22] By challenging dominant assumptions and relationships, such an approach ultimately aims to not just describe the way things are but to denaturalize and ultimately transform the status quo.

Every theoretical framework has strengths and weaknesses that illuminate certain aspects of social phenomena while deemphasizing others. A political economic analysis is an explicitly structural approach to understanding dominant social relationships and institutions. One of its strengths is that it facilitates collective action by ascertaining the big picture—the forest and perhaps not as much the trees. In confronting the journalism crisis, this framework historicizes our problems with misinformation as the culmination of explicit policy choices, always subject to political struggle, with open-ended possibilities. By framing these challenges as supply-side problems that all of society must confront—problems that are contingent, not inevitable, and open to human intervention—this analysis situates journalism as susceptible to human agency and social change.

In laying out core concerns about journalism and democracy, the book moves thematically across several broad areas. Chapter 1 focuses on the historical and normative roots of US journalism, with an emphasis on the commercial logics that were internalized early in the press system's formation. Chapter 2 focuses on the recent history and missed opportunities in contemporary debates about the future of news. Chapter 3 looks at the ongoing degradations of digital news, with an emphasis on potential alternatives. Chapter 4 examines structural threats to journalism, especially the negative impacts that platform monopolies such as Facebook have on journalism. Chapter 5 discusses the roots of "US media exceptionalism" and discusses public alternatives to commercial news in historical and global contexts. The conclusion returns to the big picture and addresses the question: What is to be done?

In addressing these concerns and questions, I make seven basic arguments:

1. Commercial journalism has always been in crisis.
2. The nature of this crisis is deeply structural and requires a systemic fix.
3. The journalism crisis is a threat to democracy.
4. This threat amounts to a major social problem that requires public policy interventions.
5. These policies should be founded on a social democratic vision of media.
6. The best hope for public service journalism is a public media option.
7. This crisis is an opportunity; it allows us to reimagine what journalism could be.

By focusing on the ongoing structural collapse of commercial journalism, this book seeks to contextualize the crisis as symptomatic of long-term historical contradictions baked into the heart of the US commercial news media system. In addition to teasing out the various pathologies and social implications of this transformation, this book attempts to reframe the debate about journalism's future as a public policy problem. I conclude the book with recommendations for systemic reform. In doing so, my hope is to help jump-start a long overdue conversation about the severity of the journalism crisis and what we as a society must do about it. It is time to reenvision what journalism should be.

1

Historical Roots of US Press Freedoms and Failures

Few freedoms in the United States are as cherished as freedom of the press. Sanctified by the First Amendment, press freedoms are inviolable in the eyes of most Americans. "Power of the press" narratives loom large in the social imaginary, from the muckrakers of yore to the Pentagon papers of the Nixon era. In recent years, popular films such as *Spotlight* and *The Post* have further romanticized the image of the dogged reporter digging for the truth, holding power to account. Our current political moment has ushered in a new-found appreciation for journalism among many Americans—though certainly not all. Yet despite the rhetorical power and emotional pull of these convictions, most Americans do not spend much time thinking about the policies, laws, and institutions that maintain their freedom of the press. Nor do they ask the critical question: freedom of the press for *whom*?

The US press system is strikingly different from that in other democracies in one key respect: It is extremely commercialized. Far more reliant on advertising revenue than most news industries around the world, US journalism is subjected to unmitigated commercial pressures. This unfettered commercialism has made US journalism exceptional in subtle yet significant ways.[1] Since the 1800s, the US press has simultaneously functioned as a business enterprise and a public good. As a commodity, it has been pegged to the capitalist market, generating tremendous profits for a relatively small number of owners and investors. As a public service, it has, at its best, strengthened democracy. Public service journalism typically aspires to inform, enlighten, keep a check on the powerful, and provide a forum for diverse views and voices. However, profit motives drive commercial media to entertain, sell advertising, satisfy shareholders, and make as much money as possible. These two sides of US journalism within a commercial system—the one, a vital public service; the other, a commodity

Democracy Without Journalism?. Victor Pickard, Oxford University Press (2020). © Victor Pickard
DOI: 10.1093/oso/9780190946753.001.0001

bought and sold on the market to make profit—have been in conflict since the 1800s.

Ever since the press commercialized, reformers have sought to protect journalism's public service mission from profit imperatives that threaten democratic objectives. Many of the ideals and codes of professional journalism in the United States developed in direct response to these pressures. The goal was to buffer newsgathering from the anti-democratic and corrosive effects of commercialism, or, at a minimum, to create a veneer of objectivity and social responsibility. Yet in many ways these journalistic ideals are an outgrowth of, rather than protection from, commercial influence. This inherent contradiction has prompted radical criticism, reform efforts, and experimental alternatives from the beginning. For as long as media have been commercialized, social critics and media reformers have risen to challenge it.

This chapter looks at how these long-standing tensions between journalism's profit-seeking and public-service objectives help explain the contemporary journalism crisis. The collapse of journalism's business model was not simply caused by new digital technologies; rather, this crisis is the culmination of long-term, systemic problems present since commercial journalism's birth. Put differently, commercial journalism has *always* been in crisis. The origins of this crisis trace back to the normative and historical foundations of US journalism, which themselves are bound up with the rise of classical liberalism.

Democratic Principles of the Press

Many of the democratic principles we associate with the press trace back to the emergence of classical liberalism. This ideological formation, which celebrates equality, tolerance, and diversity of views,[2] emerged in seventeenth-century Britain and France as a response to state tyranny and infringements on individual freedoms.[3] Classical liberals sought to resist censorship, expand freedom of choice, and protect civil liberties under the rule of law.[4] John Milton's foundational text, the *Areopagitica*, inspired the classical liberal notion that the best idea naturally rises to the fore when diverse views and voices are given their full airing.[5] Another seminal work, John Stuart Mill's *On Liberty*, celebrated such individual liberties as freedom of expression and advanced a utilitarian notion that the greatest amount of freedom for individuals, barring harm to others, serves the greater good.[6] He wrote that "unity of opinion, unless resulting from the fullest and freest comparison of opposite opinions, is not desirable, and diversity not an evil, but a good."[7] In other words, all voices and views deserve a fair hearing—not just for the sake of free speech and expression, but also to ensure that people have access to diverse information. Liberal thinkers drew from formulations such as these to uphold an ideal of the press that encouraged diversity of ideas and vibrant debate.

These texts prefigured the "marketplace of ideas" motif, which did not crystalize until much later. US Supreme Court Justice Oliver Wendell Holmes argued in a famous dissenting opinion in 1919 that the "ultimate good desired is better reached by free trade in ideas—that the best test of truth is the power of the thought to get itself accepted in the competition of the market."[8] Subsequently, the "competition of the market" became the "marketplace of ideas," a phrase that connotes an open domain for free-flowing information and expression. Few metaphors have held such power in describing a democratic ideal.[9] Invoking the "market" made the phrase even more poignant—and also problematic. As the historian Sam Lebovic notes, there were "deep ironies" in the fact that this concept ascended at the very moment that the market was corrupting media institutions to become more concentrated, consumer-based, and commercialized—and less hospitable to a teeming marketplace of diverse voices and views.[10] Nonetheless, the "Milton-Holmes" approach to press freedom laid the foundations for what became known as the "libertarian theory of the press," with the "marketplace of ideas" serving as its apt slogan.[11] Indeed, in key respects, liberal and libertarian press theories are interchangeable, as each focuses on individual freedoms and a general deference to the market.

Classical liberalism's contradictions come into focus when we scrutinize news media's underlying—and often-unexamined—normative ideals. For example, the "marketplace of ideas" model suggests that the commercial media system is a meritocracy in which the best idea wins public approval, with the implication that capitalist competition best serves democratic communication. Emphasizing fairness and equality of opportunity, this metaphor assumes a relatively level playing field that naturally encourages egalitarianism. However, liberal constructions, including the very notion of "public spheres," often suffer from blind spots when it comes to structural inequities. This is especially true regarding inequalities that emerge from the actual capitalist market, which liberalism often treats as a neutral arbiter. Liberalism's inability to effectively address structural exclusions—such as racism, classism, and sexism—renders it less compatible with more radical conceptions of redistributive justice.[12]

Liberalism also privileges individuals' private property rights over the collective needs of society. In media policy, this prioritization has historically led to a laissez-faire arrangement that treats media as private commodities whose value is dictated by the market. Such an approach does not privilege diverse voices, representations, and perspectives. Nor does it guarantee media access for all communities and social groups. While liberalism/libertarianism is quick to recognize government censorship as a serious problem for a free press, it tends to ignore recurring omissions and constraints caused by "market censorship."[13]

Liberalism's abiding faith in the market as the best vehicle for a democratic media system has spurred radical criticism in the United States since the 1800s. Liberal/libertarian theories of the press, in other words, primarily focus on protecting the press from government intervention rather than ensuring that people have access to the press. The imperfect dichotomy of positive (freedom to) and negative (freedom from) liberties brings into focus how traditional liberals typically worry about protecting individual freedom from government tyranny, but often have less to say about enhancing positive liberties. The latter might include broadening media ownership, expanding the breadth of views and voices represented in news media, and opening up access to communication systems and infrastructures to include more members of society, especially those groups who are most often marginalized. These tensions between liberal ideals for what the press should do in a democratic society and the structural constraints imposed by the market have existed since the early republic.

Normative Foundations of the US Press

In foundational narratives of the US press, few individuals figure as prominently as Thomas Jefferson. His well-known aphorisms about the vital necessity of newspapers for a self-governing society comprise a "greatest hits" playlist for why democracy depends on a well-informed populace. In one of his most famous statements about the press, Jefferson reasoned:

> The basis of our governments being the opinion of the people, the very first object should be to keep that right; and were it left to me to decide whether

we should have a government without newspapers or newspapers without a government, I should not hesitate a moment to prefer the latter. *But I should mean that every man should receive those papers and be capable of reading them.* (Emphasis added.)[14]

The last part of this quote, which emphasizes the need for access to—and not simply the existence of—the press, is often conveniently forgotten. However, Jefferson emphasized the importance of an institutionally supported and accessible press because he saw the maintenance of a free and open media system as an essential prerequisite for democratic society.[15]

Other founders of the US republic generally shared Jefferson's view that self-governance was predicated on society having access to reliable information, which in turn was predicated on a vibrant news media system. For example, James Madison famously said that "A popular Government, without popular information, or *the means of acquiring it*, is but a Prologue to a Farce or a Tragedy; or perhaps both" (emphasis added).[16] Both Jefferson and Madison emphasized the necessary condition of ensuring *access* to information. Understood in this way, the press provides an essential infrastructure for democratic society.

These sentiments are even enshrined in the US Constitution, which provides special consideration and inalienable protections to news institutions, the only industry to receive such treatment. The First Amendment to the Constitution states, "Congress shall make no law . . . abridging the freedom of speech, or of the press." Legal theorists and historians have long debated the intended meaning of the "or of the press" clause, which seems to distinguish it from "freedom of speech."[17] The leading First Amendment scholar, Steven Shiffrin, notes that while the Supreme Court has denied that the press clause confers special privileges on the press, existing jurisprudence and case law suggests otherwise. Shiffrin points out that "the *New York Times* is not a fertilizer factory" and should not be treated as if it were an ordinary business. Moreover, some historical analyses suggest that, by the time the First Amendment was adopted, the founders saw the press as an autonomous institution whose need for special protections exceeded individual speech freedoms.[18]

This interpretation again underscores the need for institutional support of the press, as well as the importance of public access to it. Key figures of the early American Republic, including Benjamin Franklin, suggested that individuals should have a positive right to express themselves in the press, that viewpoint diversity and equality in the press were important, and that newspapers were communal goods, not simply private property.[19] This position represents what the historian Robert Martin refers to as the "open press doctrine," which extended well beyond simply preventing state interference in news media to consider the press's obligations to society, such as providing diverse sources of information.[20] When the founders drafted the First Amendment, Martin observes, such normative ideals were as much "in the air" as were libertarian concerns about governmental overreach.[21]

The belief that Americans must have access to reliable and diverse information—and that the government had an affirmative duty to help provide it—justified the US government's investment in the country's first major communications network: the postal system. In its early days, this system served primarily as a news-delivery infrastructure—private letters were secondary. As much as 70 percent of mail delivered in the 1790s, and 95 percent in the 1830s, consisted of newspapers.[22] In the first major US media policy debate, the founders of the US government argued decisively that the postal system should not have to pay for itself—a rejection of what the historian Richard John terms a "fiscal rationale."[23] Rather, these visionaries privileged the postal system's *educational* purpose over economic considerations, and thus determined to heavily subsidize it.[24] Given the postal system's vital function in society as a core communication infrastructure, these early political leaders regarded the notion that it should be self-supporting as nonsensical.[25]

These debates, so timely for today's discussion about the proper relationship between media and government, show that the founders were not in thrall to market fundamentalism. Because the postal system served a higher civic purpose as a news and information infrastructure upon which a self-governing populace depended, policymakers determined that the state would directly subsidize the dissemination of newspapers with low postal rates. Remarkably, the debate on postal policy ranged between those (such as George Washington) who believed postal fees should be entirely waived for all news material and those (such as James Madison) who thought the system should just be heavily subsidized. The latter position ultimately prevailed and was inscribed into law with the Post Office Act of 1792.[26] This government-funded infrastructure—including a vast network of postal roads—would quickly expand to become the largest employer in the United States.[27] As one popular history of the post office described it, the newly created "postal commons" served as the "central nervous system to circulate news throughout the new body politic."[28] This system depended on massive government subsidies worth billions of dollars today.

Despite its long history of investing in communication systems, many assume that the US government has no legitimate role in subsidizing such infrastructure. In part, this belief stems from the misconception that state tyranny is the primary impediment to actualizing democratic ideals rather than the private tyranny of concentrated corporate power. In the classical liberal conception of the press, we need only worry about government infringing on our First Amendment rights. But as the press became highly commercialized, broader and subtler structural impediments to the free press emerged. These constraints continue to haunt US news media today. A longer historical view helps bring into focus such structural contradictions—as well as the radical criticism that arose to confront them.

The Commercialization of the US Press

The 1800s witnessed a gradual structural transformation of the press as the "partisan press" model began to fade. In its place emerged commercialized papers largely dependent on advertising revenue. The press historian Gerald Baldasty notes that the profound shift in the underlying logic of news production to a profit motive not only altered newspaper content but also changed how newspaper publishers and editors saw their own role in society and their relationship to readers. Whereas previously they saw their readers as essentially voters, by the end of the nineteenth century, they saw them primarily as consumers. This vision of the "commercialized reader" became central to news production.[29]

This shift to an advertising revenue model ultimately shrank the ideological range of opinion published in newspapers. The media historian John Nerone describes the "depoliticizing effect of commercialism" in both the US and British press systems as they became more reliant on advertising.[30] Even though the newly commercialized newspapers depended on a larger readership, advertisers had no desire to promote working-class political and economic interests. Instead, as Nerone observes, it "became common for mass-circulation media to simultaneously attract working-class audiences and promote reactionary politics," via trivial, sensational, and even untrue reporting.[31] These strategies of attracting audience attention for advertisers worked to promote a particular view of society and mobilized audiences according to specific affects and allegiances that often worked against progressive narratives of working class solidarity, the ravages of capitalism, and wealth redistribution. The media scholars James Curran and Jane Seaton have noted a similar ideological shift after the British press commercialized. Driven by the profit motive and concomitant need to expand and reach larger audiences, the market achieved what no government could by ensuring the demise of radical newspapers who could not afford the rising costs of production.[32] Tracing similar ideological policing, C. Edwin Baker argued that advertisers provided a "subsidy" for journalism while simultaneously acting as the "most consistent and the most pernicious 'censors' of media content."[33]

These structural changes unfolded differently and unevenly across newspapers, but general patterns emerged. While party patronage and partisanship did not disappear all at once, a creeping commercial logic changed the nature of news in profound ways, replacing party loyalty with economic imperatives. Toward the end of the nineteenth century, profit-seeking publishers and investors sought to expand their readership to entice advertisers. These efforts led to what we might call "clickbait" today: an emphasis on the sensational, the dramatic, and the garish. Newspapers increasingly filled their column inches with various kinds of "lowbrow" entertainment, such as crime stories and pictures of scantily clad women, and reporting that tended toward exaggerated and even fabricated accounts—a style that would become known as "yellow journalism."

By the late 1800s, such commercial excesses had become more pronounced as publishers sought ever-larger readerships that appealed to advertisers. Although publishers hoped to generate handsome sums of money, competition was fierce. One historian of this period has noted that media markets were "oversaturated; revenues were down; pay [for journalists] was poor; and publishers were locked in circulation battles, working to one-up one another for more subscribers—even if it meant engaging in some unsavory practices." Under these conditions, reporters internalized publisher's commercial logic and adhered to one rule: "do whatever it takes to get the story—even if it meant making things up."[34]

These trends were especially pronounced in some of the country's most successful newspapers. For example, in their 1898 coverage of the USS *Maine*, a US Navy battleship that exploded off the coast of Havana, Cuba, killing more than 250 Americans, both Joseph Pulitzer's *New York World* and William Randolph Hearst *New York Journal* immediately attributed the act to the Spanish and ginned up support for military action with

"Remember the *Maine*" sloganeering. Although their role in instigating the Spanish American War is often overblown, newspaper coverage was typically reactionary and lurid.[35]

This style of reportage, however, would begin to backfire. The rise of yellow journalism incited public reaction against the news media's commercial excesses. Initially, the greatest outcry came from the elite professional press, but growing disgust toward sensationalist papers soon spread among the broader public, especially as journalists began to target their own industry for malfeasance. Some public libraries and civic associations even threatened boycotts against the worst culprits, including the aforementioned *New York World* and *New York Journal*.[36] Against this rising tide of press criticism, the newspaper industry began to adopt professional norms to help inoculate the press against more structural interventions, especially government regulation. But this process of professionalization would come only after decades of pressure from the public and from news workers themselves.

Early Radical Criticism of a Commercialized Press

The first wave of twentieth-century media criticism reacted against the many commercial excesses of advertising-driven newspapers.[37] This criticism came from a number of sources, especially the radical press, which was experiencing its high-water mark of popularity. In 1910, the socialist weekly *Appeal to Reason* enjoyed an astounding readership of 750,000. Combined with other smaller outlets, the overall readership of radical newspapers at that time was approximately two million people.[38] These outlets ruthlessly critiqued the commercial press for its profit-driven venality and for serving as a capitalist mouthpiece.

These conflicts at times escaped the printed page. Objectivity in the early 1900s was still far from a standard journalistic norm, and many commercial newspapers openly espoused strong ideological positions.[39] In the early 1900s, the *Los Angeles Times* unremittingly editorialized against labor unions, the push for an eight-hour workday, and the closed shop.[40] "This city is unique in having driven to bay the snarling pack of union labor wolves that have infested many other cities of the land and have snapped their red-seeking jaws over the fallen form of industrial freedom," asserted one editorial.[41] The *Los Angeles Times* publisher, Harrison Gray Otis (referred to as "General Otis" due to his military background) saw himself leading an all-out class war against labor unions. He stockpiled weapons at his printing plant and forced his employees—whom he referred to as his "phalanx"—to drill with rifles. Otis drove around town in a touring car equipped with a brass cannon mounted to the front and an ammunition box hinged to the back. Class antagonism reached a head in 1910 when the anarchist McNamara brothers bombed the *Los Angeles Times* building, an event that gripped national attention for years.[42]

Liberal reformers, meanwhile, challenged the concentrated wealth and political corruption associated with commercial newspaper publishing. These crusading "muckrakers," including Ida Tarbell, Lincoln Steffens, and Upton Sinclair, famously exposed various forms of predation, fraud, and unsafe practices in industry after industry—including their own.[43] Their investigative reporting led to necessary regulatory reforms in food, drug, meatpacking, and other sectors, and even helped break up some of the Gilded Age's all-powerful monopolies, such as Standard Oil. These reporters typically published long exposés in outlets such as *McClure's Magazine* and *Collier's Weekly*.[44]

Early twentieth-century intellectuals also contributed to reformist projects and poignant media criticism. The celebrated philosopher John Dewey's classic essay, "Our Unfree Press," criticized commercialism's deleterious effects on the entire press system, including "upon the judgment of what news is, upon the selection and elimination of matter that is published, upon the treatment of news in both editorial and news columns."[45] This corrupted system, Dewey argued, rendered impossible "genuine intellectual freedom and social responsibility." Yet publishers' insistence that "government is the chief enemy to be dreaded" allowed them to normalize and even romanticize their profit motives as the "glory . . . of rugged individualism in a laissez-faire system." They rationalized that "private profit" was "the best way of rendering social and public service." While this view mistakenly conflated a commercialized media system with core American press freedoms, Dewey noted that a different logic might support a "cooperative" system "controlled in the interest of all." However, publishers' extreme reactions even to minor suggested reforms indicated their steadfast commitment to preserving the commercial system, regardless of the damage it might cause to democratic society.[46]

Dewey's frequent interlocutor, the famous journalist Walter Lippmann, offered some similar press criticisms, albeit likely motivated by the desire to prevent more interventionist government regulation.[47] Nonetheless, he clearly believed that the commercial press was unable to produce the quantity or quality of information that readers required to make sense of their complex social world. "Increasingly," he wrote, people "are baffled because the facts are not available; and they are wondering whether government by consent can survive in a time when *the manufacture of consent is an unregulated private enterprise*" (emphasis added). He concluded that the "present crisis of western democracy is a crisis in journalism."[48] Lippmann attributed this early crisis in journalism to the news media's increasingly commercial nature and believed that professional norms for accuracy were necessary but insufficient to address the scale of the problem. Reforming the press would, in Lippmann's view, require constant public pressure.

Upton Sinclair's 1919 muckraking book *The Brass Check* shared some of these concerns while leveling a more radical critique.[49] Named after the token that brothel customers purchased for sexual services, Sinclair's book argued that the commercial press debased everyone involved. Citing numerous examples of political bias—especially against socialist causes— Sinclair saw commercial journalism's structural flaws in terms of class conflict, with capitalist values pervading all aspects of news production throughout the entire press system. "In every newspaper-office in America," he wrote, exists "the same struggle between the business-office and the news-department."[50] According to Sinclair, a capitalist press was simply incompatible with democratic principles. He believed the entire institution should be de-commercialized and democratized, with ownership residing at the local community level.

Other radical critics worried about the rise of one-newspaper towns.[51] Oswald Garrison Villard, the publisher of the *Nation* and future author of the book *The Disappearing Daily*, wrote in the *Atlantic Monthly*: "If no good American can read of cities having only one newspaper without concern, it does not add any comfort to know that it would take millions to found a new paper . . . in our largest cities."[52] While it seemed that press freedoms increasingly were reserved only for those wealthy enough to own a newspaper, many other critics focused on advertising's pernicious effects on the press. Hamilton Holt, managing editor of the *Independent* and long-time advocate for press reform, argued that, thanks to advertising, "journalism is no longer a profession, but a commercial enterprise."[53] Similarly, Will Irwin, an author and muckraking journalist, condemned "The direct control of the advertiser," arguing that "commercial publishers of million dollar newspapers must recognize this influence whether they like it or not."[54] Writing in the

1930s, James Rorty called advertising's ideological power—and the title of his well-known book—"Our Master's Voice."[55]

This radical media criticism continued through the Great Depression and President Franklin Roosevelt's New Deal.[56] Harold Ickes, Roosevelt's first secretary of the interior, continued the structural critique that journalism's problems stemmed from the commercial press's profit imperatives and class allegiances. In his book *America's House of Lords*, he argued that the publishers who "belong to the moneyed class and whose primary objective is to make profits" could never provide the journalism that democratic society needs.[57]

Few media critics from this period loom as large as George Seldes, a predecessor to the legendary muckraking journalist I.F. Stone. Seldes wrote two books highly critical of the newspaper business, *Freedom of the Press* and *Lords of the Press*.[58] He also launched the weekly *In Fact* in 1940, which was subtitled with the tag line: "An Antidote to Falsehoods in the Daily Press." The four-page muckraking newsletter, devoted to press criticism and investigative reporting, exposed the growing influence of corporate power in US society, including its ownership of much of the US news media system. Both publicly and in private letters, Seldes acknowledged that he launched *In Fact* to provide a truthful alternative to the "commercial press." In a letter to his readers announcing that he would be suspending the journal, he noted: "We were the only publication in the country devoted to printing the important news the commercial press suppressed, distorted, faked or buried. We were the only publication in the country exposing reaction—which is the step before fascism."[59] Although his newsletter's circulation peaked at one hundred and seventy-six thousand subscribers in 1947, Seldes's outspoken opposition to corporate power left him exposed to attacks by anti-Communists in the late 1940s. When subscriptions plummeted, he was forced to close his paper in 1950.[60]

Several years later, I.F. Stone, who credited Seldes as the "father of the alternative press," picked up where he left off with his own news weekly. In describing his and Seldes's tradition of adversarial journalism, Stone was adamant that it was "very much in the best American tradition" because "journalism is not a business . . . just a way of making money . . . it's a major part of a free society . . . [just as] Jefferson intended it to be."[61] Stone passionately believed that the press should never be reduced to a mere commodity or solely a for-profit enterprise.

For both Seldes and Stone, the rise of media monopolies posed one of the greatest threats to freedom of the press in the United States. Since the early 1900s, newspaper chains had exploited economies of scale and cut costs by centralizing editorial authority, consolidating various administrative functions, and relying on syndicated content. Edward Scripps, who already by 1914 owned twenty-three papers with their own news service, mastered this business formula through vertical integration, low-cost production, and market segmentation.[62] By the middle of the twentieth century, media monopolies had eliminated competition in many cities, leading to fewer total newspapers and less local reporting. This, in turn, left fewer voices and viewpoints in circulation, all while amplifying powerful economic and political interests.[63] Even worse, as the press transformed into a big business, commercial pressures magnified into what one critic called a "brutal monopoly" that served the interests of the "fascist fringe," including the media mogul William Randolph Hearst.[64] In this context, activists and reformers of all stripes proposed structural alternatives.

Alternative Models to the Commercial Press

During the first half of the twentieth century, public disdain toward the commercial press created fertile ground for experiments with alternative models.[65] In addition to alternative weeklies pioneered by the likes of Seldes and Stone, other reformers experimented with advertising-free dailies. Two ad-less, subscriber-supported newspapers merit particular note, one each in the Progressive and New Deal eras. Chicago's the *Day Book*, founded by the publisher Scripps in 1911, focused on working class issues and was launched as a direct response to the over-commercialization of newspapers and a perceived lack of independence. New York's *PM*, founded by the journalist Ralph Ingersoll in 1940, was closely aligned with President Franklin Roosevelt's New Deal project and was a steadfast champion of the labor movement.[66]

Despite promising beginnings, these pioneering newspapers ultimately folded for want of adequate funding. In the case of the *Day Book*, which lasted six years, a sudden increase in the cost of paper accelerated the collapse of what was potentially a sustainable model. The *PM*, which closed after eight years of publication, suffered from some mismanagement, but also experienced similar red-baiting and political shifts that undermined radical journalists such as Seldes. Although they ultimately failed, both publications maintained enthusiastic audiences until their end.

Municipal-owned newspapers offered another alternative in the Progressive Era. The *Los Angeles Municipal News* launched in April 1912 following a December 1911 majority vote on a city ordinance to establish the paper.[67] Early on, George Dunlop, the newspaper's original architect and one of its three commissioners/publishers, posed the rhetorical question: "can commercial journalism make good, or must we look for the public newspaper?"[68] He believed public newspapers offered the best hope for democracy, and he helped set up the model in direct opposition to the commercial press. The municipal newspaper experiment reflected the growing conviction that a commercial model of the press could never rise above profit pressures and status quo allegiances to serve democratic imperatives.

Widely seen as a local protest against the excesses of sensationalism and yellow journalism, the *Los Angeles Municipal News* enjoyed much community support and initially seemed successful.[69] The paper's distribution of sixty thousand copies was financed by the city and governed by a municipal newspaper commission, the latter comprised of three citizen volunteers appointed by the mayor to four-year terms. The newspaper guaranteed an equal amount of weekly column space to any political party that received a certain percentage of the vote, including the Democratic, Republican, Socialist, and Socialist Labor parties. Newspaper carriers delivered the eight-to-twelve-page paper free of charge to residences, or people could subscribe to it via mail for one penny.[70] The inaugural editorial of this "people's newspaper" stated that it was "the first municipal newspaper in the world . . . owned by the people of the community in which it is printed." It described its mission as being "created by the people, for the people, and built for them under their control. It is in this sense unique."[71] The newspaper's masthead declared simply and boldly: "a newspaper owned by the people."

The *Los Angeles Municipal News* focused on hard news, including government operations, the proceedings of various agencies, and public school events. However, it also reported on popular culture, including women's fashion and music. Its editorials typically focused on city government problems and citizen responsibilities. The paper included equal treatment of arguments for or against specific city ordinances being proposed to voters. While it did accept local commercial advertisements, it also offered free classified advertisements to individuals for jobs and other important information.

This model's supporters argued that all major cities should have publicly owned daily newspapers to compete with the commercial press. Reformers across the country watched the Los Angeles experiment closely. One article noted:

> In view of the growing realization on the part of the public that the commercialization of the great daily newspapers of the country presents one of the most serious problems connected with the movement toward democracy, the career of this newspaper owned by the taxpayers will be watched with interest everywhere.[72]

But despite widespread enthusiasm, the experiment was short-lived. Feeling threatened by the *Los Angeles Municipal News*, the commercial newspapers in Los Angeles, including the *Los Angeles Times*, banded together to oppose the initiative. When public funding for the newspaper appeared on the ballot again in 1913, it was voted down in an election with very low turnout. Many supporters believed the paper fell victim to a misinformation campaign fueled by the ideological opposition of the commercial publishers. In addition to voter apathy and other problems that beset newspaper delivery early on, the editor blamed an "antagonism, carefully and consistently fostered by the private press and its representatives," that impeded progress and discouraged erstwhile supporters.[73]

Toward the end of its final run, the paper announced on the top of its front page in big capital letters "THE MUNICIPAL NEWSPAPER IDEA CANNOT BE KILLED." Although the paper conceded that the "first municipal newspaper passes into history," it was undeterred in promoting the idea that citizens needed access to a newspaper that was not simply the "private property of some millionaire," but offered a "service . . . for all and not for a few."[74] The editor urged other cities to not be dissuaded from launching similar newspapers that informed people about city government and the policy positions held by a wide range of political parties. One nonpartisan—though sympathetic—post mortem described the paper as a "successful experiment" brought down by "active determined opposition" from the city's local capitalists, demonstrating the need for more such newspapers to fight political corruption and expand "civic service" and "impartial information" similar to that of schools and libraries.[75] Voted into existence by residents and supported by local taxes, the municipal paper stands testament to a largely forgotten alternative to the commercial newspaper.[76]

One of the most profound structural challenges to the commercial journalism model came from journalists themselves when they unionized.
Founded in 1933, the Newspaper Guild fueled its campaigns to reform
the newspaper industry with a radical critique of the commercial media
system.[77] Under the leadership of the journalist and editor Heywood Broun,
news workers organized themselves to challenge the industry's commercial logic, especially around issues of ownership and control. The guild's
objectives ranged from calls for increased wages for news workers to more
radical proposals for newspapers to be owned and controlled by journalists
themselves. Guild members disseminated their arguments and positions—
steeped in class conflict—via their newspaper the *Guild Reporter*. Their activism quickly grew militant, including a two-year strike against William
Randolph Hearst-owned papers in Chicago.[78]

Beyond fighting for better work conditions, the guild saw itself as directly
confronting the fundamental commercial logic driving newspapers. Ben
Scott, a leading historian of the guild, has noted that its members "explicitly understood their efforts as rooted in core principles of the public's First
Amendment rights." They saw themselves as part of something much bigger,
a social democratic project then sweeping the country. "This was not a side
road adjacent to the main currents of political and economic history during
the 1930s," Scott argues. "The Guild was in the midst of the industrial union
movement, wrapped up in the biggest New Deal reforms, and grappling with
a powerful, rising force in American political economy."[79] By establishing
strict autonomy from newspaper publishers and external political and economic pressures, the guild attempted to create a truly democratic institution, embracing professional norms that embodied a more radical notion of
journalism's role within a society. Its ultimate goal was nothing less than to
redefine American notions of freedom of the press.

A rapid and successful unionization drive indicated that this project
deeply resonated with working journalists. The guild aligned itself with the
feisty leftist Congress of Industrial Organizations and quickly began setting up chapters across the country. In the span of just five years, the union
had forty-seven signed contracts and nearly seventeen thousand members
from three hundred papers.[80] By the end of the 1930s, over half of all
working journalists belonged to the guild, with even higher membership
percentages at the big metro dailies.[81] These union members played a key
role in expanding craft unions while bolstering class-consciousness among
all media workers.[82]

The Newspaper Guild, like many other leftist organizations, came under intense political pressure in the late 1940s. Years of red-baiting made the union's membership skittish, and communists were purged from its ranks. One leading press historian argues that red-baiting within the guild had a far-reaching effect, even defining "journalistic objectivity and the media's obligation to the public in nationalist, anti-radical terms."[83] Nonetheless, the movement still had some fight left in it, even as the guild became more accommodating of the commercial order. In the mid-to-late 1940s, the guild continued to inject radical media criticism into the nation's political discourse as a growing reform coalition advanced major regulatory and legal challenges to the commercial press.

The Crystallization of Modern US Journalism

Many contemporary ideological assumptions about the nature of the press in the United States crystallized through a cluster of policy battles in the 1940s. This moment was a critical juncture when social movements, media institutions, and regulators struggled over defining news media's role in democracy. The statements and actions of government regulators, media critics, and labor unions attest to a society-wide debate about the nature of the press, calling into question the presumed natural, laissez-faire arrangement between the US government and the press that remains intact to this day.[84]

While the Newspaper Guild and other radical activists challenged newspapers over fundamental questions of ownership and control from below, New Deal liberals hatched plans to rein in the industry from above, at the policy level. These actions began in the late 1930s and carried on into the late 1940s. In 1938, President Roosevelt made the unusual move of issuing a five-page letter to the *St. Louis Dispatch* that questioned whether a profit-driven model was compatible with freedom of the press. He called for a more progressive vision for media, articulating Americans' freedom to access quality news.[85] That same year, the Department of Justice (DOJ) quietly began collecting information on print media concentration for a secret report focused on "restraints of trade in the newspaper industry."[86]

The report noted that the news industry "was ripe for a thorough governmental investigation and possible intervention." Because the news industry is already "under general suspicion by the public," the report argued, if they were to further expose its "notorious" monopolistic infractions, "their mere

recitation should forever lay low the shibboleth of 'freedom of the press.'"
Stating that the newspaper industry had become a "big business" that
suppressed competition, the report observed that only the extremely wealthy
could afford to establish and maintain a new paper (in fact, by the 1940s
no one had launched a new profitable US daily newspaper in decades).[87] It
found that newspaper publishers were only "concerned with making money"
and their coverage was deeply prejudiced against labor protections and other
New Deal initiatives. Describing a "pervasive system of censorship" by a
small number of companies that monopolized much of the newspaper industry, the report concluded that without immediate government intervention, the newspaper industry would also "own and control most of the radio
stations in the country."[88]

Several years later, the DOJ targeted the newspaper industry under the
Sherman Antitrust Act and sued the Associated Press (AP), accusing it of
hindering trade by refusing wire services to the liberal *Chicago Sun* while
maintaining an exclusive market contract with the conservative *Chicago
Tribune*, owned by the far-right publisher Colonel Robert McCormick. The
1943 court case became a confrontation between a more expansive, "positive" concept of press freedom that emphasized citizens' rights to access diverse opinions and sources of news, and a libertarian "negative" argument
that the press's First Amendment rights exempted the newspaper industry
from antitrust interventions. A lively national debate ensued among op-
posing intellectual camps, but the positive view ultimately prevailed in a federal district court's split decision.

Judge Learned Hand argued that the democratic imperatives of the press
not only superseded newspapers' economic interests but also fell under the
protection of the First Amendment because "that industry serves one of the
most vital of all general interests."[89] Namely, Hand reasoned, the press should
be dedicated to disseminating information "from as many different sources,
and with as many different facets and colors as is possible." The *Chicago Sun's*
rights to the wire fell under First Amendment protections because the "right
conclusions are more likely to be gathered out of a multitude of tongues,
than through any kind of authoritative process." Judge Hand famously concluded: "To many this is, and always will be, folly; but we have staked upon it
our all."

The AP lost again two years later in its appeal to the Supreme Court. Justice
Hugo Black upheld strong positive freedoms in the majority's opinion, stating
that the First Amendment assumes that "the widest possible dissemination of

information from diverse and antagonistic sources is essential to the welfare of the public." Because "a free press is a condition of free society," he wrote, "freedom to publish means freedom for all and not for some." Delineating a progressive role for government, the decision clearly articulated the necessity of state-guaranteed public interest protections: "Freedom of the press from governmental interference under the First Amendment does not sanction repression of that freedom by private interests." Nothing in the First Amendment prevented the government from maintaining the conditions necessary for a healthy press system. "It would be strange indeed," Justice Black wrote, "if the grave concern for freedom of the press which prompted adoption of the First Amendment should be read as a command that the government was without power to protect that freedom."[90] In his concurring opinion, Justice Frankfurter went even further to underscore that journalism was not a commodity "like peanuts or potatoes" that is valued by "having merely a commercial aspect." Rather, the press is an essential public service that is "indispensable to the workings of our democratic society," and therefore deserving of special "considerations."[91]

These opinions affirmed three key points. First, when democratic imperatives were at stake, media institutions were fair game for government intervention and could not hide behind the First Amendment. Second, the press's commercial concerns were not as important as its democratic obligations to the public. And third, the press was invested with special public-service attributes; it was not a mere commodity and therefore should not be treated as one under the law. Ultimately, the public's positive rights to a diverse media system are more precious than publishers' negative individual rights shielding them from government regulation.

The legislative branch, too, turned its regulatory eye to the newspaper industry in the mid-1940s. Congressional critics began probing newspapers' monopolistic practices and issuing reports that focused on media consolidation, the prohibitive costs of starting up a new newspaper, the loss of competition and localism, and the effects that these developments had on democracy. Concerns about the rise of one-newspaper towns led to a major congressional study in the mid-1940s titled, "Survival of a Free Competitive Press: The Small Newspaper, Democracy's Grass Roots." Democratic Senator James Murray released the seventy-one-page report and called for more federal oversight of the newspaper industry, including congressional hearings on how newspaper ownership concentration was hurting small publishers. Murray's committee saw democracy itself at risk: Given that the "future of the small press business is linked with the future of . . . political democracy" and that the "traditionally valued American system of small competing press units is now in such serious jeopardy," the situation "warrant[ed] the immediate attention of Congress."[92]

Congressional Democrats had planned on more hearings about possible government intervention into the media landscape, but these plans were jettisoned after Democrats lost the House to a Republican wave in the 1946 midterm elections. The Republican-controlled congress shifted attention away from the threat of media monopolies to focus on newsprint shortages, and Murray's report soon fell into obscurity.[93] Nonetheless, while the congressional investigation into the disappearance of small newspapers did not amount to a serious policy intervention, this regulatory activism and key court decisions alerted the commercial press that it needed to either self-reform or risk losing its privileged autonomy from public oversight. Media owners could no longer simply hide behind the First Amendment.

The Rise of Professionalism

The professionalism of news work in the early twentieth century largely arose in response to growing public criticism. Newspaper publishers and editors were concerned that untrustworthy journalism, sensationalism, and an overall lack of legitimacy would ultimately diminish their commercial prospects. In an effort to repair their damaged credibility, they embraced the trappings of balance and objectivity. A hallmark of this professionalism was to provide fact-based, dispassionate news that was ostensibly neutral and unbiased in its coverage. Journalists could achieve this kind of reportage by relying heavily on official sources without taking a strong position on political issues—or by avoiding controversial issues altogether.

Papers also began imposing a strict boundary between the news and business sides of their operations. This firewall between "church and state" would presumably shield journalism from commercial pressures. Although always a porous barrier, journalists came to see this protocol as one of their most sacred tenets. Losing this "Chinese Wall," it was widely believed, would threaten their credibility and independence. According to legend, the Chicago Tribune Tower even maintained separate elevators for business and editorial staff to prevent undue communication between the two types of personnel.[94]

These norms and ethical codes helped stabilize a newspaper market undergoing systemic change at the turn of the twentieth century. They also became the founding doctrine taught in the major journalism schools that were all being established at this time—themselves another avenue to professionalizing journalism. Toward the end of his life, Joseph Pulitzer endowed Columbia University with funding for a journalism school specifically to train reporters to cultivate an "anti-commercial" attitude.[95] Publishers like Pulitzer seemed to acknowledge that they would need to contain—or at least camouflage—their commercial imperatives if they wished to retain legitimacy, stave off government intervention, and continue to reap commercial rewards. As the twentieth century progressed, the US press system transitioned from the excesses of yellow journalism into a more respectable news organ.

The journalistic norm of objectivity became a cornerstone of this professionalization project. Dominant interpretations of this phenomenon often describe it as a cultural shift that reflected a broader democratization of US society and changing attitudes among journalists about their social standing.[96] However, a growing number of revisionist historians have underscored the economic origins of the objectivity norm. Drawing from a more political economic approach, their interpretation does not see the development of modern journalism as reflecting an increasingly enlightened mainstream culture. Instead, these scholars argue that professional codes ultimately aimed to satisfy advertisers' and newspaper publishers' commercial imperatives.[97] The consensus history, in contrast, tends to naturalize processes of commercialization while downplaying conflict around journalism's normative role. Such a whiggish narrative of cultural progression in US journalism history risks erasing age-old public debates and ongoing reform efforts over the commercial press system's fundamental design and democratic role.

Without this context of earlier conflict between competing visions of journalism, we are less likely to understand today's journalism crisis as a culmination of long historical processes and endemic tensions in the commercial press. Moreover, the professionalization process did not come to full fruition until after World War II. The period leading up to what Nerone calls the "High Modern Moment" has been described as a transitional phase of "proto-professionalization" during which journalists gradually took on a tone of objective authority.[98] This professionalization project was primarily an attempt to negotiate key tensions arising from commercial pressures. It served as a form of soft self-regulation by which journalists can exert subtle but significant agency over their reporting. Curran describes this system as "a great media experiment" in which commercial journalism tries to negate the market's adverse effects by developing "a tradition of professionalism among journalists" who endeavor to be "accurate, impartial, and informative."[99] To the extent that this experiment has succeeded, it serves as a reminder that commercial news institutions are indeed capable of producing high-quality journalism. But throughout its history, too often we see the telltale signs of a failed commercial experiment in which negative externalities far outweigh positive ones.

Concerns about these structural failures had begun to materialize in the 1940s. Toward the end of WWII, magazine publisher Henry Luce sponsored a commission tasked with defining the proper role of media in a democracy.[100] Formally known as the Commission on Freedom of the Press, the Hutchins Commission (named after its chair, University of Chicago president Robert Hutchins) helped establish the ethical foundations for the modern US press system.[101] Its members focused on two implicit questions: What is the role of media in a democratic society, and how should that role be ensured? They grappled with these questions over numerous meetings and consultations with a wide range of experts, ultimately producing six book-length studies on the US media system.

Early in its deliberations, the renowned legal theorist Zechariah Chafee described one of the commission's central tasks as deciding "whether the giants should be slain or persuaded to be good."[102] The implication was that the "giants" (large media institutions) could be dismantled if they failed to adhere to basic ethical guidelines. But the newspaper industry fiercely opposed even light oversight, arguing that regulation was antithetical to US press freedoms. Struggling to agree on the meaning of press freedom, after a long debate the commissioners concluded that news media institutions should practice social responsibility but remain self-regulated with the government intervening only sparingly and in very limited ways.

However, archival evidence from unpublished reports and transcripts suggests a less well-known story. At various points in their deliberations, the commissioners considered a number of more radical alternatives before ultimately jettisoning them. They discussed structural reforms such as subsidizing news institutions in one-newspaper communities, launching local citizen newspaper councils, and treating the press as a utility or common carrier that guaranteed access to critical information. The commissioners declared that the news should not be left solely in the hands of private companies and discussed how a federal agency modeled after the Federal Communications Commission (FCC) could regulate newspaper content. They also proposed breaking up newspaper chains and preventing new ones from forming. Archibald MacLeish, the most radical voice on the commission and the primary author of their main report, argued forcibly for a democratized news media system that guaranteed public access—otherwise, he argued, the very principle of freedom of the press was farcical.

Out of fear of sounding like socialists, however, the Hutchins Commission gradually fell back on calls for self-regulation, while leaving the door open for such government interventions as antitrust proceedings. It also called for such uncontroversial measures as requiring the press to cover important issues of the day. In the viciously anti-Communist climate of the late 1940s, the established press rejected even these fairly innocuous calls for reform as radical. Ironically, the norm-setting codes of professionalization that the landmark commission established helped shield the industry from subsequent reform. The commission ultimately elevated an intellectual rationale for self-regulation based on a libertarian understanding of the First Amendment that placed the press's freedom from government interference above citizens' rights to a democratic press—an interpretation that the Supreme Court had only recently dismissed.

In 1956, the foundational book *Four Theories of the Press* codified these media ethics as the "social responsibility" model.[103] Drawing some of its core precepts from the Hutchins Commission, this book became required reading in many US journalism schools for generations of students, shaping their thinking about the roles and responsibilities of the press.[104] The book discussed four press models—authoritarian, Soviet, libertarian, and social responsibility—with the latter held up as the gold standard for ethical journalism. In many ways, however, "social responsibility" was merely a rebranding of the libertarian model. The newspaper economist Robert Picard has argued that an overlooked fifth model would be a "democratic socialist" model like that practiced in the Nordic countries.[105] This model, similar to a "social democratic" approach to journalism, legitimates a proactive role for the state in guaranteeing public service journalism.[106] In the 1950s, though, the social democratic approach was clearly off the table. The US media industry was spared significant structural reform—only to erupt in crisis once again in the early decades of the twenty-first century.

Despite a growing grassroots press reform movement and challenges from all three branches of government, an industry-friendly version of "freedom of the press" emerged triumphant at a historical juncture in the 1940s. Notions of journalistic professionalism legitimated this project, seeking to stave off regulatory intervention, appease the public, and ensure significant profits for media owners. This lightly regulated commercial model that the United States pursued has remained the dominant paradigm for US news media for the past six decades. However, significant exceptions have emerged—such as the Public Broadcasting Act of 1967, which I turn to in chapter 5. Moreover, the long tradition of government support for news media—for instance, postal subsidies—suggest that this was not a foreordained outcome. Key court decisions in the 1940s planted seeds for an alternative vision of the First Amendment, one that protected positive rights of access to a diverse news media system. Even the Hutchins Commission's watered-down proposals contained potential avenues for a more robust freedom of the press, leaving the door open to state intervention if the commercial press were to fail in its responsibilities.

Nonetheless, the corporate libertarian arrangement that emerged from the 1940s continues to frame many of our conversations and assumptions surrounding today's journalism crisis. This is especially true of the notion that government should maintain a laissez-faire position toward media institutions—even if this notion contradicts the history of the government's involvement with the press. And while this dominant model would become normalized and take on an air of inevitability, the commercial nature of the press has continued to galvanize criticism in our modern era.

Modern Media Criticism

The heavily commercialized media system that we largely take for granted today was possible only because earlier reform movements to democratize the media failed. A social democratic vision of the media collapsed in the face of red-baiting and market fundamentalism, and few structural challenges to the dominant model have emerged since the 1940s. Nonetheless, journalistic professionalism and the embrace of "social responsibility" did not simply mollify critics, despite a widely held belief that the postwar period was a "golden age" for investigative journalism. Many structural problems in the commercial press continued, and even a casual glance at public criticism suggests that these flaws did not go unnoticed.

Moreover, academic studies from recent decades empirically substantiate many radical critiques from this earlier period. Taken together, these studies present accumulating evidence that commercial values shape media content over time in predictable patterns according to constraints and tensions associated with market-driven news values. While social science analyses of media are generally hesitant to ascribe strong media effects or suggest fundamental flaws in the underlying economic system—often reflecting a similar commitment to "objectivity" and the status quo as professional journalism— even mainstream scholarship has empirically borne out many of the radical claims of the Progressive and New Deal era media critiques.

For example, much scholarship confirms that one of the most pronounced weaknesses in the US news media system is an over-reliance on official sources.[107] The fear of appearing controversial and jeopardizing access to elite sources often leads journalists to reproduce official accounts. This tendency was cast into stark relief in news coverage during the build-up to the Iraq War in 2003. When asked at a Harvard forum about press performance from this time—what is seen now as a major press failure—the famous news anchor Dan Rather conceded that "more questions should have been asked." But then he said: "Look, when a president of the United States, any president, Republican or Democrat, says these are the facts, there is heavy prejudice, including my own, to give him the benefit of any doubt, and for that I do not apologize."[108] While this arrangement has come under considerable strain during the Trump era, journalists have often been overly credulous toward elite accounts, creating a media environment through which misleading information is easily amplified. Content analyses bear this out by showing how US news media echo presidential rhetoric that is strategically crafted to discourage public debate.[109] Given the tendency of the US news media to report official messages almost verbatim (even when they are criticizing official claims, such as those made by President Trump), this style of reporting easily propagates misinformation about a wide range of crucially important issues—from the case for war to the causes of climate change.

Other research suggests that the press implicitly indexes its coverage to the parameters of elite opinion.[110] According to this "index model," if consensus exists among elites, regardless of grassroots opposition to the status quo, little dissent may enter into mainstream news discourse. To make sense of why mainstream journalism failed to ask tough questions in the run up to the Iraq

War, *Washington Post* columnist David Ignatius explained, "journalists were victims of their own professionalism. Because there was little criticism of the war from prominent Democrats and foreign policy analysts, journalistic rules meant we shouldn't create a debate on our own."[111] Despite opposition voiced by numerous international experts, more than a hundred members of Congress, and millions of protestors around the world who took to the streets to challenge the case for the Iraq War, major news media uncritically accepted and repeated official rationales in stenographic fashion. Journalism professor Jeff Cohen, the former senior producer of MSNBC's Phil Donahue show, offers a stark example of media's profound bias against anti-war voices. He carefully documented his firsthand account of how MSNBC instructed him and his colleagues that, for every anti-war guest they had on the show, they had to balance that person with two pro-war guests. MSNBC eventually fired Donahue for his anti-war views.[112]

While blatant cases of overt corporate censorship are rare, more subtle effects of commercialism on news coverage are often discernible.[113] For example, commercial imperatives may skew news discourse through "news framing," namely "persistent selection, emphasis, and exclusion."[114] Political communication scholar Robert Entman suggests that "frames have at least four places in the communication process: the communicator, the text, the receiver, and the culture," which work together to select aspects of a perceived reality and make them more salient to promoting a particular moral evaluation.[115] This framework provides a template for assembling facts, quotations, and other story elements in a news article, encouraging specific types of narration and orienting audiences toward particular interpretations of the news.[116] These framing studies help bring into focus the varied ways that media maintain official narratives. One study recasts the traditional "watchdog" role of the press as a "guard dog" that protects the legitimacy of status quo power structures from dissent.[117] Similar research suggests that the press tacitly "manages" who gets to speak in news stories and what issues are covered.[118] Media sociologist Todd Gitlin argues that commercial media do not actually manufacture the status quo, but rather reproduce and relay elite ideology and—to a much lesser extent—messages from dissident interest groups and social movements.[119]

Other critics level a more structural critique by focusing on commercial restraints within the press system. In their view, recurring omissions in media coverage point to endemic flaws, ranging from corporate media ownership to extreme commercial pressures on news production. Most of this criticism looks beyond individual reporters and seeks to explain the patterns of disinformation and misinformation in the news by examining the larger power relations within which the news industry is embedded. Understood this way, controversial reporting that alienates elites and scares away advertisers is antithetical to advancing profit goals.

Encapsulating many of these themes, Ed Herman and Noam Chomsky's famous "Propaganda Model" provides a conceptual framework—of what they refer to as a "guided market system"—for understanding how news coverage selectively filters out some bodies of evidence while privileging others. Their model suggests that framing patterns, journalistic routines, and news values can be attributed to five filters present in commercial media: corporate ownership; advertising; reliance on official sources; flak from interest groups (predominantly right-wing); and anti-communism (anti-terrorism in more recent formulations), or anti- whomever or whatever the official enemy is at a particular historical moment. These filters combine to create specific, and largely predictable, patterns in press coverage that link up with other trends noted by scholars, from the rise of journalistic professionalization to news norms guided by the sole criterion of shareholders' profits.[120]

Left-of-center critics have raised thoughtful and nuanced criticism of the propaganda model over the years. Herman addressed some of this criticism directly in a classic essay published in the *Monthly Review*. In critiquing professional news norms, he points to commercial constraints:

Professionalism and objectivity rules are fuzzy, flexible, and superficial manifestations of deeper power and control relationships. Professionalism arose in journalism in the years when the newspaper business was becoming less competitive and more dependent on advertising. Professionalism was not an antagonistic movement by the workers against the press owners, but was actively encouraged by many of the latter. It gave a badge of legitimacy to journalism, ostensibly assuring readers that the news would not be influenced by the biases of owners, advertisers, or the journalists themselves. In certain circumstances it has provided a degree of autonomy, but professionalism has also internalized some of the commercial values that media owners hold most dear, like relying on inexpensive official sources as the credible news source.[121]

These critical frameworks all have strengths and weaknesses, obscuring some aspects of our media system while illuminating others. What is striking, however, is the consistency of this criticism over time. Media criticism has gained new relevance and resonance in the age of Trump, but the media failures they describe—whether misinformation within social media or sensationalism in mainstream news media—are not new problems. A historical analysis brings into clear focus how these structural problems are actually continuities—not disjunctures—within commercial media systems. The sooner we recognize these long-standing structural problems, the sooner we can strike at the root problem and create real systemic alternatives to a failing commercial news model.

What This Historical Context Tells Us

By focusing on commercial journalism's structural contradictions, the history outlined in this chapter differs in some key respects from standard media histories. This long history of media criticism and reform efforts reveals recurring challenges to the commercial model of the press and the unremitting vision for structural alternatives. This history also suggests that our normative foundations and democratic theories of the press are not natural or static, but rather contingent on previous conflicts over journalism's role in society.

The counter-narrative that I sketch here questions the often-implicit assumption that the default position for the press in the United States has always been a version of the liberal/libertarian model. To the contrary, history shows us a long—if uneven and often besieged—tradition of radical media criticism, affirmative government media policy, and alternative media models that directly challenged the commercial model of the press. Earlier reformers understood that the root of journalism's endemic problems stemmed from the commercial logic that drove much of the US press system.

The radical tradition of US media criticism emerged as a response to the press system's deeper structural problems. These problems became especially pronounced during journalism crises in the Progressive Era and again in the New Deal era, characterized by simultaneous developments in the modern commercial press, contradictions between public service and private profits, and the professionalization of journalism. This historical trajectory exposes journalism's structural vulnerabilities, suggesting that crisis is baked into the commercial press system's very DNA. The market has been an unreliable provider for the public service journalism that democracy requires. But within dominant discourses about journalism, it has been almost verboten to point that out.[122]

Before we expand the parameters of the debate around journalism's future, we must situate our media system's structural design as a core problem for democratic society. We must bring into focus journalism's normative foundations, economic structures, and policies that often evade scholarly scrutiny.[123] In particular, we must underscore that public service journalism—reporting that focuses on local coverage, watchdogging those in power, and giving voice to the many silenced in society—has always been in tension with commercial imperatives. Despite this often-obscured relationship, the United States has essentially conducted a hundred and fifty-year experiment in commercial journalism by treating news as both a commodity and a public service. With the latter function driven into the ground by the market, this experiment has largely failed.

The next chapter will look at the most recent moment when these structural contradictions flared up: the modern journalism crisis that metastasized in 2009. During this time, critics, commentators, and regulators once again challenged the press's normative foundations and democratic responsibilities, in the process affirming many age-old critiques of commercial news media. For decades, a highly profitable business model based on advertising revenues overshadowed these tensions. But as this model collapsed during the financial freefall of 2008–2009, commercial journalism's long-standing structural tensions erupted into full view.

2

The Early Crisis and Missed Opportunities

At the height of the contemporary press crisis in 2009, the US Senate Commerce Committee held a hearing on the future of journalism. The discussions that day showcased central divisions within future-of-news debates, as well as major models for reform. Senator John Kerry opened the hearing with a dramatic statement: "Today it is fair to say that newspapers look like an endangered species." The air hung solemnly over this opening remark, and people in the packed room shuffled uneasily in their seats, unsure how the conversation would unfold. Senator Kerry acknowledged this uncertainty as he invoked a question on many attendees' minds: "Why is the government interested in this, and what are we looking at?" Then he answered:

> Well, the fact is that we do have a responsibility for the licensing of broadcasts, we have a responsibility for the regulatory oversight of ownership of cable, satellite, and other issues with respect to communications. And needless to say, how the American people get their information, what the structure of ownership is, is of enormous interest to all of us, because it is the foundation of our democracy.[1]

The assumption that government has a duty to maintain and protect our news media receded as the discussion focused more on the nature of the journalism crisis and potential solutions. But it remained a crucial subtext throughout the hearing.

One of the witnesses invited to testify was David Simon, a former *Baltimore Sun* reporter and the creator of the television series *The Wire*. Simon offered a colorful synopsis of the journalism crisis, highlighting the industry's business model and the role of corporate greed:

> From the captains of the newspaper industry, you may hear a certain martyrology, a claim that they were heroically serving democracy, only to be undone by a cataclysmic shift in technology. From those speaking on behalf of new media, Web blogs, and that which goes Twitter, you will be treated to

Democracy Without Journalism?. Victor Pickard, Oxford University Press (2020). © Victor Pickard
DOI: 10.1093/oso/9780190946753.001.0001

assurances that American journalism has a perfectly fine future online and that a great democratization is taking place.[2]

Simon was having none of it, casting "a plague on both their houses." He warned: "Unless a new economic model is achieved, [journalism] will not be reborn on the Web or anywhere else." For Simon, the much-heralded blogosphere did not evidence a brave new future for journalism. Instead, "it leaches [its] reporting from mainstream news publications, whereupon aggregating websites and bloggers contribute little more than repetition, commentary, and froth." The very phrase "citizen journalist," he argued, was Orwellian. A "neighbor who is a good listener and cares about people is a good neighbor. He is not in any sense a citizen social worker. Just as a neighbor with a garden hose and good intentions is not a citizen firefighter." "To say so," according to Simon, "is a heedless insult to trained social workers and firefighters."[3]

Wall Street-owned newspaper chains' "shortsighted arrogance" was also a key part of the problem. Simon noted that the *Baltimore Sun* eliminated scores of reporters while it was achieving 37 percent profits. "In short," Simon concluded, "my industry butchered itself . . . [by following] the same unfettered, free-market logic that has proven so disastrous for so many American industries." This was, according to Simon, US newspapers' original sin. When local family-owned newspapers consolidated into publicly owned newspaper chains, "an essential trust, between journalism and the community served by that journalism was betrayed."[4]

Two of the other witnesses, New America Foundation president and award-winning journalist Steve Coll and the former newspaper editor and Knight Foundation president Alberto Albarguen, agreed with much of Simon's analysis, emphasizing the need for nonprofit and public media models. However, a lively disagreement broke out between Simon, who argued that paywall subscription models were the way forward, and Arianna Huffington, who offered a more sanguine view of citizen journalism's democratic potential.

Huffington believed that blogs would more than compensate for what was being lost, pointing to her own *Huffington Post* as an exemplar. In her view, Luddite concerns about digital journalism's viability resembled the mindset of "scribes working with stone tablets" during the advent of the printing press. Declaring with great confidence that "Journalism will not only survive, it will thrive," Huffington enthused about the power of linking stories and driving traffic. She cited the media pundit Jeff Jarvis, who argued that the new "link economy" would quickly replace the "content economy."[5] She also invoked the Harvard business school professor Clayton Christensen's ideas around "disruptive innovation" and suggested that Google was developing advertising platforms that would help news organizations monetize their online content.[6] Simon, responding to some of these claims, replied (to much laughter): "The day I run into a *Huffington Post* reporter at a Baltimore Zoning Board hearing is the day that I will be confident that we've actually reached some sort of equilibrium." Until then, Simon believed, bloggers would never replace beat reporters.

These four positions—citizen journalism, subscription/paywalls, nonprofit models, and public models—roughly map onto the major prescriptions for alternative models to advertising-dependent news, a topic I will return to in the next chapter. That these four models are still among the most commonly proposed alternatives to advertising-dependent journalism attests to the hearing's prescience—as well as to the stubborn consistency of the structural crisis and the paucity of new ideas. Despite some debate over the discussants' preferred alternatives, it also was striking that nearly all of them saw the status quo as untenable. With its core business model coming apart, everyone agreed that journalism would never be the same. But what would come next remained unclear.

The House of Representatives' hearing about journalism's future was more explicitly activist and sympathetic to government intervention.[7] The assumption that the United States has never had, and should never countenance, government intervention in news media systems was roundly refuted by several witnesses, especially the law professor C. Edwin Baker. Putting the journalism crisis in historical context, Baker argued that the founders of the American Republic recognized early on that the market would *never* provide adequate support for the news and information that a democracy required. Reminding his audience of the founders' support for postal subsidies to guarantee wide dissemination of news—equaling roughly $6 billion in 2009 dollars—Baker proposed targeted subsidies in the form of tax credits to news organizations for half of their journalists' salaries. Such subsidies would remove the incentive for newspapers to lay off journalists and would lead to higher quality news reporting.[8] Most of the other witnesses agreed with Baker's assessment, arguing for aggressive government intervention, including a variety of media subsidies for public service journalism.

The very existence of both of these hearings implies that at least some policymakers believed government had, and has, an important role to play in ensuring public access to a vibrant press. In its willingness to address matters of political economy, however, the House hearing proved the exception to a conversation that rarely acknowledged, let alone addressed, the structural causes of the crisis in journalism. Despite the sense of urgency in 2009, the US government still has taken no meaningful action to address the ongoing journalism crisis. This tremendous "policy failure," as I termed it in my previous book, deserves much more attention.[9] Clues that help explain this inaction appear in those early months of the modern journalism crisis. In this chapter, I explore how Americans' inability to move beyond a libertarian discourse has limited our capacity to envision and enact alternatives to a broken media system.

Origins of the Crisis

To understand such a strange political moment, it is worth pausing to consider why newspapers were suddenly collapsing. Although the newspaper industry had been, by some measures, in slow decline for decades, four major factors sparked its abrupt descent in 2008–2009.[10] First, as I will discuss later in this chapter, for more than a century the US press system has been inordinately dependent on advertising revenue, leaving it vulnerable to economic and technological disruptions. This preexisting structural condition differed from many other news industries around the world.

Second, the news industry suffered from self-inflicted wounds. Many newspapers were over-leveraged, with many already carrying extensive debts from earlier buying sprees.[11] Instead of reinvesting profit margins of 25 percent or more back into newsrooms, these papers' investors had grown accustomed to acquiring new assets in anticipation of big payouts—decisions that often turned into devastating losses. To give just one example, the *New York Times* bought the *Boston Globe* in 1993 for $1.1 billion, among the highest prices ever paid for a newspaper. It sold the paper in 2013 at about a 93 percent loss.[12]

These media companies, in other words, had already been neglecting their newsrooms for years before the third contributing factor hit: the 2008 financial crisis. The worst economic downturn since the Great Depression eighty years prior, the crisis hit many industries hard, but especially those with structural vulnerabilities. Furthermore, there was no social safety net for this massive market failure; public media (such as NPR and PBS) and the non-profit sector were woefully unprepared to step into the breach.

The fourth and most noted contributing factor to the journalism crisis was a new set of economic relationships ushered in by digital media. While news organizations increasingly invested in digital content, online ads generated a mere fraction of revenue compared to their paper-based counterparts. With the loss of local advertising monopolies, the business model for journalism suddenly collapsed. A particularly major blow was the loss of classified ad revenue. With websites such as Craigslist offering free classified ads, newspapers held no hope of ever returning to the heady days of making advertising money hand over fist. A study by the Pew Internet and American Life Project found that classified advertising revenue fell by approximately $7 billion between 2005 and 2009.[13] An oft-cited study shows the detrimental effects that Craigslist alone had on newsrooms, costing the newspaper industry $5 billion between 2000 and 2007 in lost classified ad revenue.[14]

Of course, to blame the journalism crisis largely on Craigslist—as some have done—is to overlook key contextual factors.[15] Local newspapers had grown accustomed to exploiting their market power and charging exorbitant monopoly prices for advertising. If anyone wanted to advertise to a given population, they had little choice but to go through a local newspaper or other local media. With the shift to digital, however, newspapers faced tremendous competition and struggled to monetize their online content. Making matters worse, newspapers ruthlessly disinvested in news and cut costs as they chased the increasingly elusive goal of maintaining obscene profits. Many outlets reduced or entirely dismantled their foreign, Washington, and statehouse bureaus. More generally, the immediate effects of this economic shift, exacerbated by the financial downturn, was the dramatic loss of news jobs.

Employment across much of the news media industry was hurting, but newspaper jobs were in free fall, shedding thousands of positions between 2008 and 2009. Advertising revenues and circulation numbers plummeted. In 2008, the value of newspaper stock dropped by a stunning 83 percent. In a six-month period, the one hundred-and-seventy-eight-year-old *Detroit Free Press* cut home delivery to three times a week; the one-hundred-and-forty-six-year-old *Seattle Post-Intelligencer* went online only, cutting all but a handful of employees; the one-hundred-year-old *Christian Science Monitor* went online only; and the one-hundred-and-fifty-year-old *Rocky Mountain News* shut down. With many other papers in various stages of bankruptcy, some media commentators warned—correctly, as it turned out—that a major city would soon not have a daily newspaper. Within the next two years, Detroit, Cleveland, and New Orleans would all lack daily papers.[16]

As almost daily news accounts around the country documented the industry's downward spiral—including the website Paper Cuts that kept a constant tally of lost jobs—the growing panic about the future of journalism was palpable. With this multiplying "body count" as a backdrop, bold actions were demanded, experts were assembled, and a raft of reports were published. The seemingly progressive politics of newly elected President Barack Obama led many observers to hope that good government would devise reasonable plans for tackling the crisis—even, perhaps, launching a new New Deal of government activism. Many (myself included) dared to dream that those in government would recognize the limits of a laissez-faire approach to the market and step in to preserve public service journalism from the ravages of capitalism. Once unassailable verities about the magic of the market had suddenly collapsed; even former Federal Reserve Chairman Alan Greenspan announced publicly, shortly after the financial crisis began, that he had been tragically mistaken to assume that markets were self-correcting.[17] At last, we thought, clear-headedness would prevail over the libertarian madness that had driven our economy into a ditch. Progressive change seemed imminent.

Subsequent events did not transpire in the way many of us had hoped or expected. The alarm bells quieted, plans for bold reforms receded, and the status quo quietly but assuredly reasserted itself. Nevertheless, it is important to recall that none of this was inevitable; it could have gone quite differently.

Immediate Responses to the Crisis

Given the resignation that many feel today, it is easy to forget the sense of great urgency when the journalism crisis first erupted in 2008 and 2009. The fear of institutional collapse especially gripped Washington, DC, where I was working during that time as a research fellow, first for a major think tank and later for a leading media reform organization, focusing specifically on policy approaches to the journalism crisis. It was remarkable to witness firsthand various transformations as our nation's politics seemingly underwent a paradigm shift. With the economy imploding and the Obama administration in the White House, policy ideas previously relegated to the discursive margins were now bandied about within mainstream circles.

During what appeared to be a political and intellectual realignment, early 2009 witnessed a rare window of opportunity for government interventions in redesigning the nation's media system.[18] Policymakers frantically turned to media reformers and scholars (even historians!) for advice on how to address the structural collapse of ad-supported journalism. Policy experts dusted off old books and articles to resuscitate arguments about the dangers of unregulated commercial systems. Politicians began proposing policy options not entirely under the sway of market fundamentalism. Lessons from our grandparents' generation came roaring back.

Amid this tumult, an inchoate policy agenda quickly emerged, one that sought to unhook news and information from commercial pressures. To give one example, Senator Ben Cardin sponsored the Newspaper Revitalization Act of 2009, which offered tax benefits to news organizations as well as to the philanthropies that donate to them.[19] His bill proposed revising sections of the Internal Revenue Code to qualify newspapers as nonprofits with an "educational purpose." The bill would have also exempted qualifying newspapers from paying corporate taxes on their advertising revenue and would allow donations to these newspapers to count as tax-deductible charitable contributions. Although well intentioned, the Cardin bill fell short in some key areas. While it mandated that qualifying newspapers contain local, national, and international news stories of interest to the general public, the bill seemed to preclude funding for smaller community-oriented papers and other news organizations. Nonetheless, it was a remarkable bill despite its failure to gain any traction in Congress. After being referred to committee, it never received a vote—and now has been almost entirely forgotten.

A raft of major policy reports also came out during this early stage of the journalism crisis,[20] many endorsing an aggressive agenda for press subsidies, an expanded public media system, and other measures that legitimated an activist state in support of public service journalism. A report published by the leading media reform organization Free Press (I was the lead author of this study) was the first out of the gate.[21] It helped set the tone for prescribing a number of structural policy interventions, including new ownership models (such as low profit and nonprofit), new tax incentives (such as a minority media tax certificate), a journalism jobs program, a journalism research and development fund, and subsidies for a robust new public media system.

While many of these reports came from foundations, think tanks, and scholars, government regulatory agencies also felt pressured to act. The

Federal Trade Commission (FTC) was at the forefront of these discussions, launching a series of high-profile workshops on "How Will Journalism Survive the Internet Age?"[22] A number of invited speakers and consultants— including Robert McChesney and C. Edwin Baker—advocated for aggressive structural interventions in response to a systemic journalism crisis. These discussions informed the FTC's draft report, which considered a wide range of direct and indirect subsidies for journalism.[23] The discussion draft, however, encountered fierce backlash the moment it was issued. It especially drew the ire of conservatives and libertarians who were newly emboldened by the ascendant Tea Party movement. After much bad press and political pressure, the report was set aside to languish—an outcome that arguably had a chilling effect on subsequent reports.[24]

As foundations, advocacy groups, and government agencies began responding with high-profile hearings and reports, the FCC joined the fray by announcing an inquiry into the future of journalism. Its interim chair, Commissioner Michael Copps, helped initiate a discussion that would later become a months-long, expansive study on the state of US news media. Commissioner Copps, who refers to President Franklin D. Roosevelt as a personal hero, was one of the most progressive commissioners ever to have served on the FCC.[25] He was sympathetic to an aggressive public policy program for addressing structural problems in commercial news media. Given the growing severity of the crisis, media reformers and the D.C.-based public interest community held high hopes for this greatly anticipated report. Copps himself hoped it would deliver "hard-hitting action recommendations that can be implemented before the end of this year. A report falling short of that," he warned, "will have failed the public interest."[26]

As we shall see, the report certainly fell short. Nonetheless, it is instructive to examine what this report found and prescribed—and, more importantly, what it did not. The report's framing of the crisis and its many blind spots hold clues as to why there has been no policy response to the US journalism crisis.

The FCC Report

The FCC did not formally launch its study on the future of journalism, the "Information Needs of Communities," until the fall of 2009.[27] By that time, a more industry-friendly FCC chairman, Julius Genachowski, had taken the agency's helm. Chairman Genachowski commissioned his one-time Columbia classmate Steven Waldman, former editor of the *Washington Monthly* and co-founder of *Beliefnet*, to author the report. Early on, Waldman initiated a kind of "listening tour," meeting with various scholars and practitioners to discuss the journalism crisis.[28]

The comprehensiveness of the FCC's research was truly admirable. They ultimately conducted more than six hundred interviews with people from a diverse range of professions, including journalists, scholars, industry representatives, lawyers, activists, philanthropists, government officials, and many others.[29] The FCC also held full-day workshops focusing on questions related to the future of journalism and media ownership and examined more than a thousand submitted public comments. FCC staff conducted an extensive literature review of other reports and studies on the future of journalism. An informal working group of respected scholars and consultants conducted research and contributed studies on specific subjects.

The FCC released the report in early June 2011. Weighing in at 468 pages, it contained a vast review of scholarship on the journalism crisis. Although it overlooked some political economic scholarship, the study did not hedge in its critical analysis of the depth of the crisis. Using employment census data from the American Society of News Editors (ASNE), the FCC concluded that the decline in jobs from 2006 to 2010 was particularly alarming: "In just four years, newspaper employment fell from 55,000 to roughly 41,600—about where it was before Watergate."[30] Page after page of the report documented in critical detail how market downturns had devastated the press, causing a wide array of social harms. Financially struggling news organizations were increasingly cutting costs, resulting in "less time to investigate, to question, to take a story to the next level." Fewer reporters to work on labor-intensive and investigative stories led to lower-quality journalism and "less daily beat reporting about municipal government, schools, the environment, local businesses, and other topics that impact Americans' future, their safety, their livelihood, and their everyday life." The report grimly observed that "the dramatic newspaper industry cutbacks appear to have caused genuine harm to US citizens and local communities."[31]

Like the 1940s Hutchins Report that came before it, the FCC report offered a timely critique of overall press performance as well as a trenchant analysis of structural problems, such as a loss of "local accountability reporting."[32] Parts of the report seemed to reject market fundamentalism with references to public goods, even mentioning the term "market failure," albeit tucked away in an endnote.[33] Yet, as was also the case with the Hutchins Commission, there was a glaring disconnect between the report's diagnosis of what was wrong and its proposed solutions. Most problematically, the report ruled significant policy intervention out of bounds from the start: "In crafting recommendations, this report started with the overriding premise that the First Amendment circumscribes the role government can play in improving local news. Beyond that, sound policy would recognize that *government is simply not the main player in this drama*" (emphasis added).[34] The report reiterated this statement several times, almost like a catechism. Its language reflected the market-libertarian paradigm that established the parameters of permissible policy reform and left little room for government intervention. The report even cautioned that a study about the media crafted by a government agency "could be met with suspicion," since it is the media's job to examine government and not the other way around.[35] Such an ideologically loaded stance conveniently ignored the long history of the US government's affirmative role in maintaining a healthy news media system, from creating the postal system to subsidizing the development of the internet. This unfortunate framing constrained the report from the get-go.

The report did state that the FCC "has not only the authority but the affirmative duty to look at these issues." But even this move was framed as a *deregulatory* intervention, arguing that it would amount to "public policy malpractice for the [FCC] to simply assume that the current (voluminous) set of public policies about communications—some crafted before there was an internet—are well suited for the twentieth century." Because the media landscape was changing "so rapidly and so dramatically," the FCC would examine "whether its assumptions and rules are still operating." It also cautioned that identifying "a particular problem does not mean that we believe the FCC has the responsibility or authority to solve it . . . In some cases, the role of this report is simply to describe things—to stimulate discussion and to suggest new paradigms for understanding local media markets."[36] The report made clear that, beyond outlining problems and removing "obstacles confronting those working to solve the problems of providing robust local news and information," there was little for government to do. It declared that most "solutions to today's media problems will be found by entrepreneurs, reporters, and creative citizens, not legislators or agencies." The report asserted that "Government cannot 'save journalism'" because the "media landscape is evolving so rapidly that heavy-handed regulatory intervention dictating media company behavior could backfire, distorting markets in un-helpful ways."[37]

The FCC carefully hewed to a non-interventionist approach to the jour-nalism crisis and instead placed its trust in the market. This strategy, how-ever, had significant limitations. One of the few media scholars to scrutinize the FCC report, Christopher Ali, notes that its limitations became clear when the report raised a key question and then failed to address it: "Markets usu-ally respond to consumer demand. But what happens if consumers don't demand something they essentially need?"[38] This question encapsulates a core tension within the FCC report and within modern liberal thought more broadly: relying on the market to provide public service journalism ignores both the public-good nature of news media and the market's inability to pro-duce such goods in sufficient quality or quantity.

Despite the report's reluctance to argue for affirmative government inter-vention, it did not hesitate to recommend deregulation, including the removal of the much-maligned and long-defunct Fairness Doctrine, which had man-dated that broadcasters air contrasting views on controversial and socially significant issues. According to the report, staff researchers came to realize that remnants of the Fairness Doctrine—repealed since 1987—remained on the books. Thus, they felt compelled to "eliminate any outstanding uncer-tainty about our intentions—about the localism proceeding, about enhanced disclosure, and about the Fairness Doctrine. We therefore recommend that the Commission consider cleaning up its books by repealing what's left of the Fairness Doctrine."[39] It is curious that they were moved to suggest such actions since the already-dead Fairness Doctrine posed little threat to an-yone, but it seems consistent with the report's overall deregulatory thrust.

To be fair, the FCC report was prescient in underscoring the depth of the local journalism crisis, and it offered an incisive analysis of the social implications of losing local accountability reporting. Furthermore, had it pushed for more aggressive policy interventions, it likely would have been attacked in the same fashion as the FTC report had been. In a recent conver-sation, Waldman reflected that he did not want the report—if the percep-tion were that the FCC aimed to reregulate media industries—to "become a political football" and overshadow the important research his team had conducted for nearly two years.[40] Given the shifting political landscape at the time, this caution may have seemed tactful and prudent. Perceived constraints—especially from the perspective of Waldman's boss, the rela-tively conservative FCC Chairman Genachowski (who himself may have been reading signals from the White House)—as well as compromises that inevitably come with a group project, also may have contributed to such modest recommendations. The report's four proposals mostly called for using more precise measurements and language in defining and regulating news media.[41] A more meaningful policy reform that the report did advance was to require local television stations to post transparency records online about political advertising purchased on their channels.[42]

Overall, however, the report's concrete policy proposals were tepid. First Amendment absolutism lurked just below the surface, with narrow definitions of press freedoms mostly benefiting corporations' negative liberties instead of communities' and the public's positive liberties. The report valorized the private sector's role in supporting journalism: "With a terrain more hospitable to local media innovation, the private sector—both for-profit and nonprofit entities—can increase the production of local programming, including accountability reporting." It implied that if we simply let the private sector operate freely, "The resulting media system could be the best the nation has ever had."[43] In reaching these conclusions, the FCC report's default position of accommodating the market would not have sat well if it had engaged more with critical scholarship. For example, there is no citation or mention of C. Edwin Baker, who had, prior to his sudden death in late 2009, written extensively about the future of news media and its relationship to markets and democracy.[44] Two scholars who remained engaged with the FCC's ongoing policy work, noted that "None of the conclusions or recommendations in any way questioned—or suggested alterations to—the status quo." The report devoted much research to illustrating "the magnitude of the changes, challenges, and problems" facing journalism, yet "concluded with a set of relatively inconsequential policy recommendations."[45]

Immediate reactions to the report zeroed in on some of these weaknesses. Given its lack of structural analysis and prescriptions for public policy interventions, leading progressives such as Michael Copps (no longer chair, but still an FCC commissioner at the time) decried what they saw as a huge missed opportunity. In his official FCC statement, Copps observed that, while the report seemed "aware of a serious problem," it lacked any serious recommendations for strong programs that could immediately begin undoing "generations of media injustice."[46] More specifically, he felt it focused too "little attention on what proactively reform-minded FCCs, like the ones we had back in the 1940s, can do when they put their minds—and a majority vote—to it." Instead, Copps was "sorely disappointed by the timidity of the recommendations given the breadth of the immediate problems the Report itself tees up."

In contrast to his more diffident colleagues at the FCC, Copps presented a bold counter-narrative for government's necessary role in supporting a healthy news media system:

> There are two schools of thought on what role government should play in providing the infrastructure to inform our citizens. One school would say let's leave this important task up to the free market and deregulate the entities that serve this purpose. This school has been in charge of the classroom for most of the past 30 years. We have been through an ongoing orgy of private sector consolidation with a few mega-media companies buying up small, independent broadcast stations and newspapers and then downsizing—and often shuttering—newsrooms and firing journalists in order to pay the huge debts these merger transactions always entail. The private sector found a willing accomplice in an FCC that was only too happy to bless it all and encourage even more, almost never saying "No" to whatever merger the financial wizards could conjure up. To make things even worse, successive iterations of FCCs vanquished from the books most of the public-interest rules and guidelines that could have imposed some discipline on broadcasting run rampant.

Challenging the First Amendment absolutism proudly championed by those who saw little role for government in protecting the Fourth Estate, Copps invoked the actual authors of the First Amendment who saw government provision of postal roads and subsidized delivery of newspapers as a "perfectly legitimate public policy." Seeking to reclaim this progressive vision of the First Amendment, Copps exhorted his fellow reformers to not "cower in the corner when the Do-Nothings try to shout us down."[47] This vision of positive rights to essential services such as a democracy-enabling press system was a cornerstone of Copps's envisioned alternative. In an essay published just weeks before the release of the FCC report, Copps implored the public to demand a healthy media system, for it was government's duty to protect the "conduit and shaper of our democratic dialogue."[48]

Elsewhere, immediate reactions among media reformers and journalists were swift and damning. Free Press issued a press release calling the report a "major disappointment," charging that it embraces "policies that would make this problem even worse" such as abandoning the rule "that requires broadcasters to report how much or how little local news and pro-gramming they air."[49] Ryan Blethen of the *Seattle Times* wrote: "It is as if the authors . . . did not know what fixes needed to be made so they put forward the easiest and mostly meaningless solutions for the FCC."[50] Similarly, media analyst Rick Edmond observed that despite some strong analysis, when it came to recommending what the FCC or Congress could actually do, "they pretty much punt."[51] Speaking to this regulatory retreat, a *Wall Street Journal* story interpreted the FCC report as an indication that "government's interest in helping the newspaper industry appears to be waning."[52] Media critic Eric Alterman lamented, that the report's "proposed solutions are actually more amenable to conservatives than to liberals or even moderates."[53]

As if to prove this last point, it is telling that the report received its most positive responses from the trade press and from free market ideologues. The well-known libertarian Adam Thierer reported that his first reac-tion to the FCC report was relief: "For those of us who care about the First Amendment, media freedom, and free market experimentation with new media business models, it feels like we've dodged a major bullet." He con-gratulated Steve Waldman for his "impressive achievement" and expressed delight that the report was "far removed from the radical Free Press/McChesney agenda that guided the FTC's controversial report."[54] Likewise, the Republican-appointed FCC commissioner Robert McDowell assured readers that the report would not lead to new FCC rules, but instead would stimulate "deregulatory action that better fits a competitive and dynamic marketplace."[55]

During a debriefing phone call a few days after the long-awaited report was issued, public interest advocates confronted Waldman (I was on the call), de-manding to know why the report expressed such an impoverished notion of government support for journalism. Waldman defended the study's laissez-faire approach by arguing that more aggressive policy intervention was in-appropriate for two reasons: First, because the government should not be choosing winners in the market, and, second, because the First Amendment forbade it. What is remarkable about this defense is that it perfectly captures something that C. Edwin Baker once said to me over lunch, just weeks be-fore he passed away. "Two arguments," he said, "that media owners typically use to fend off regulation. One is that government must always stay out of markets. And the other is that the First Amendment forbids it." Indeed, the arguments that Waldman invoked in his defense reflect a tacit libertarianism that leaves little room for meaningful public policy interventions. Ultimately, the FCC report's implicit message is that the market caused this crisis, and the market will solve it.

We Are All Libertarians Now

While the FCC report internalized the logic of market libertarianism, reformers nonetheless tried their best to build on some of the report's recommendations. They seized on the report's otherwise critical analysis of journalism's dire predicament to vindicate arguments they had been making for many years. And they pressed the FCC to be more proactive in studying the problem and suggesting policy interventions. The FCC eventually issued a public call for a new study in February 2012 that sought to find out how Americans meet their critical information needs and whether the existing "media ecosystem" serves them.

In addition to identifying barriers to obtaining such information, the FCC mined relevant studies to arrive at a working definition of "critical information needs." Commissioner Mignon Clyburn, who was the interim FCC Chair, made clear that she hoped this study would help support the FCC's efforts in boosting minority and female media ownership.[56] A group of reform-minded scholars comprising the Communications Policy Research Network (CPRN) won the bid to carry out the study.[57] Ultimately, the scholars produced a large-scale literature review that clearly defined journalism as a public good vulnerable to specific market failures. They drew from this report to identify eight critical information needs, ranging from emergency communication infrastructure to having reliable access to political information.[58] The study also called for more research to assess whether these needs were actually being met.

Mark Lloyd—a media historian, public interest advocate, and former FCC Associate General Counsel (focusing on diversity and localism) who was deeply involved in these policy debates as a core member of the CPRN research team—has chronicled the entire episode in fine detail.[59] As an expert agency, he notes, studying problems in our communication systems, identifying barriers to critical information needs, and formulating policy responses is well within the FCC's established purview—in fact, the Commission arguably had both a congressional and a court obligation to do so. Accordingly, the FCC followed through on the CPRN's recommendations to conduct a new study to assess the public's critical information by collecting and analyzing relevant data. Lloyd observed that all too often this research is limited to "questionnaires posed to FCC-regulated media and telecommunications industries and tallying up the replies." However, he noted that once in a great while the "Commission actually seeks information about how its 'public interest' policies and various licensees actually serve the public."[60]

This was the case when the CPRN and the FCC sought to understand whether media outlets were providing critical information needs to representative communities. After a long debate over who would lead this study—and despite industry interests continuously trying to derail the process—a new report was proposed to further study "critical information needs." The study aimed to conduct a "media market census" based on all media content in a designated market, including broadcast news, newspapers, and local internet news. The study would also include a voluntary survey of local media providers to gather information pertaining to ownership characteristics, employment, and barriers to entry. This "community ecology" study would canvas the general population to survey actual and perceived critical information needs, including in-depth neighborhood interviews.[61]

As soon as these plans became public, however, the right-wing press—with an assist from conservatives in Congress and at the FCC—immediately condemned the FCC's proposed study on communities' information needs. First, Tucker Carlson's *Daily Caller* published an article (drawing from an industry-inspired critique), with the headline: "FCC to Police News Media, Question Reporters in Wide-Ranging Content Survey."[62] Then a group of Republican members of Congress wrote a letter to FCC Chairman Tom Wheeler condemning the report, referring to it in their press release as a "Fairness Doctrine 2.0."[63] (In the conservative imagination, the Fairness Doctrine represents extreme government interference in the nation's communication systems.[64]) This letter was soon followed by an op-ed in the *Wall Street Journal* by then-Commissioner Ajit Pai (Pai later became FCC chair in 2016), who also likened the study's aims to that of the Fairness Doctrine and charged the FCC with taking the country "down the same dangerous path."[65]

Pai's op-ed unleashed an onslaught from conservative media. Lloyd recalls: "Soon scores of conservative radio hosts and other right-wing bloggers were spreading the word that the White House was ordering the FCC to police newsrooms and that this amounted to a return of the Fairness Doctrine." Some of these false stories targeted the CPRN professors' home academic institutions, which "resulted in a barrage of threatening calls and emails from angry citizens," according to Lloyd. Fox News even devoted an entire prime time segment on the FCC's supposed plan to police newsrooms.[66] In response to this pressure, the FCC first distanced itself from and then completely disavowed the study.[67] One CPRN member wrote in a subsequent op-ed that such hyperbolic accounts were toxic to the nation's policy discourse: "To conservative media from Fox News to Rush Limbaugh, [the proposed study] was an attempt to reintroduce the now-lapsed Fairness Doctrine and for President Obama to take control of America's newsrooms."[68]

This episode shows how the FCC's efforts to merely study these issues in greater depth posed a threat to established commercial interests. These media industries and their proxies—including the Republican-appointed FCC commissioners—felt compelled to delegitimate the very idea of collecting and analyzing data that might reveal deficiencies in the commercial media system. Simply gathering information on critical information needs—topics such as civic participation, consumer welfare, and public safety—triggered industry associations to question the constitutionality of such endeavors. The fear, of course, is that verifying such deficiencies might mandate government regulation and therefore threaten commercial media firms' prerogative to put profits above democracy.

But this episode also casts into stark relief another contributing factor to the status quo: how quickly liberals shade into libertarians when pressed on their allegiance to market fundamentalism and First Amendment absolutism. Indeed, the speed with which liberal policymakers and intellectuals caved to right-wing accusations of heavy-handed government speaks volumes about the relationship of policy discourse and power. On the rare occasions when liberal policymakers call for governmental affirmative action to guarantee media access to communities underserved by the market-driven media system, they quickly fall back on libertarian talking points the moment commercial forces push back. Until we find a way to inoculate progressive policy discourse from such attacks, many of our media crises will only worsen.

This failure to confront the journalism crisis with any meaningful policy response is reminiscent of previous failed reform efforts, such as the 1940s Hutchins Commission. Then as now, policy discourses defined US news media's structural problems as beyond government's reach. Both in the 1940s and today, society's response to a journalism crisis spurred discussions about media's normative role in a democratic society and the government's regulatory role in guaranteeing a healthy press system. Both the Hutchins and FCC reports leveled a strong structural critique about the commercial news media system's failures, and both reports concluded with only weak reform proposals that essentially punted on confronting these failures' structural roots—only to ensure their likely re-emergence in subsequent years.

This recurring pattern of policy failure recalls the phrase "nervous liberals" featured in media historian Brett Gary's book of the same title.[69] Gary used the phrase (first articulated by the Hutchins Commission's Archibald MacLeish) to describe postwar liberals whose selective adherence to First Amendment freedoms allowed them to switch seamlessly from targeting fascists during World War II to blacklisting leftists during the Cold War. These intellectuals compromised democratic principles for war-related imperatives in fighting a homegrown nativist movement in the United States and a fascist threat abroad. Supported by Rockefeller grants, many of these men were pioneers in the field of communication who became willing conscripts in the propaganda wars against perceived domestic and foreign threats.

Over the decades, liberal policymakers and intellectuals have consistently applied classical democratic theories—the stuff of "public spheres" and "marketplaces of ideas"—to a commercial media system that systematically underserves these ideals. In theorizing this failure, liberal thinkers sometimes arrive at a structural critique of a market-driven media system. However, once they find themselves arriving at the kinds of social democratic conclusions that would necessitate government intervention in media markets, they tend to retreat to extolling the comfortable sanctities of the market and its propensity for innovation and efficiency. Any concession that government may need to intervene in the face of overt market failure must be accompanied with sufficient caveats and qualifiers that dissuade accusations of statism, authoritarianism, and anti-capitalism. These are the nervous liberals—liberals made nervous by their own conclusions.

Meanwhile, the political and ideological landscape of the early Obama years quickly shifted, closing the discursive window of opportunity for structural reform. Conservative and liberal policymakers alike concluded that little could be done at the policy level to support journalism. By shying away from bold interventions and focusing instead on small-bore, market-friendly proposals, initiatives such as the FCC report were emblematic of this policy inaction. Ultimately, policymakers did little to confront the underlying structural causes of the commercial journalism crisis. Today we all reap what was sown by these earlier policy decisions and indecisions.

These patterns of critique and inaction bring into focus what I refer to as the "discursive capture" of policy discussions in the United States about the proper relationship between media and government.[70] This discursive paradigm is constrained by an implicit market fundamentalism that renders government incapable of intervening against significant social problems—such as the collapse of the Fourth Estate. Certain logics and value systems become so internalized that claims and arguments falling outside acceptable bounds become unthinkable. Over time, it leads to policy narratives with predictable silences that banish specific ideas from permissible discourse.[71] The result of these silences is a shrunken political imaginary about what is politically possible and desirable.

We will have to overcome these ideological blinders if we are to confront the "systemic market failure" that is driving journalism into the ground. We must first challenge the discursive constraints that limit how we talk and think about the role of journalism in a democratic society. Doing so penetrates to the core logic of liberalism—a logic that consistently conflates the "marketplace of ideas" with the commercial marketplace. In the remainder of this chapter, I will focus on some of the discourses surrounding journalism—what I suggest is a "market ontology" that delimits how we think about journalism—as well as antidotes to help guide us out of these discursive constraints.

Economic and Regulatory Discourses About Journalism

Discourses around US journalism are shot through with libertarian assumptions. This ideological orientation supports a "corporate libertarian" paradigm that sees the market as an expression of democratic choice and freedom, assumes technologies are inherently liberating, and renders government intervention illegitimate. The triumph of this policy discourse has helped perpetuate a commercial media system subject to little public oversight and few challenges from noncommercial media. This framework, which crystallized in the 1940s, largely remains the dominant paradigm for US media policy today.[72]

This paradigm helps explain the United States' remarkable policy failure in addressing the journalism crisis. It assumes that government has little legitimate role in intervening in media markets, which, as we saw in the last chapter, is an ahistorical, libertarian myth. This assumption ignores the fact that those suffering the most from these structural shifts are not large media corporations, but rather news workers who have lost their jobs and communities who no longer receive adequate news and information. This discourse, which combines a terrific excitement about digital publishing models with a deep trust in the market, tacitly assumes that technological fixes, the charity of benevolent billionaires, and bold entrepreneurialism—with the market as final arbiter—will somehow produce the journalism that democracy requires. We must unpack these narratives if we hope to weaken their hold on society's assumptions about journalism's future.

Crisis Narratives

In many ways, the crisis in journalism is as much about how we think and talk about journalism as it is about the institution itself. Few would dispute that journalism is undergoing a structural transformation in the United States. Yet narratives about journalism's future vary, with some scholars questioning whether "crisis" is even an apt way to describe its current state.[73] Most observers agree, however, that old business models are failing. Commentators typically ascribe this phenomenon to various factors: the inexorable march of new technology, the culmination of endemic structural flaws in the US news media system, a shift in how people (especially young people) consume the news, a loss of trust in mainstream news institutions, unforeseen financial downturns, media consolidation, or a mixture of all of the above. These differing emphases have produced a diversity of narratives about the crisis.

Since 2009, commentators have offered wildly variable predictions on how the journalism crisis will unfold. Some scholars have viewed this crisis as a kind of progression in which journalism is "evolving" into something entirely different, or "adapting" to a new "post-industrial" phase.[74] In the earliest period of the crisis, some observers even expressed optimism that journalism would emerge from the crisis leaner, nimbler, and tech savvier. Others assumed that the market and new technologies would eventually remedy the situation.[75] In recent years, however, this optimism has gradually given way to a growing resignation that nothing can be done to end journalism's demise.

These positions connect with particular discursive frames or "crisis origin" narratives. For example, business stories reduce the problem to a lack of profitability, while technological stories see a tale of progress and necessary die-off as the old print dinosaurs fade and new digital media ascend.[76] De-emphasizing journalism's indispensable public service mission, these narratives rarely frame a free press as an essential precondition of democratic governance. For commentators who operate within this ideological frame, the notion that government might subsidize public service journalism, for example, is immediately rejected as a "bailout" or "hand out" to incumbent news organizations. These kinds of narratives also often mistakenly assume that the present form of mainstream commercial media reflects popular taste.

Other crisis narratives use metaphors, such as a "perfect storm," that depict news organizations as history's innocent victims, caught unawares by the internet's wrath and economic shifts.[77] Yet other observers favor the metaphor of "self-inflicted wounds," blaming the crisis on corporate consolidators who impoverished newspapers and accumulated significant debt loads during buying sprees. In their myopic pursuit for unsustainable profits, media institutions privileged short-term gains instead of re-investing revenues into news operations and new technologies.[78]

That the journalism crisis resulted in part from news organizations' own mismanagement is arguably true. But it is wrong to assume, as many have, that media giants stuck their heads in the sand while new technologies snuck up on them. News organizations have been grappling with digital technologies for many years—albeit, often to cut labor costs—and tried but mostly failed to monetize their online content. Historical scholarship shows that newspapers experimented with different types of digital tools in the 1980s and 1990s.[79] Rather than just incompetence, their failure to monetize digital content suggests that digital technologies alone cannot overcome the growing economic gap between the capital needed to support news labor and the decreasing revenues generated by digital advertising.

Narratives about news organizations' incompetence often miss the bigger picture: this is a systemic crisis. The problems facing journalism are not simply the result of a few bad decisions or the ineptitude of traditional news organizations. Moreover, this crisis pertains not solely to newspapers but to newsrooms and newsgathering writ large. In other words, the crisis is not about the future of newspapers—it is about the viability of public service journalism. Unfortunately, we rarely hear discussions about the future of news framed in this way. Instead, by attributing the crisis in journalism to news organizations' incompetence, technological disruption, and business evolution, most crisis narratives divert potential policy responses to the journalism crisis.

Meanwhile, as news media institutions continue to search desperately for new commercial models, one central fact usually remains unsaid: There is precious little evidence to suggest that market-based initiatives and new media technologies can effectively replace everything being lost with the downfall of traditional news outlets. It is doubtful that new commercial models will *ever* be able to fill the vacuum created by the gradual implosion of our primary newsgathering organizations. But this distinct possibility is almost never pointed out. If we were instead to take this premise as our starting point—that the market cannot save journalism—we can begin to confront the depth of the crisis head-on by discussing true structural alternatives such as *noncommercial* models.

Discursive Capture, Market Ontology, and Policy Failure

The inaction toward confronting the journalism crisis stems from society's failure to see it as a public policy problem. "Future of journalism" discussions unfold within a constrained discourse that limits the range of policy responses. The discussions within these frameworks typically fail to acknowledge the structural problems facing media institutions. As I mentioned earlier, this is an example of "discursive capture" characterized by a "market ontology" that treats the journalism crisis as a problem of supply and demand, consumer preference, and profitability.[80]

In the United States, market fundamentalism prefigures how we think and talk about journalism. This discursive framework contains certain assumptions that depoliticize journalistic institutions, practices, and policies. For example, when we speak of news markets as responding to the straightforward calculus of supply and demand, we are treating news as a simple commodity, bought and sold on the market, rather than as a vital public service. This implies that, if journalism is unprofitable for publishers and media owners (usually a handful of wealthy white men), then we should simply let it wither away. Of course, supply and demand in the unfettered free market does not always reflect accurate assessments of social value or privilege concerns about what best serves democracy.

Reducing the journalism crisis to a supply and demand problem—although compelling in its elegant simplicity—risks naturalizing a commercial system of market transactions that treats media like a standard economic "widget" governed by consumer behavior.[81] News media are of course not simply widgets; they play a special role in a democratic society. But we nevertheless often talk about our information systems as if news were a "product" indistinguishable from other goods, like shoes or toothpaste. According to this market ontology, if news media consumers (or advertisers) are not willing to pay enough for journalism to make it profitable, we should resign ourselves to its inevitable decline. This discursive framework treats journalism as primarily a business, which presupposes a commercial relationship that treats newsreaders as only consumers, not citizens of a polity.

Another organizing discourse depicts the institutional collapse of journalism as beyond our control, like a natural disaster or an act of God. Media theorists such as Clay Shirky see newspapers' demise as simply the stuff of revolution, when "old stuff gets broken faster than the new stuff is put in its place."[82] According to this view, a period of painful transition naturally leads to something better, and it would be sheer folly to intervene as a society to preserve old institutions being crushed by the inexorable force of history. Such Schumpeterian "creative destruction" is at once awful and awesome, and presumably beyond the reach of human agency and intervention. We simply have to get out of the way and wait for what evolves organically. This seemingly radical argument is actually quite conservative, in that it essentially defers to the market and other powerful interests to decide what kind of journalism all of society should receive.

A related assumption holds that market forces and new technologies will somehow combine to guide us out of this predicament. Paradoxically, even though many see the internet (as opposed to an overreliance on advertising) as the primary impetus for the journalism crisis, they also see digital technology as journalism's savior. To be sure, new technologies and their affordances can greatly reduce barriers to entry, expand access to and participation in news production, and facilitate news dissemination. But these potentials can only be realized if public input and sound public policy prioritize them. Trusting in the market to automatically provide the news media that our democracy requires has always been, and is especially now, a risky proposal.

A kind of "digital exuberance" further obfuscates the structural roots of the journalism crisis, leaving market fundamentalism unchallenged and dismissing the possibility of collective action through policy interventions. This leads to ongoing policy failure and, ultimately, policy "drift." Jacob Hacker and Paul Pierson describe this concept as "systematic, prolonged failures of government to respond to the shifting realities of a dynamic economy."[83] For the journalism crisis, this drift amounts to ongoing disinvestment in news production and the dismantling of news institutions.

Collectively, these tropes reflect a "discursive capture" in which the possibilities for reforming the press are constrained by market-dictated parameters. Whether intended or not, this "market ontology" bounds discussions on the future of journalism. Within a market ontology, the journalism crisis is understood as something resulting from a lack of demand, changing modes of news consumption, and technological disruption. But these explanations elide a more basic story: We are witnessing an already-flawed commercial press system disintegrate as it migrates to a digital format where it cannot sufficiently monetize online content. Fortunately, there are antidotes for this market fundamentalism.

Economic Theories of Journalism: Public Goods and Market Failures

Ironically, mainstream neoclassical economic theory—which aims to understand how capitalist markets operate—can help us escape the confines of market ontology. Because even within such orthodox economic theory there is a recognition of the market's limitations. These understandings can help us make sense of media markets' inability to adequately finance and provide the high-quality news and information that democratic society requires.[84] Rather than thinking of journalism as a product to be bought and sold, we might instead think of it as a public good that society needs.

News and Information = Public Goods

News and information produced by journalism are in fact public goods.[85] According to a definition from neoclassical economics, public goods are non-rivalrous (one person's consumption of the good does not detract from another's) and nonexcludable (it is difficult to exclude free riders from consuming the good). Both of these conditions attach to digital media.

Countless people can access online news at once without detracting from others' ability to do so. Even when newspapers charge fees for accessing their online content, readers find ways to either circumvent the paywall or glean the information from another source. These qualities separate news media and information from other commodities within a capitalistic economy and make it exceedingly difficult to support them through standard market mechanisms.[86] For example, public affairs programming has traditionally not been a viable commercial product on its own and has required funding by the state, patrons, or advertising.[87]

News and information are not only public goods in an economic sense; they also serve "the public good" in a socially beneficial sense. Thus, journalism's value to society transcends the revenue that it generates. Put differently, journalism produces *positive externalities* (benefits that accrue to parties outside of direct economic transactions)—such as maintaining an informed populace—that are vitally important for a healthy democratic society. Many public goods—clean air, open space, artificial light, and knowledge, to name only a few—all produce tremendous positive externalities. A classic example of a public good is a lighthouse, which is a kind of essential infrastructure that ships need to navigate coastlines, but no cost-effective way exists to make people pay for it. Instead, people will "free ride," which takes away market incentives to provide the good.[88] Society requires these goods, but individuals typically undervalue them because they are unable or unwilling to pay for their full costs, which leads to the market under-producing them.

News and information should be further qualified as "merit goods" whose production should not depend on popular choice or "consumer sovereignty" but rather on social need.[89] Christopher Ali, a leading scholar on the subject, notes that "merit goods are based on a normative assumption that the good should be provided regardless of consumption habits."[90] Regardless of what the market or individual consumers demand, society as a whole benefits when local journalists report on school board hearings or highway infrastructure—decidedly unsexy stories that do not make for good clickbait. Nonetheless, this kind of information is vitally important for democratic societies. Such news media qualifies as a merit good because individual consumers, left to their own devices, are likely to underinvest in it. The media expert Karol Jakubowicz offers the example of commercial radio not producing the quality fare that democracy requires: "Good broadcasting is a 'merit' good—just as with education, training, or health," which means "consumers, if left to themselves, tend to take less care to obtain it than is in their own long-term interests."[91] Instead of leaving such decisions up to the market or individual consumer preferences, prioritizing merit goods places social value on social *needs* instead of individual *wants*.[92]

High-quality journalism—like many public goods that exhibit positive externalities—has rarely been supported by direct market transactions. News media traditionally have been funded by other means, such as public subsidies or, to some degree, advertising revenue.[93] The cultural and social benefits of high-quality news and information often far exceed their pecuniary value. Even members of society who are not directly paying for these services still benefit from their role in disseminating information about important socio-political issues. But unless commercial providers are incentivized or simply mandated by government to address those public needs, they do not reliably provide such content. Simply put: Producing high-quality information is often an unprofitable enterprise for media outlets. Many countries therefore ensure its availability via nonmarket-based mechanisms such as regulations and subsidies that range from public service broadcasting to content requirements.[94]

Given the structural constraints of market-driven media, public media can cover issues and regions ignored by commercial media.[95] For example, public media can focus on providing public affairs and cultural programming; serving the needs of children, ethnic minorities, communities of color, and other frequently underserved groups; as well as delivering services to rural areas that are commercially unviable. Studies show that a widely available public broadcasting system can actually reduce the overall cost of programs available to the public.[96] Universal access to high-quality news content is a social priority, but the market often fails to support this vital infrastructure for democratic society. This situation amounts to various kinds of "market failure" in our media institutions.[97]

Journalism Crisis = Market Failure

The crisis in journalism is more than an instance of failing to invest in a public good. A structural analysis suggests that the contemporary crisis in journalism should be considered an active market failure. The concept "market failure," a term I have used several times thus far, generally denotes the market's inability to efficiently allocate socially necessary goods and services. Market failures often arise when private firms do not adequately fund critical infrastructures and social services because the anticipated returns do not justify the expenditures.[98] Market failure is also exacerbated when consumers fail to pay for such services' full societal benefit. In the United States, large-scale public investments, for instance, in education, a national highway system, and other essential services and infrastructures have traditionally been justified through the language of market failure. For example, universal service in telecommunications is socially desirable but economically inefficient, particularly in sparsely populated areas, resulting in an urban-rural divide. For that reason, government may provide subsidies in the form of tax benefits to telecommunication companies to encourage universal access.

Commercial media models are particularly prone to market failure because news rarely pays for itself. For the past one hundred and fifty years, news media have been supported by what was essentially an advertising subsidy. Advertisers were not paying for news media directly; instead they were paying to have access to audiences' eyes and ears. News was a by-product—a positive externality—from the primary exchange between media owners and advertisers.[99] Advertisers were never especially concerned about whether their revenues supported foreign bureaus or good local news; they were chasing consumers. Large conglomerates, for their part, often have a fiduciary duty to maximize shareholder value. Therefore, it is entirely rational, given their economic incentives, for commercial media firms to underinvest in systems, infrastructures, and content that do not provide adequate—and often short-term—returns. In other words: What is good for the news business is often suboptimal for democracy.

Many democratic societies have long used a market failure rationale to maintain healthy public media systems, especially public broadcasting services. Policy regimes in these countries recognize that commercial media markets tend toward concentration and produce both negative and positive externalities that require government regulation.[100] In recent decades, however, the growing ascendency of a neoliberal political economy—one marked by privatization, deregulation, and increased commercialization of core social institutions—has weakened such policy arrangements and amplified market failure in many countries.[101]

Market failure is a central cause of the lack of quality journalism and the ongoing disinvestment in news production. While these trends are occurring around the world, they are especially evident in the United States. As I will further delineate in the next chapter, US news institutions—especially the newspaper industry—have witnessed a declining number of journalists, revenues, and circulation. Bankruptcies are on the rise, with leading metro dailies reducing or ending home deliveries as they convert to primarily web-based outlets. In addition to the underproduction of news media, limited accessible broadband internet services in poor and rural areas—sometimes referred to as "digital redlining"—is another market failure.

Various kinds of market failures that specifically affect media industries stem from structural problems, including oligopolistic concentration.[102] Profit-maximizing behavior can be particularly problematic in noncompetitive markets if it results in too little production and consumption because the price is set above marginal cost. Uncompetitive markets may lead to the abuse of market power and other perverse incentives that work against the maximization of social welfare, resulting in a media system's degradation. Another kind of market failure affecting news media access and dissemination is a lack of interconnection between communication networks, a longstanding problem for telecommunication, broadband, and cable television networks.

Specific challenges also arise because commercial media often involve two-sided markets since news products are sold to both advertisers and consumers. Commercial media often provide free or low-cost content to attract audiences' attention to sell to advertisers. Historically, this arrangement has invited market failure because advertising revenue typically outweighs the value of consumer payments (e.g., subscriptions), which privileges advertiser needs over those of audiences. Therefore, maximizing advertising revenue in turn incentivizes ownership concentration and consolidation because large media institutions can better reach mass audiences.[103] Other drawbacks stemming from dependence on advertising revenue are that advertising is biased against strongly held preferences by a statistical minority, and advertisers do not care about the utility derived by viewers, just the fact of exposure.[104] Another kind of media market failure arises from the economies of scale and scope, including high first-copy costs that disproportionately advantage large incumbents. Given the diminishing costs and increasing profits associated with making copies of media products, large companies benefit from being able to afford the higher costs for first copies of original news content, with subsequent mass production at much lower costs.[105]

Many of the scenarios described here represent what I refer to as "systemic market failure." In other words, these failures are endemic to commercial media. They are always present and can never be fully eliminated (unless media are taken out of the market entirely), but smart public policy can help control for them. Different market structures may experience different failures to varying degrees, and various incentives and subsidies can be built into a policy system to help minimize or offset these problems. A number of creative methods exist that can help compensate for democratic deficits created by the decline of commercial news media.[106] Systemic market failure has created a wide range of problems, from the loss of local journalism to a lack of affordable and accessible internet services. For too long, we have let market fundamentalism prevent discussion of potential government responses. The crisis in US journalism is rapidly approaching a "point of no return." Now is the time to push for nonmarket alternatives.

Beyond Market Failure

Using "market failure" as the central framework for understanding the journalism crisis should not imply that under normal circumstances, the market is working just fine. Again, these problems evidence *systemic* market failure— a few tweaks here and there would not return journalism to its former health. Market failure has never been fully eradicated in commercial news media systems, and the US experiment of expecting a commercial press to provide public service journalism has always been a fraught enterprise. After 2008, long-standing structural tensions within the system metastasized. The current crisis presents a tantalizing opportunity for structural change—an opportunity that thus far has been squandered. The journalism crisis must be recontextualized and reframed in a way that moves the debate toward implementing structural alternatives that can sustain independent journalism. Before doing so, however, we must first explore, in more detail, just how the contemporary journalism crisis is manifesting in newsrooms across the country. The next chapter explores these issues alongside the strengths and weaknesses of major alternatives to the advertising revenue model for journalism.

3

How Commercialism Degrades Journalism

While journalism's downward slide has only worsened, the initial alarm bells have long since receded. Since 2009, the phrase "journalism crisis" has faded from conversation, and some commentators even risked optimism. In 2014, the venerable Pew Research Center enthusiastically reported that "digital native" news outlets had created five thousand new jobs.[1] Others celebrated the flexibility of digital journalism and the expansion of "explanatory" and "long form" journalism. One group of scholars chided "materialists" for fixating on economic factors like the loss of journalism jobs and, as they put it, overly "gloomy predictions." The authors called for a more "open-ended and also more hopeful argument," with a focus on the "cultural codes driving new journalistic practices allow[ing] creative pathways to be discovered for sustaining journalistic commitments through digital technology and new organizational forms."[2] A different kind of wishful thinking occurred immediately after the 2016 presidential election, when a "Trump Bump" propelled a sudden spike in newspaper subscriptions. Some observers thought we had turned a corner; surely, now, journalism would begin to rebound.[3]

Each case proved to be a false dawn. The print news industry's downward death-spiral continues unabated. While new digital models such as *BuzzFeed, Vox,* and *Vice* initially inspired much hope that they would come to replace the old journalism, nearly all major indicators now show a troubling and indisputable decline in terms of both quantity and quality. These ongoing trends make it all but certain that by the time this book is published, journalism' decline will have only quickened.[4]

Commercial media in the United States have always been structurally flawed, but Americans usually had access to some form of local news. This increasingly is no longer the case, and the loss of local journalism is just one symptom of a dysfunctional news media system. In the following sections, I trace the degradations that manifest with the structural collapse of commercial journalism.[5] I describe how the media landscape has shifted in

Democracy Without Journalism?. Victor Pickard, Oxford University Press (2020). © Victor Pickard
DOI: 10.1093/oso/9780190946753.001.0001

recent years, and how experts, journalists, and the broader US public have fallen prey to rarely examined assumptions and misconceptions about journalism. The situation is not entirely hopeless: the last third of the chapter discusses alternatives to advertising-dependent news media. I argue that we have already lost precious time desperately searching for entrepreneurial and technological fixes instead of crafting public policies to directly confront the crisis. As a first step toward reforming it, we must appraise the design flaws in the existing commercial media system.

The New US Media Landscape

While newspapers' digital advertising revenue has grown in recent years, this uptick does not come close to compensating for the enormous losses in traditional advertising revenue. The Pew Research Center's reports have consistently cast these trends into stark relief over many years. As early as 2012, a Pew study found that, since 2003, declines of up to 50 percent in print advertising revenue were barely offset by gains in online advertising revenue. Losses outnumbered gains by ten to one.[6] Since then, these trends have continued and worsened for most newspapers, with digital advertising failing to make up for lost revenues from print advertising and subscriptions.[7] With print advertising revenue permanently gone, has anything taken its place?[8]

Digital Start-Ups

In recent years, a new crop of digital start-ups—including the previously mentioned *BuzzFeed, Vox,* and *Vice*—have burst on to the media scene. On the surface, their appearance seemed to suggest a greater abundance of media outlets and consumer choices. But the gloss of diversity masks an underlying uniformity in media ownership and control. A number of scholars and journalists have pointed out that in many media sectors, ownership concentration is actually *increasing*, and many of these new entities are owned or supported by the very legacy media companies they purportedly displace.[9] Indeed, old media and telecommunication giants, including AT&T, Verizon, Disney, Comcast, Time Warner, and others, have quietly invested millions of dollars into these new outlets, sometimes even buying them outright. Netflix, Google, Amazon, and Apple are also increasingly moving into content production and distribution.[10] Meanwhile, big media companies continue to get bigger via endless mergers and acquisitions.[11] In recent years, regulators have green-lighted several mega-mergers—such as AT&T and Time Warner and Disney and 21st Century Fox—to create media behemoths. While new players occasionally gain footholds on the internet, scholarship has long shown that established media corporations dominate online traffic and audience attention (I expand on this point in the next chapter). This concentration of power challenges the notion that the digital media landscape has elevated new voices and viewpoints.[12]

Despite significant investment from legacy media and venture capitalists, digital start-ups turned out to be a kind of financial bubble that has steadily deflated since 2017. Since then, leading digital news outlets have significantly missed quarterly profit expectations, lost the backing of venture capital, and laid off many reporters.[13] To give just a few examples of this decline: In early 2018, *Vox* laid off fifty staffers, representing 5 percent of its workforce.[14] During consecutive weeks in early 2019, *Buzzfeed* and *Vice* each laid off well over two hundred reporters, respectively 15 and 10 percent of their work forces.[15] With digital advertising revenue increasingly scarce for all outlets other than Google and Facebook, it seems increasingly likely that these previously celebrated digital outlets lack economic viability for the long term, especially at their current size.

The rise and fall of another celebrated digital newcomer, *Gawker*, brings into focus troubling vulnerabilities in the new digital media ecosystem.[16] *Gawker* appeared to be an exemplar of a new kind of journalism, one that could skewer elites as it reaped the fruits of digital advertising. While *Gawker* tended toward sensationalistic and tawdry coverage, it was also capable of hard-hitting reporting. Its general irreverence toward the powerful and famous led to some independent investigative journalism over the years, such as reporting the scandal in which retired General David Petraeus, then director of the Central Intelligence Agency, leaked classified information to his mistress.[17] Gawker was also the first major digital media company to unionize.[18]

Then along came Peter Thiel, a libertarian billionaire out of Silicon Valley. Thiel, reportedly seeking vengeance for an earlier piece in *Gawker* about his sexual orientation, bankrolled a libel lawsuit by retired professional wrestler Hulk Hogan, who himself had been the target of an earlier exposé. The litigation forced *Gawker* into bankruptcy. As a former *Gawker* editor succinctly put it, the news site folded simply because "one wealthy person maliciously set out to destroy it, spending millions of dollars in secret," demonstrating that there is "no freedom in this world but power and money."[19] Beyond raising troubling questions about threats to press freedoms, the *Gawker* affair revealed US journalism's powerlessness in the face of billionaires and corporations. Monied interests are increasingly determining what is publishable and what we can see and say in the media.[20] Journalism requires considerable resources and institutional support, yet good journalism will inevitably anger the powerful. What happened to *Gawker* could conceivably happen to any media outlet—especially smaller, independent organizations without access to the finances necessary to fend off lawsuits. Such inequities portend a dark future of deferential journalism and unassailable power. Signs of economic weakness are no less grim in legacy media.

Legacy Newspapers

The US newspaper industry has been in dramatic freefall in recent years, but some patterns have been unfolding for decades. While for many years the overall number of US daily newspapers remained relatively stable, the number of independent papers fell by nearly 50 percent from 1955–1985 as large newspaper chains acquired them, one by one.[21] Such chains were already a growing concern by the late nineteenth century, but wealthy individuals or families owned and controlled most major magazines and newspapers. From roughly 1965 to 2005, however, media ownership increasingly transitioned to publicly traded companies that expanded into large chains.[22] Newspapers' value increased as they transitioned from family-owned to publicly traded companies with shareholders, which in turn incentivized owners to sell their controlling shares to newspaper chains for high profits.[23] These chains rapidly expanded as they acquired previously independent newspaper companies. For example, Gannett, one of the largest chains, owns *USA Today* and more than one hundred other daily newspapers.[24]

While a private company can decide to de-emphasize profits, a publicly traded company is legally obliged to maximize shareholder value. Moreover, by the 1990s, investors were increasingly expecting short-term returns. Escalating pressure for strong quarterly earnings encouraged companies to cut costs to inflate profits instead of reinvesting in newsgathering capacities for the long term.[25] This focus on commercial value often conflicts with journalism's professional standards, democratic concerns, and commitments to local communities. Some newspapers have mitigated these commercial pressures through different ownership structures. For example, after the *Washington Post* went public in 1971, the longtime family owners (the Grahams) continued to control voting stock. Similarly, the *New York Times* has for many years maintained a two-tiered stock ownership structure that gives the Sulzberger family some degree of control.[26] Such safeguards can buffer news organizations, allowing publishers to absorb short-term losses and avoid cost-cutting measures. Thus, in some cases, private ownership might liberate news organizations from Wall Street's imperatives.[27]

Private ownership, however, can also expose media outlets to the same pressures as publicly traded companies. In addition to problems with hidden political agendas and a lack of transparency, this ownership structure's venality can far surpass other models. Exhibit A is one of the fastest-growing forms of media ownership: the private equity firm. Seven such investment groups own over a thousand US newspapers (nearly 15 percent of all US papers).[28] Half of the ten largest newspaper owners in the United States are now investment firms, including New Media/Gatehouse, which is in the process of merging with Gannett to create a newspaper "megachain," and Digital First Media, which is notorious for acquiring and stripping down papers.[29] As Daniel Kishi, the associate editor of the *American Conservative* notes, these newspaper chains' absentee owners make decisions that "no longer reflect long-term sustainability, but instead seek to maximize a short-term return on investment."[30]

Because their primary loyalties are to their shareholders and not to local communities, these investment firms can aggressively buy up and then bleed out already-suffering newspaper companies before harvesting them for parts. An exposé in the *Nation* revealed that Wall Street tycoon Randall Smith, owner of the hedge fund Digital First Media, acquired and gutted scores of hometown papers across the United States to amass the $57 million he spent on sixteen mansions in Palm Beach, Florida. The article argued that such firms qualify as "vulture funds" because they target bankrupt and struggling companies "to invest in at rock-bottom prices." After finding ways "to squeeze out maximum profit, from cutting costs to collecting debt repayments at high interest rates . . . they leave the bones behind as they fly off in search of the next opportunity."[31] The newspaper economist Ken Doctor noted that Alden Global Capital, the majority owner of Digital First, was "wrecking" local journalism as it pulled in a whopping 17 percent operating margin and profits of almost $160 million in its 2017 fiscal year—far beyond what its peers were accumulating.[32] The *Washington Post* reported that the hedge fund's "mercenary strategy" entailed first slashing photographers, reporters, and editors, and then selling off newspapers' real estate, including their office buildings and printing plants.[33]

In the spring of 2018, this predatory behavior culminated with *Denver Post* journalists staging an "open revolt" against their owner, Digital First.[34] They published a brave editorial indicting the hedge fund for mismanaging the paper, lamenting that "the fracturing of newsrooms" has encouraged "political interests to lavish investments in echo-chamber outlets that merely seek to report from biased perspectives, leaving the hollowed-out shells of newsrooms loyal to traditional journalistic values to find their voice in the maelstrom." If newsroom owners see profits as their only goal, the editorial continued, "quality, reliability, and accountability suffer." Therefore, "The course correction" for "communities across the land" requires "owners committed to serving their readers and viewers and users." If, as many assume, the *Denver Post* soon becomes "rotting bones," a "major city in an important political region will find itself without a newspaper."[35]

Fears that had once seemed hyperbolic are now a distinct reality. In 2009, before the *Rocky Mountain News* closed, Denver had around six hundred print journalists. After this recent round of layoffs, the city had fewer than seventy reporters.[36] Going forward, the situation in Denver is a case study of what happens when society treats newsrooms like devalued commodities instead of essential public services. These ownership trends have escalated over the past several decades, further reducing accountability to the local communities that newspapers purportedly serve. And this situation will likely only worsen in the coming years as investment firms, understanding there is no long-term profitable future for newspapers, will continue to bleed them dry. In early 2019, Digital First sought to also acquire the Gannett newspaper chain, which caused universal condemnation.[37]

Over the past decade, newspapers' era of high profits ended dramatically, as advertising revenue rapidly declined and the dominant commercial model collapsed. This has been a staggering descent for an industry that was, until relatively recently, making obscene amounts of money. In the 1980s and 1990s, most large newspaper companies had profit margins exceeding 20 percent; advertising revenue continued to climb steadily into the 2000s. Indeed, until about 2005, newspaper companies were incredibly profitable, maintaining 20 to 30—sometimes as high as 40—percent profit margins.[38]

But because US newspapers relied on advertising revenue for roughly 80 percent of their aggregate revenues, they were particularly vulnerable to specific kinds of market fluctuations and failures.[39] This structural vulnerability
helps explain why the US newspaper industry is suffering more than many of
its international counterparts.

Death by a Thousand Paper Cuts

While several high-profile newspaper closures have received the most
attention—especially in the few remaining two-paper cities—the journalism
crisis has hurt all papers. Leading national papers such as the *New York Times*
and the *Washington Post* have bounced back—even reporting profits in recent years.[40] Indeed, the divide between the haves and have-nots is evident
with the big three—the *New York Times*, the *Washington Post*, and the *Wall
Street Journal*—prospering, while nearly all other newspapers flounder.[41]
Smaller-circulation papers serving mid-sized cities, community papers, and
large metro areas outside of Washington and New York have all continued to
lose paid circulation for years.[42] As circulation falls, the number of bankruptcies climbs. Among the nation's top one hundred newspapers, twenty-two
filed for bankruptcy between 2005 and 2015.[43]

A number of these outlets—again, these are newspapers that ranked in
the top one hundred by circulation only fifteen years ago—have ceased
publication entirely, merged with other newspapers, reduced home delivery, or have gone online-only, cutting all but a handful of staff. As a result, residents of major US cities, including Birmingham, Cleveland,
Detroit, and Pittsburgh, no longer have a daily home-delivered newspaper.
When newspapers cease their print operation and go online-only, much
of their audience simply disappears—or at least their audience's *attention*
disappears—as their degraded product is forced to compete with innumerable online content creators. A study that examined the British general-
interest newspaper the *Independent*, for example, found that the total time
its audience spent with its content fell by 81 percent after the transition to a
web-based format, suggesting significant differences in the habits of online
and print readers.[44] A related problem is that once a paper goes online in
the United States, it immediately runs up against a still-significant digital
divide (a point I return to in the next chapter). One study found that after

a century-old, small-town paper closed, residents faced many problems accessing the new digital-only alternative, which eventually succumbed to public pressure and began printing hard copies of its paper.[45] Newspapers' digital transition has also led to a decrease in the quality of information that they publish. A study led by media studies scholar Vicki Mayer tracked the content of the *Times-Picayune* newspaper from before it reduced home delivery through its move to an online-only newspaper in 2011, finding that the web-based version of the newspaper featured more soft news stories and contained fewer sources.[46]

The number of papers cutting home delivery or going online-only will undoubtedly expand in the coming years, as will bankruptcies. In 2017, high-profile papers, such as Alaska's largest newspaper and an award-winning newspaper in West Virginia, have gone bankrupt.[47] More recently, the hundred-and-fifty-year old *Reading Eagle* in Pennsylvania filed for bankruptcy.[48] No evidence suggests that the trend of bankruptcy and online-only publication is slowing down; if anything, it is only accelerating.[49] The long-time journalism observer and director of the Nieman Journalism Lab, Joshua Benton, astutely observes that "the story of the last decade-plus hasn't been about mass *closures*—it's been about mass *shrinkage*."[50] While actual closures have been relatively modest and consistent (so far), he observes that with each year "just about every daily paper has gotten smaller—smaller newsroom, smaller budgets, smaller print runs, smaller page counts . . . It's death by a thousand paper cuts." With daily print newspaper subscribers either moving to digital formats or literally dying off, he argues, the inevitable not-too-distant future will see the "print costs" and "print revenues" lines on an accountant's projection sheet intersect. At that point, Benton notes, "it'll be time to stop the presses for good." Newspapers will then face the option of either going online-only or shutting down entirely.

Many newspapers have responded to these economic pressures with aggressive layoffs. The American Society of News Editors estimated that from 2005 to 2015 the number of people employed by the news industry declined by nearly 40 percent.[51] In 2016, the organization announced it would stop estimating the number of jobs lost. Similarly, the Bureau of Labor Statistics found that newspaper publishers have lost over half of their employees since 2001.[52]

Another much-maligned contributor to journalism's demise is Craigslist and its free classified advertising model, which singlehandedly wiped out a major revenue source for newspapers. However, this blow to newspapers' business model was only one visible manifestation of a deeper problem, a pre-existing structural vulnerability with the commercial model. Even if Craigslist never existed, there is simply no reliable business model as readers and advertisers move online where the vast majority of digital advertising revenue—again, only a fraction of its print counterpart—is siphoned off to online platforms and search engines that host links to the original news content. Monopolistic internet firms such as Google and Facebook increasingly serve as consumers' point of entry to this news content. This "duopoly" is now collecting around 85 percent of every new dollar spent on digital advertising.[53] With the newspaper industry losing tens of billions of dollars in annual advertising revenue since 2000, it is safe to assume that these revenue streams will never return.

Newspaper companies have attempted to compensate for lost revenues by ruthlessly cutting costs, but it is unclear how much more there is to cut. Cost-cutting is a short-term tactic with long-term negative consequences. The media economist Ken Doctor notes that, as a general strategy, cost-cutting measures create a vicious cycle: "As publishers cut back on newsprint, cutting sections and pages, they worsened their value proposition with their best and most loyal, high-paying customers: their print subscribers." As newspapers continue to decrease in quality—filling their pages with more advertising, syndicated news, and fluffy human-interest stories—the incentive for actually buying a paper attenuates over time. Doctor warns, "Even subscribers who were loyal for decades are cancelling."[54] And there is evidence to bear this out. Public opinion data suggest that US readers have noticed the industry's cutbacks and responded accordingly by no longer paying for these services. For example, a 2013 Pew study found that 31 percent of people surveyed reported deserting a particular news outlet because of its degraded news and information.[55]

This death spiral seemingly has no end. As I noted in the introduction to this book, in 2016, after showing how daily circulation, advertising revenue, and newsroom staffing had all significantly fallen since the previous year, the Pew Research Center concluded that the industry may have crossed "a point of no return."[56] If the collapse of journalism is truly imminent, it is a serious social problem worthy of a national conversation, but no such conversation has occurred. In the meantime, deep structural pathologies endemic to commercial journalism are manifesting in a myriad of ways, all to democracy's detriment.

Symptoms of Journalism's Degradation

With the slow-but-sure collapse of its business model, a number of symptoms have become increasingly visible, especially as some news organizations double down on an ever-failing advertising revenue model. These problems fall into several categories: specific social harms associated with new virulent types of advertising; the rise of news deserts and news divides; and an overall growing precarity in news labor.

The Harms of Digital Advertising

News organizations continue to seek ways to maximize advertising revenue, even as its efficacy becomes increasingly dubious. This endless pursuit of increasingly elusive profits encourages "clickbait," a slavish devotion to news metrics, and other practices that further degrade journalism. The rise of clickbait recalls similar problems associated with yellow journalism 125 years ago. One prominent historian of this period has noted how journalists wrote stories "as 'written bait,' to make the public take in ads."[57] Similar practices today reflect digital news outlets' need to tailor their content in ways that capture users' attention and generate advertising revenue.[58]

Recent research indicates that commercial news organizations are relying on social media—especially Facebook—to reach audiences.[59] Increasingly, monopolistic internet firms such as Google and Facebook serve as consumers' point of entry. This shift has reshaped journalism in profound ways.[60] Journalism's overreliance on Facebook, in particular, has several troubling consequences. In an interview with the Shorenstein Center, the media studies scholar Siva Vaidhyanathan noted, "Editors and designers are constantly making decisions based on what works on Facebook, so they choose images and write headlines to pander to Facebook's algorithms and the behavior of Facebook users." According to Vaidhyanathan, "the more that journalists pander to Facebook . . . the more that Facebook becomes the governing mechanism to journalism." At the same time, he notes, journalists feed the beast that is cutting off their sustenance. While Facebook pockets most of the money, "journalistic outlets create more content for Facebook and sometimes pay Facebook to promote it. It's all absurd."[61]

Vaidhyanathan and other critics point out that this exploitative relationship pervades every aspect of news labor and content—from the nature of media work to how journalists frame stories. Reporters internalize an almost-instinctual awareness that some stories and images are better suited than others for capturing attention on Facebook. Facebook's position as the sole portal to millions of readers forces journalists—many of whom are facing intense job insecurity—into tailoring their reporting according to clickbait criteria. Moreover, editors reinforce this unhealthy dependence by constantly informing reporters how their work is performing on Facebook so that journalists have real-time analytics flashing across their screens. Some newsrooms even display wall-mounted data dashboards—essentially scoreboards—displaying the social media metrics of specific stories, creating a perverse obsession over audience analytics provided by platforms such as Chartbeat, Parse.ly or Google analytics.[62] These dynamics encourage journalists to produce controversial and sensational content, priming more people to engage with and argue over stories. Generating controversy in turn generates more advertising revenue—which mostly goes to Facebook instead of the journalists who create the content.[63]

Online news outlets increasingly rely on these metrics to provide incessant feedback about how well particular stories fare on social media. Although the constant measurement has had a detrimental effect on journalistic routines, some observers have rosily suggested that this practice allows journalists to become more attuned and responsive to their audiences' desires—in a sense, democratizing the news. However, others have shown that the use of news metrics can be stressful and demoralizing for journalists. Media sociologist Caitlin Petre argues that such metrics are a vivid manifestation of how intensified commercial pressures are restructuring newsrooms in profound ways. She found that these audience analytics extract increased productivity in news workers while overshadowing other kinds of evaluations—such as normative objectives for advancing a social mission—that are not easily measurable.[64] Other analyses reveal how such metrics ultimately force reporters to pander to their readers' passing whims, treating audiences as apolitical entertainment seekers rather than engaged citizens of a democratic society. One careful study on the ethics of web metrics for journalism systematically shows how this market-based approach to journalism privileges soft news, conflates consumer choice with democratic needs, and reduces audience engagement to a commercial transaction. The study concludes by reminding us that "journalism serves a purpose above and beyond its immediate commercial audience."[65]

Digital advertising degrades journalism beyond the search for clickbait and eyeballs. Even more troubling than the constant bombardment of annoying pop-up ads is news organizations' frequent practice of deceptive and invasive forms of advertising. "Native advertising," a phrase sometimes used interchangeably with "branded journalism" and "sponsored content," has become a revenue mainstay for both new digital outlets such as *Buzzfeed* and older, more established magazines, such as the *Atlantic*. Blurring the divide between news and advertising, these practices range from the mostly innocuous "infomercial" to a more problematic variety of corporate propaganda. Whereas news organizations historically worked with outside advertising firms, today's media companies are increasingly crafting their own advertising in-house to better coordinate with their news content. At the behest of particular brands, *Buzzfeed*'s own "BuzzFeed Creative," a prominent source of the company's revenue, is dedicated to creating custom video and list-style advertising that resembles its editorial content.[66] An exposé of *New York Times*' shop T Brand Studio revealed that advertisers are constantly pushing the *Times* to coordinate "with the newsroom in deeper and more complex ways" and that publishers are partnering with advertisers to customize content "without being transparent to readers about these deals."[67]

In some ways, so-called "native advertising" is as old as commercial advertising. One of the first policy battles over misinformation, the Newspaper Publicity Act of 1912, focused on "disguised advertisements" in newspapers.[68] Early commercial radio broadcasters surreptitiously advertised products during its regular programming, which was sponsored by specific companies (hence the term "soap operas"), sometimes even running radio advertisements that mimicked newscasts.[69] Nonetheless, the acceptable norms for bounding advertising have shifted dramatically in recent years as media companies seek new revenue sources. While the ethical barrier between journalism's editorial and advertising divisions—metaphorically called the church/state divide and the much-vaunted "Chinese wall"—was always imperfect, this construct has abruptly collapsed.

To give a sense of how quickly this shift occurred, consider an incident from the spring of 2009. The *Los Angeles Times* caused a huge controversy when it crafted a front-page advertisement about NBC's show "Southland" that resembled a news column. At the time, readers widely ridiculed the decision, seeing it as a shocking move by one of the nation's major reputable papers. The *New York Times* reported that it "raised questions about how far newspapers would go to please advertisers."[70] From today's perspective, we can see that it was a harbinger of things to come. Within a few years, such practices had become the new normal, with media organizations blurring the boundaries between news and advertising, and corporations even creating their own media outlets. The *Washington Post* reported that "Dozens of companies, including Boeing, General Electric, Pepsi, American Express and Verizon Wireless, are becoming their own publishers, creating and distributing 'content'—articles, videos, photos—that would be right at home in a traditional newspaper, magazine, or TV program." The article noted that this new kind of publishing "doesn't just blur the line between journalism and product promotion—it all but obliterates it." The article quoted a Verizon spokesman who said: "We don't see our jobs as being P.R. people anymore. We see our jobs as publishers . . . [who] compete against [the news]."[71] Verizon's short-lived faux news outlet "SugarString" did exactly that by providing its own version of "brand publishing" that tried to pass as just another tech-focused news outlet—though it reportedly forbade its writers to discuss such politically fraught topics as net neutrality and government surveillance.[72]

These increasingly common forms of advertising are deeply problematic.[73] They deliberately blur the distinction between news and advertising, with the difference typically indicated only in small print. However, studies consistently show that the majority of readers miss such statements and are unaware that they are reading advertising-driven content.[74] Ethical concerns about misinformation, public trust, and social responsibility are rising to the fore, especially as native advertising becomes more prevalent. Media studies scholar Mara Einstein, who has researched this process extensively, finds that "covert selling" within online news media is now rampant.[75] Bob Garfield, another vocal critic, notes that native advertising amounts to a "Faustian bargain," nothing more than "the latest gimmick for infusing a dying old industry (and a sickly new one) with desperately needed cash."[76]

In 2015, the FTC briefly scrutinized such practices, but the agency has taken little concrete action beyond providing guidelines and calling for greater self-regulation.[77] Native advertising's defenders argue that readers are generally not concerned about where content comes from, as long as it is good, informative, or funny. Despite such self-serving rationalizations, obfuscating the source of news content—a telltale sign of propaganda—is always dangerous for a democratic society. Deception is inherent to this kind of advertising. Determining appropriate standards—or whether such advertising should be allowed at all—requires public scrutiny and debate.

Online media, like print media before them, continue to face various types of market censorship stemming from advertisers' influence on news content and commentary. This long-standing tension broke through the surface when *Buzzfeed* took down an article written by a journalist who had criticized a Dove advertising campaign. Management removed the article because it ran afoul of the perceived interests of Dove's parent company Unilever, a major advertiser on *Buzzfeed*. The editor determined that the critical article had the wrong "tone" for the section in which it was published.[78] This "Dovegate" episode gives the lie to the argument that we have nothing to fear from advertisers' influence on digital journalism. Beyond misleading readers, native advertising may subtly skew media content in general toward pro-corporate narratives.

The Dove episode stands out for its overt censorship, but the increasingly cozy relationship between advertisers and news organizations invites less obvious forms of self-censorship and editorial decisions that distort public discourse around important and controversial issues. Journalists may learn not to take on stories that they know will challenge the commercial interests of their news organization. As the distinctions between advertising and news operations continue to blur, and the marketing office has more sway over news reporting, we can expect more of these controversies in the future. This shift in the economics of digital news should force journalists—and society as a whole—to have a serious conversation about the changing relationship between legitimate news and advertising.

Advertising that relies on invasive behavioral tracking and surveillance is arguably even more ethically dubious than these already troubling practices. A study I conducted with computer scientist Tim Libert shows how news organizations are among the worst culprits in exposing their digital readers to third-party advertisers and data brokers. We found that browsing news-related websites exposed readers to more than twice as much tracking as the rest of the web, with an average of nineteen third parties compared to an overall average on non-news websites of eight third parties.[79] On the day that we conducted our study, the *New York Times* subjected readers—most likely without their knowledge—to forty-four third-parties.[80]

This invisible network of trackers routinely captures information from internet users as they visit news sites, allowing companies to create consumer profiles by monitoring which pages its readers visit. While many of these sites may be innocuous, it is likely that some are not, and oversight is almost non-existent. We found that in some cases, news sites leaked readers' information to such data brokers as Experian and Acxiom. These companies sell personal information and bundle people into consumer "segments," with categories ranging from "Power Elite" and "American Royalty" to "Small Town Shallow Pockets" and "Urban Survivors."[81] Without proper regulation that mandates disclosure and transparency, these companies can effectively use consumer data however they wish. Although these firms typically claim not to sell "personally identifiable information," there are well-founded fears that "anonymous" data can be combined with other information, such as email addresses, that link back to real names. In addition to violating personal privacy protections, this kind of data manipulation can be used to target specific demographics and discriminate against minorities and other vulnerable groups. Nonetheless, the vast majority of readers make these transactions unwittingly, routinely sacrificing their privacy to read news for "free."[82]

Libert and I likened surveillance-funded journalism to a villainous "clown car" of trackers driving into your living room to issue an endless parade of marketers hopping out and competing with each other to peek over your shoulder while you read news online.[83] Some readers have defended themselves by deploying ad-blocking software. In response, publishers have decried ad blockers as "unethical," even arguing that blocking ads is equivalent to stealing content—that, by not allowing themselves to be subject to advertising, readers are not "paying" for journalism. The CEO of the Interactive Advertising Bureau has claimed that "ad blocking is robbery" that could lead to an "internet apocalypse." Nonetheless, twenty-six percent of users reportedly are now blocking ads.[84] By attempting to block the blockers, publishers instigated an unwinnable war with readers.

The future of such unethical advertising may become even more insidious as news organizations develop more covert and sophisticated methods, such as targeting people based on their emotions.[85] Data scientists are designing predictive algorithms for news publishers based on the findings that articles eliciting feelings of "love, sadness and fear, performed significantly better than articles that were not."[86] With an increasing number of news outlets tailoring advertising to mesh with "psychographic" instead of demographic information, Emily Bell, director of the Tow Center for Digital Journalism, rightly notes that the "implications of targeting based on mood and attitude remain troublingly creepy."[87] Once again, these practices suggest that the digital advertising industry deserves much closer regulatory oversight.

Despite all of the evidence that the digital advertising model was unsustainable, many news organizations have doubled-down on a failed revenue strategy in recent years. At times, media companies have seemed to shift from advertising-supported journalism to journalism-supported advertising. While some news organizations are supposedly trying to rely less on digital advertising revenue, these practices remain a persistent scourge in need of public discussion and regulatory intervention. Given that behavioral advertising and surveillance have become the commercial internet's core business model, it is deeply problematic that the future of the press has been pegged to such unprincipled practices.

Precarity of Journalistic Labor

As news organizations cut costs and chase ever-diminishing revenues, increasing austerity translates to not only fewer jobs, but also lower-paid jobs with fewer—if any—benefits. Deteriorating news work conditions are rising in tandem with an increasing dependency on volunteer and casualized labor. In the midst of all of this, newsrooms are asking journalists to do more with less time and fewer resources. Dean Starkman famously likened this news work to the "hamster wheel," and others have referred to it as the "hamsterization" of journalism, by which news workers have to continuously take on more digital labor. This growing precarity has been accompanied by a wide variety of new methods to phase out full-time journalists, including a greater reliance on freelancers, interns, and even robots.[88] Meanwhile, business advisers and media pundits counsel news organizations to be more nimble, lean, and efficient. Tapping into libertarian ideas that the market is infallible and government has no role in ameliorating social problems, such discourses mask the material reality of economic distress and worsening work conditions.

The casualization of journalistic labor has also created legions of semi-employed news workers who must spend much of their time simply looking for short-term writing gigs. What communication scholar Nicole Cohen calls "entrepreneurial journalism" has become the only option for many struggling freelancers. Discourse around this phenomenon, she writes, "promotes a notion of the enterprising individual journalist forging a career for herself through practices of self-branding and self-employment and learning to be adaptable, flexible, and self-sufficient."[89] This growing reliance on short-term assignments and piecework creates many new challenges for journalists around contracts that often devalue their labor and deprive them of copyright protections for their work.[90]

Growing casualization and precarity in news labor is also becoming more prevalent in international journalism. When news organizations dismantle foreign bureaus and disinvest in international news coverage, they must rely more on stringers and freelance reporters who receive little institutional and financial support.[91] Much of what we know about the Middle East and other dangerous war zones around the world comes from brave freelance reporters and photojournalists on the frontlines of conflict. Yet this kind of journalism has become increasingly difficult and dangerous, with many freelance journalists taken captive, injured, or killed each year.[92] The beheading of journalist James Foley was one particularly gruesome case that attracted much public attention, but a little-discussed context was that he was a freelancer working under precarious conditions.[93]

With no clear career paths in traditional journalism, many would-be or former journalists are turning to public relations or other kinds of corporate communications jobs, which usually come with greater job security and higher pay. Just a decade ago, the ratio of public relations workers to journalists was already an alarming three to one. By 2014, the ratio was a staggering five to one, with more recent calculations placing it at six to one. It is hard to blame journalists when, on average, they earn two-thirds of what those in public relations make.[94]

As with many social maladies, these deteriorating working conditions for journalists disproportionately affect people of color and women.[95] For example, multiple inequity studies of major newspapers found glaring pay gaps within newsrooms between men and women and whites and people of color. At the *New York Times*, on average women make 91 percent of the men's salaries, while people of color make 88 percent of what their white colleagues make in the newsroom.[96] Another study by the Women's Media Center found significant gender disparities in bylines, with men writing 69 percent of newswire bylines (AP and Reuters), 60 percent of online news, and 59 percent of print news.[97] Stronger public interest protections—including those that incentivize newsrooms to look like the communities they are serving—could reduce these racial and gender divides.

In recent years, increasing numbers of journalists, particularly those working in digital newsrooms, have unionized in attempts to push back against many of these trends. Over the past several years, such digital outlets as *HuffPost, Salon, Slate, Daily Beast, Intercept, Root, Vice, Vox* and many others have unionized—all told, more than two thousand editorial employees.[98] At the time of this writing, news media workers have won union recognition at about thirty digital news sites and a handful of traditional newsrooms since 2015.[99] They have achieved this through a combination of traditional and new organizing strategies.[100] These trends draw from a long history of labor activism in newsrooms, going back to the Newspaper Guild in the 1930s. Then as now, unions are an important bulwark against commercial logics that commodify journalism and treat workers like hamsters in running wheels, forced to pursue impossible profits.

Loss of Public Service Journalism and the Rise of News Deserts

Concern about the loss of particular kinds of valuable journalism has grown more acute as commercial pressures continue to hollow out media institutions. These widening gaps in reporting, or "news deserts," often afflict news beats at the state and local levels, where entire geographic areas and particular policy issues lack coverage.[101] Examining data from a variety of sources, Penelope Muse Abernathy, an expert on journalism and digital media economics at the University of North Carolina, has found that about 1,800 local papers have closed or merged since 2004, leaving significant expanses of the United States with little local coverage.[102] She continues to track the expansion of these deserts, finding that (as of 2018) 171 US counties do not have a local newspaper and nearly half of all counties have only one paper (often a weekly).[103] Furthermore, she argues, the papers that survive are mostly run by skeleton crews of downsized staff who barely keep afloat what are essentially "ghost newspapers."[104]

Moreover, research shows that even purportedly local news is often not local at all. A comprehensive study of community newspapers across the country led by Philip Napoli shows that only 17 percent of stories published by local outlets actually cover events that occurred in close proximity to the paper's home.[105] Over half of these news reports originated elsewhere, often provided by a wire service such as the AP. Napoli found that segments of local television news are often derived from repurposed content originally produced by a parent network. The study also found an overall lack of substance, with only 56 percent of all local reports addressing a critical informational need, such as reports on infrastructure and crime coverage. Much reporting instead focused on sports stories and celebrity gossip, and only 11 percent of examined news stories could be considered locally produced, original, and addressing substantive public interest-oriented news. Of the one hundred communities that the researchers examined in a week-long period, twenty received no local news stories, twelve received no original stories, and eight received no stories addressing critical information needs.[106] These findings are also consistent with studies showing an alarming loss of statehouse reporters. For example in 2014, 86 percent of local television stations lacked a single reporter at the state capitol.[107]

Another destructive trend is the dismantling of newspapers' Washington bureaus. Erica Martinson was the sole reporter for the *Anchorage Daily News* Washington Bureau when she was laid off on September 11, 2018. Martinson had covered important stories about how federal laws passed in DC would affect the people of Alaska, including whether the Alaska delegation was voting for bills that would cost local jobs. The last reporter for the entire state of Alaska covering political news in Washington is Liz Ruskin, a public radio reporter. Upon hearing the news of Erica's dismissal, Ruskin said she by herself could never "replace the reach of a state's paper of record."[108]

It is difficult to ascertain exactly what is not being covered and what we are losing as a society when journalism withers away. But numerous cases of key journalists and entire news teams losing their jobs indicates their irreplaceability, especially during times of crisis when they are most needed. For example, by the time Hurricane Florence touched down in the Carolinas in the fall of 2018, the *Raleigh News Observer* had been reduced to a mere shell of its former self. The same paper that won accolades and was a Pulitzer Prize finalist for its coverage of Hurricane Floyd nineteen years earlier had lost 75 percent of the reporters it had in 1999 when Hurricane Florence struck. Such a decreased capacity greatly hindered journalists' ability to cover the storm and its aftermath.[109]

Similar deficits have emerged even in large cities such as New York City. After *The Daily News* laid off half its newsroom in July 2018, the vast borough of Brooklyn no longer received daily coverage. Although, as the *Atlantic* reported, a group of scrappy community journalists are trying to cover the area, their efforts are no substitute for having dedicated reporters on the daily beat. The month after the *Daily News* collapsed, the famous *Village Voice* shuttered its online publication, having closed its print operations the year before. The previous November, the billionaire owner of *Gothamist* and *DNA info*, Joe Ricketts, shut down the outlets just days after both newsrooms had voted to unionize.[110]

One of the economic challenges facing local news in small towns and large cities alike is that, beyond the immediate locale, there often is not a large enough audience to financially support local coverage, especially as it is cut back and further diminished. Nonetheless, lack of profitability should not dictate its existence. Local reporters play the vitally important role of "bearing witness" and it is socially beneficial to have them posted in all neighborhoods. Just having reporters on the scene can change the way that authorities operate, making them more accountable, especially in situations involving marginalized populations who often lack institutional support and political representation. This "observer effect" helps journalists advocate for vulnerable segments of the public.[111] With issues such as police brutality, unfair housing policies, health and safety, and other critically important types of information, such reporting is invaluable for local communities, particularly those who historically have been disempowered.

These concerns are especially poignant given that news deficits disproportionately affect communities of color and lower socioeconomic neighborhoods. Media researcher Alex Williams has studied a phenomenon he refers to as "news redlining," in which news gaps reflect pre-existing economic and racial inequities.[112] Similarly, another study found "journalism divides" that reflected patterns akin to "digital divides" in which low-income groups, communities of color, and rural locales were far more disadvantaged in terms of access to reliable local news relative to other segments of the population.[113] Other scholars have found similar information inequalities present in poor communities, which translates to lower quantities and qualities of "accountability journalism" for low-income Americans, rendering them more susceptible to deception.[114] Ultimately, these divides do not simply reflect pre-existing inequities, but also reinforce and reproduce them.

While growing swaths of Americans lack access to high-quality journalism, it is readily available for those who can afford it. This widening gap is especially true for policy reporting. At a time when cash-strapped newspapers are dismantling their Washington bureaus, specialized trade publications and members-only niche outlets are flourishing in the nation's capital. These publications rely on elite clientele—often companies and law firms—who are willing to pay thousands of dollars for subscriptions. A *Washington Monthly* article noted that while this high-quality information is fenced off behind paywalls, the seemingly ubiquitous political news flashing across the screens of televisions and devices that most Americans consume almost never focuses on how power actually operates. Stories that do cover power include the "day-to-day inner workings of government—the slow, steady development of policy in Congress, in the administration, and in the independent regulatory agencies, and how those policies are implemented." This kind of news media coverage should inform everyone's voting habits, but it is available only for those who can pay hefty fees, while becoming increasingly scarce for everyone else. The article concludes with a grim observation: "Policy journalism in Washington is thriving. It's just not being written for you, and you're probably never going to read it."[115]

Despite all these problems and injustices, newspapers continue to play a vitally central role within the entire US media system—even as the market afflicts profound violence on the industry. With the growing demolition of advertising-supported news, the ongoing search for new profitable business models has eluded even the most entrepreneurial start-ups. Nevertheless, regardless of whether public service journalism is profitable, democracy still depends on it. For over a decade, this quandary has driven a desperate search for alternative funding mechanisms for journalism.

Alternatives to the Advertising Revenue Model

Back in 2011—already several years into the modern journalism crisis—Robert McChesney and I gathered together essays by leading analysts to make sense of the crisis and propose solutions. From this collection, cheerfully titled *Will the Last Reporter Please Turn out the Lights*, four general models emerged: paywalls; citizen journalism; support from benevolent billionaires, foundations, or nonprofits; and public media. Many of these areas overlap—nonprofit models, for example, can be supported by paying members, backed by foundations, and run by citizens—and the categories have morphed and evolved. Today, few people would still suggest that citizen journalism in the form of blogs or social media can sufficiently supplant older forms of journalism. And it now makes sense to talk about "membership models" as something distinct from paywalls. Nonetheless, this typology has remained remarkably constant overall. I address each model in the following sections.

Paywalls

A paywall acts as a barrier between an internet user and a news organization's online content.[116] To access the content, users must purchase a digital subscription. While most newspapers only began experimenting with this model in the past decade, *The Wall Street Journal* launched the first paywall in 1997. Although this early initiative was successful—at least partly because it provided expert financial news to an elite audience—many news outlets hesitated to launch paywalls, fearing they would reduce online readership and digital advertising revenue. In 2009, writer David Simon urged publishers to embrace the model, arguing that otherwise newspapers were sure to face "the slow strangulation of paid, professional journalism."[117]

Since the modern journalism crisis erupted over a decade ago, newspapers have increasingly turned to this digital subscription model to compensate for dwindling advertising revenue. With consecutive years being declared "the year of the paywall," at least one commentator referred to paywalls as a "Hail Mary pass" for the industry's survival, and many analysts see the digital subscription model as newspapers' last chance at viability.[118] Various types of publications—from large national newspapers such as the *New York Times* to smaller papers such as Rhode Island's *Newport Daily News*—increasingly implement paywalls. The record thus far has been decidedly mixed; the evidence does not bode well for digital subscriptions saving the entire US newspaper industry.[119] Most outlets that deploy paywalls find that the revenues have not come close to offsetting the tremendous losses of print advertising. While national papers such as the *New York Times* have made tremendous gains in digital subscription revenue, most US newspapers still rely on other means of support.[120]

Ultimately, paywalls seem to work to varying degrees for some niche news outlets, major magazines, and large national newspapers. However, for most local and regional outlets they will likely provide at best only a partial solution for finding new revenue sources. Ideally, while journalists should be duly compensated for their work, paying for their labor should not rely on policing online content or encouraging an already overly commercialized media system to become even more so. Moreover, paywalls present several often-overlooked normative concerns: They diminish the positive externalities that come with free-flowing news; they disenfranchise people unable to afford the digital subscription cost; and they further inscribe commercial values into newsgathering processes by treating journalism as a commodity instead of a public service.[121]

Other variants on the paywall/digital subscription model adopt more flexible payment schemes, but all share the same conceptual weakness of not recouping enough revenue. The BlockChain model, for instance, relies on crypto currencies to support news. But the best-known example, the Civil Media Company, after much hype and anticipation, spectacularly failed to attract enough customers in the fall of 2018.[122] Another model that periodically re-emerges in future-of-news discussions is the "micropayments model"—sometimes referred to as an "iTunes model" or a "Spotify model"—that allows readers to pay for one story at a time.[123] Despite a certain intuitive plausibility, the system seems unlikely to succeed in the marketplace. It is difficult to make news stories compelling enough that people would pay for a one-off read and, unlike music, it is doubtful that many would purchase stories for repeated use. Thus far, few viable examples of this model exist.

The "events" model might be considered another variation on the theme. In recent years, a number of high-profile news organizations have begun selling tickets to special events that feature prominent journalists or discussions about particular hot topics. The *New Yorker* festival, which generates significant revenue and even features "native panels," is one of the more prominent examples of this strategy.[124] If publicly accessible, these events can help promote discussion about important issues. But this practice also raises thorny ethical questions, as it can stray toward a kind of influence peddling. Beyond cozying up too close to the rich and powerful, such events may drive discussion of important political issues out of the public sphere and into a private forum of elites.[125] For example, the *Washington Post* garnered much criticism in 2009 when then-publisher Katharine Weymouth attempted to sell access to her journalists at off-the-record dinners in her own home.[126]

The endless pursuit of commercial success incentivizes news organizations to sacrifice principles for profit, and treat journalism as a product instead of a public good or essential service. Moreover, many proponents of these revenue models assume, at least tacitly, that a new commercial formula is still out there to be discovered. Media industries, and US society in general, have yet to recognize that the massive profits of the commercial model's heyday are simply not coming back. Fortunately, the other major alternatives rely more on non-market-based support.

Citizen Journalism and Crowdfunding

One model that has receded somewhat—or morphed into other variants—
is what was once called "citizen journalism." Earlier articulations emphasized blogs and social media—and even earlier were Indymedia centers
whose slogan was "be the media"—but today this model often suggests
crowdsourcing labor and crowdfunding financial support.[127] At one time,
some citizen journalism proponents went so far as to assume that these
new models would supplant professional news organizations and therefore
we no longer needed such institutions. Clay Shirky, Yochai Benkler, and
other early proponents of crowdsourcing models believed that the internet
could be leveraged to replace professional journalism, but this view has
faded along with some of the earlier utopian discourses around the democratic promises of the internet.[128] While blogs and other citizen journalism
initiatives have made—and continue to make—important contributions,
today the focus is less on replacing professionals and more on finding ways
to help complement and fund working journalists.[129] While still mostly experimental, crowdfunding models continue to attract attention and show
some promise.[130]

One successful crowdfunded publication that has been around for decades
is the *New Internationalist* magazine based in Oxford, England. The publication has become one of the world's largest media cooperatives, with 3,467 co-
owners, including readers, writers, and supporters who bought shares as part
of a crowdfunding campaign that raised nearly $900,000.[131] Many observers
of the media landscape are hopeful that increasing numbers of news organizations will adopt this model. The New Revenue Hub, which spun out from
the *Voice of San Diego*, is now trying to help small outlets build out their own
membership programs.[132]

A variation of the crowdfunding model is the "membership model," which
relies on paying members for its revenue. Although the specifics of this
model can differ, proponents point out that it is less blunt and transactional
than the paywall model. Members often see themselves buying into a particular civic vision, and in some cases are even involved with questions of
governance and choosing what kinds of stories the news outlets cover. If a
critical mass of the public feels strongly enough about a particular kind of
journalism, the thinking goes, it will susbisidize it for the rest of us. One compelling exemplar is the Dutch journalism platform *De Correspondent*, which
began five years ago with a crowdfunding campaign to "unbreak" the news

and is devoted to in-depth, analytical coverage. Now with more than 60,000 members, it remains militantly ad-free.[133]

The US version—the *Correspondent*—was initially embraced with much fanfare. The media expert Jay Rosen, an early proponent, even discussed the venture with Trevor Noah on *The Daily Show*. However, this experiment also demonstrated how the high levels of reader trust that such models require could also be their greatest vulnerability. A controversy erupted in the spring of 2019 when it was revealed that the news organization, which had conducted an extensive fundraising campaign in the United States, would not actually open up an office in the country. Heated debates unfolded across Twitter and elsewhere, with many erstwhile supporters, even the *Correspondent*'s first US employee, feeling betrayed.[134]

Nonetheless, the membership model is worth continued experimentation. Jay Rosen rightly notes that the model was never purported to be the silver bullet solution; rather, it can be part of the answer, one that will require "trust, transparency and superb media literacy." Rosen sees its highest potential when it is part of a multi-pronged approach. For a compelling example, he points to the British *Guardian*, which combines subscription, donation, membership, and subsidy from an endowment to remain sustainable.[135]

Wealthy Benefactors

With most commercial plans failing, many media organizations are pinning their hopes on benevolent billionaires, nonprofits, and foundations. Rich benefactors like Laurene Powell Jobs, Jeff Bezos, Craig Newmark, and many others have funneled millions of dollars toward bolstering media outlets and initiatives. A number of exciting nonprofit ventures have emerged as well.[136] For example, eBay founder Pierre Omidyar has put hundreds of millions of dollars into journalism projects such as the 501(c)(3) nonprofit First Look Media, the news organization that supports the *Intercept* and its team of investigative reporters, including Glenn Greenwald and Jeremy Scahill. Omidyar has promised hundreds of millions of dollars to ensure the website's editorial independence and autonomy. The Omidyar Network's donations have also included millions for the International Consortium of Investigative Journalists (ICIJ), the small group that led the explosive Panama Papers investigation.

Another interesting venture launched in early 2016 when Gerry Lenfest, the owner of the Philadelphia Media Network (PMN)—consisting of Philadelphia's two newspapers and a news website—donated PMN to the Lenfest Institute for Journalism, a nonprofit organization with a $20 million endowment. This unique structure, technically a "public benefit corporation" (a legal designation that incentivizes publishers to make a beneficial impact on society while still being for-profit), preserves editorial influence for PMN.[137] It allows the news organization to retain its own independent board of directors while also permitting the institute to solicit grants to raise funds. The hybrid model (its ownership structure is nonprofit, but its newsrooms are still run as for-profits) shields its newsgathering from some commercial pressures.[138] For example, the model frees news organizations to reinvest in newsrooms instead of distributing all profits to shareholders. While still in a relatively experimental stage, the Lenfest Institute's unique structural attributes have yielded some significant results. The *Inquirer* has nearly doubled its investigative journalist team from seven to thirteen reporters; created a new two-year Lenfest Fellows program that places emerging journalists of color in the *Inquirer* newsroom; and contributed to a number of investigative journalism projects in Philadelphia and in the state capital of Harrisburg, including a promising project focused on collaborative reporting called Spotlight PA.[139]

As it becomes increasingly clear that no commercial future exists for newspapers, others might choose similar routes. Many observers—myself included—have long advocated for new tax laws that help incentivize newspapers to transition into non- or low-profit institutions. However, even though the IRS has increasingly granted approval to news media institutions seeking to qualify as nonprofits (and therefore permitted to receive charitable contributions and special tax protections according to a 501(c)(3) status), and the considerable wait times have gradually lessened, established newspapers have not chosen this path.[140] This might be finally changing. In a first for a legacy newspaper, the *Salt Lake Tribune* is seeking to become an official non-profit operation, a "community asset," sustained by donations. Under this new status, which first requires federal approval, a community board of directors would likely govern the paper.[141] Removing commercial pressures and bringing newsroom governance back to the community could greatly benefit the struggling newspaper industry if more papers were to follow suit.

These experiments signal a recognition that market forces alone cannot support adequate levels of journalism. Indeed, liberation from profit-maximizing imperatives gives nonprofit media outfits advantages over their commercial counterparts. Nonprofits tend to devote a considerably higher proportion of their resources to news operations compared to profit-driven media.[142] Ideally, they can focus more on neglected regions and issues, including local reporting, statehouse coverage, and hard-hitting, labor-intensive investigative news—the kind of journalism that is increasingly scarce. Some proponents see this model as the ideal antidote to the failing for-profit model. Charles Lewis, founder of the Center for Public Integrity, one of the country's oldest nonprofit investigative news organizations, and more recently the cofounder of the Institute for Nonprofit News (INN), believes these organizations will proliferate in the wake of the commercial model's collapse.[143] Evidence suggests that this sector is indeed growing, especially in the area of nonprofit digital news sites.

One extensive study conducted by the INN in the fall of 2018 found these nonprofit outlets generating annual revenues of $325 to $350 million and supporting three thousand staffers, including two thousand and two hundred journalists. This "INN index" also corroborates the advantage that nonprofit news organizations generally hold over their commercial counterparts (an advantage that is even greater for digital outlets because their production costs are significantly lower than their print counterparts). For instance, nonprofits can direct a greater share of their revenues toward editorial operations. According to the study, these sites devote two-thirds of their resources to reporting and editing, compared to about 15 to 20 percent at legacy newspapers.[144] The report concluded that these new ventures "have created a collective incubator for the future of public service journalism, finding new ways to share knowledge, include and engage people in civic life, and strengthen our communities."[145]

Many other journalistic enterprises funded by foundation grants and other nonmarket-based sources are longstanding. Prime examples include the Scott Trust, which owns the *Guardian*, a leading British newspaper, and the Poynter Institute, a nonprofit journalism education and training center that owns the *Tampa Bay Times* and supports the PolitiFact fact-checking service. Similar nonprofit models—or for-profit ventures owned by nonprofits—exist in various forms elsewhere, including the *Christian Science Monitor*, which belongs to the First Church of Christ; the Manchester, New Hampshire, *Union Leader*; the *Day* in New London, Connecticut; the *Delaware State News*; and Alabama's *Anniston Star*. Other longstanding examples of nonprofit news organizations include *Harper's Magazine*, the *Washington Monthly, Consumer Reports, Ms. Magazine*, and *Mother Jones*.

As I discuss in more detail in chapter 5, the Ford Foundation and other large grant-makers played a key role in creating US public broadcasting. More recently, foundation-funded organizations like *ProPublica* and *The Marshall Project* have flourished, winning Pulitzer Prizes and other prestigious journalism awards. *ProPublica* has even expanded to create the Local Reporting Network, a collaborative project with local outlets that has already generated an impressive body of reporting and will focus on desperately needed coverage of statehouses. In 2017, the nonprofit exemplar launched ProPublica Illinois, a Chicago-based investigative newsroom that focuses on exposing wrongdoing across the state.[146] Another much-celebrated example is the *Texas Tribune*, which relies on a mix of foundation support, membership, events, and corporate sponsorship. These institutions—along with smaller ventures such as the *Voice of San Diego* and *MinnPost*, which have been around for over a decade and depend on a mix of paid membership and charitable support, and even older initiatives such as the Center for Public Integrity and the Center for Investigative Reporting, all exemplify viable nonprofit models.

A more recent crop of local journalism initiatives have emerged in cities, such as the *City Bureau* in Chicago, the *City* in New York, and *Resolve* in Philadelphia, a collaborative reporting project that produces the economic justice-focused "Broke in Philly" initiative.[147] Other interesting experiments seek out news gaps in small communities. The Community Impact Newspaper, for example, focuses on areas outside of media-rich cities, including Houston, Austin, and Dallas.[148] The *Daily Yonder*, published on the web since 2007 by a nonprofit media and advocacy organization, covers issues important to rural communities across the United States.[149] Two local cooperative projects worthy of attention are the long-standing Banyan Project, founded by Tom Stites in Haverhill, Massachusetts, and the Info Districts program based in New Jersey.[150]

Another noteworthy initiative is Report for America (RFA), a journalism nonprofit cofounded by Steve Waldman (author of the FCC report discussed in chapter 2), and inspired by AmeriCorps and Teach for America. Having already placed several reporters in Appalachia during its pilot stage, RFA plans to deploy a thousand journalists to understaffed regional newsrooms by 2022 (it has around sixty as of 2019).[151] RFA is one of the more promising models to emerge, with a governance structure that has a double firewall between donors and journalists (neither party knows what funding is going to which specific reporting).[152] Questions remain, however, about whether RFA journalists, who residents might see as outsiders, can build trust with local communities, especially when they serve only one- or two-year contracts.[153] Yet another promising model is the American Journalism Project (AJP), a "venture philanthropy organization" focused on rebuilding local journalism and aiding civic news organizations' capacity to become self-sustainable. Cofounded by the earlier founders of the *The Texas Tribune* and *Chalkbeat*, AJP has raised $42 million thus far and has established a clear and compelling vision for promoting nonprofit journalism.[154] Universities are also gradually becoming more involved with producing original local journalism.[155]

While all of these experiments—and many others—are promising and desperately needed, they are still tiny relative to the scope of the problem. Support from foundations and benevolent billionaires is not a systemic solution to a structural crisis. Furthermore, relying on these resources for news operations exposes journalism to several specific hazards. For example, grants usually come with at least implicit expectations about what kind of news the monies will support. Even well-meaning donors typically focus on certain issues while neglecting others. Media scholar Rodney Benson's research shows that relying on foundation support may put nonprofit news outlets under "specific strings and metrics attached to grants," including sunset provisions and the expectation of demonstrable impact.[156] Such relationships rarely provide long-term financial security for struggling news organizations. Moreover, grants may lead to what journalism scholar Anya Schiffrin refers to as "media capture" by foundation donors who are guided by specific issue agendas when they support news outlets.[157] Foundations also shape "philanthro-journalism" in more subtle ways by defining the "boundaries" of journalism.[158] Some critics and scholars rightly question how different this journalism is in practice from commercialized journalism and whether it mainly serves elites.[159] But perhaps most importantly, several analyses show that there is simply not enough charitable giving to go around. A 2014 Pew research report indicated that philanthropic annual giving and capital investment in US media organizations account for only $150 million, or about 1 percent of overall financial support for news.[160] This amount may have grown in recent years, but supporting US journalism at a systemic level requires tens of billions of dollars.

Ultimately, while the foundation-support model for journalism has numerous successful exemplars that deserve case-by-case evaluation, this model also raises serious concerns. At best, billionaires and foundations can save the odd news outlet or create a few new ones, but that alone will not address the systemic problems afflicting journalism. Moreover, what might be called the "benevolent billionaire model" for supporting journalism begs the observation that not all billionaires are benevolent—some might have ulterior motives, political agendas, and conflicts of interest. The most obvious example is Sheldon Adelson, the casino mogul and conservative activist who bought the *Las Vegas Review-Journal*, Nevada's largest paper, in 2015. He kept the purchase secret at first, and his representatives reportedly pressured the newspaper's staff to cover Adelson and his allies in a positive light.[161] Notorious press barons of yore such as William Randolph Hearst and Robert McCormick often weaponized their papers to push far-right agendas, including admiration for Adolf Hitler. Clearly, many potential hazards emerge if news outlets become the playthings of billionaires.

Journalism's financial weakness renders it vulnerable to capture by commercial and political interests. Despite the industry's rapid devaluation in recent years, newspapers still hold significant political power and therefore are desirable, easy pickings for rich politicos with personal agendas. With corporate "sponsored content" and billionaire-backed news rushing into the vacuum left by professional journalism, the potential for a pay-to-play "payola society" arises in which inequalities are increasingly inscribed into its media system. In this media landscape, marred by digital divides and various kinds of news redlining, rich people and corporations can say what they want, but everyone else is censored by market forces.

Rodney Benson and I have called this formation the "oligarchy media model."[162] Although sometimes relatively benevolent, rich benefactors rarely aim to provide news access to all segments of society. Given that media owners' class interests rarely align with those of the working class and the poor—their business model tends to exclude audiences or issues that are not easily monetized, thereby skewing coverage (especially for outlets still dependent on advertisers, who typically favor content that appeals to high-earning demographics). Rather than engaging underserved readers, these billionaire-owned news organizations may actually exacerbate economic and racial divides by privileging views more in line with higher socioeconomic groups and neoliberal economic policies. This tendency is not that surprising since those who have most benefitted from a highly stratified economic system are unlikely to focus on the structural roots of inequality. It is unrealistic to expect well-heeled patrons to fund an adversarial journalism that bucks the status quo and challenges fellow elites. Furthermore, the whims of the rich and powerful are unreliable governors of public discourse.[163]

Public Media

The weaknesses in the nonprofit model bring us to the least discussed and most politically fraught model: the public media option, which relies on some form of non-market-based subsidy. Implementing public media subsidies is usually dismissed as a political nonstarter in the United States, but—as discussed in chapter 1—the idea has a long, rich history. The US government has always granted the press a special status and has often helped offset the costs of producing and disseminating the news, going back to postal and printing subsidies in the early republic. Since then, everything from broadcast-spectrum giveaways to the birth of the internet has relied on massive public subsidies. Nonetheless, media subsidies are largely seen today as deeply un-American. The United States and its media system are unique among democracies in this regard. Media organizations in all leading democratic nations around the globe benefit from significant government subsidies.[164] Moreover, reputable organizations such as Freedom House consistently rank many countries with subsidized media systems as having higher levels of press freedom compared to the United States.[165]

I return to the question of public subsidies in chapter 5. For now, suffice it to say that the 150-year-old advertising-dependent revenue model for commercial newspapers is doomed, with no obvious replacement. Why should we care? Do newspapers still matter?

Social Implications of the Journalism Crisis

Before discussing the reasons for why this crisis has been met with such policy inaction, it is worth considering why journalism matters for self-governance and a healthy democratic society. While it is axiomatic that democracy is impossible without an informed polity, a growing body of empirical research lays out practical reasons for why we still need public service journalism, especially local news. These studies, which I briefly summarize in this section, demonstrate clear material effects associated with the loss of journalism. The studies offer a sobering view of what happens to communities when local news disappears. Beyond abstract democratic theory, they underscore why we should treat the journalism crisis as a problem for public policy.

Long-standing research shows that the loss of local journalism leads to less informed voters. However, in recent years scholars have begun to detail the wide range of significant negative effects this decline has on local communities and democratic society in general.[166] These studies generally show that civic engagement declines in tandem with the loss of local news. In one often-cited study, Lee Shaker found that levels of engagement, such as getting involved with civic groups or contacting local representatives, declined significantly in Seattle and Denver after each of these cities lost one of their two major newspapers.[167] Similarly, a number of studies show that local newspaper closures lead to lower voter participation. For example, an analysis of newspaper coverage of the 2010 midterm elections found that people living in districts that lacked robust election coverage were less able to evaluate their choices for congressional representative and ultimately were less likely to vote.[168] Another study suggests that residents in communities lacking press coverage are less able to recall their representatives' names and therefore are less capable of holding them accountable. Moreover, those same representatives are less engaged in their districts and less attentive to their constituents.[169]

Economist Matthew Gentzkow and his coauthors found that "newspapers have a robust positive effect on political participation" and that reading newspapers can mobilize as many as 13 percent of nonvoters to vote.[170] A subsequent study by the same researchers shows long historical patterns of how losing local media coverage correlates with lower voter turnout.[171] Another study of mayoral elections shows that newspaper decline correlates with fewer people running for local office and less political competition.[172] Research also shows that voters in news deserts tend to base their vote more on national than local news and thus follow "partisan heuristics" that lead to increased polarization.[173]

These findings notwithstanding, many social costs of losing local journalism are harder to quantify. As mentioned in the last chapter, journalism's positive externalities carry tremendous monetary value and other incalculable benefits for all of society, especially when investigative reporting holds those in power to account and gathers new, relevant information. While it is sometimes difficult to ascertain, ample evidence suggests that those in power benefit and corruption rises when journalism disappears. The historian and sociologist Paul Starr synthesized a wide range of social science research that demonstrates a correlation between the loss of local news media and the rise of political corruption. He observed that "newspapers have been our eyes on the state, our check on private abuses, our civic alarm systems."[174] One recent study found that newspaper closures increase the likelihood of local governments expanding their borrowing costs and mismanaging taxpayers funds, presumably because of the lack of public scrutiny.[175] The loss of government monitoring from local newspaper journalists has resulted in higher costs for municipalities, greater deficits, and significant losses to local taxpayers.[176]

Whereas the loss of journalism is costly, the presence of strong reporting is conversely financially beneficial for society as a whole. The media economist Jay Hamilton calculates that each dollar spent by a newspaper on investigative reporting can save taxpayers hundreds of dollars by changing public policy and rooting out waste and corruption.[177] An illustrative example occurred several years ago, when *Mother Jones* magazine appealed directly to readers about the prohibitive economics of investigative journalism. Their award-winning story on private prisons—the result of a four-month, in-depth investigation that exposed the brutal working conditions for inmates—led to widespread praise and social benefits when the DOJ announced the end of its use of private prisons.[178] But the story also led to significant economic losses for *Mother Jones*: It cost $350,000 to produce, but the banner ads that ran with the piece generated only $5,000 in return.[179] Ideally, news organizations would not forgo such socially important journalism simply because it is unprofitable, but that is the incentive structure commercial outlets currently face.

Another direct saving to society as the result of investigative reporting occurred when the *Daily News* journalist Juan Gonzalez uncovered a group of private computer consultants ripping off taxpayers in what Preet Bharara, the US Attorney in Manhattan, dubbed the "biggest and most brazen fraud in the city's history" involving illegal kickbacks and phantom workers.[180] After reading Gonzalez's exposé, Bharara immediately went after the culprits, forcing the project's main contractor to return $500 million to New York City. Another example of investigative journalism uncovering wrongdoing and threats to public health was the Flint water crisis. Dangerous levels of lead contamination in Flint's water supply, first exposed by activist groups, were brought to public attention by a lone investigative reporter working for the American Civil Liberties Union.[181]

These are just a few examples in which time- and labor-intensive journalism yielded significant and often immeasurable savings and benefits to society. Yet such tremendous positive externalities rarely factor into economic calculations about the demands, needs, and costs of journalism. The decline in investigative reporting is especially troubling because the entire media ecosystem in the United States depends on newspapers' journalism. Other news media—broadcast television and radio, cable television, blogs, social media—infrequently produce original journalism, but rather focus on political commentary and various forms of entertainment media. To the extent that these outlets discuss hard news, their coverage often derives from stories initially reported by newspapers. Even casual observers will notice that leading cable news shows typically riff from the day's newspaper headlines. Yet newspapers' vital role as a "news feeder" to the entire media ecosystem is often underappreciated.

A Pew report documented this dependence on newspaper journalism through an exhaustive analysis of Baltimore's media ecology in a single week in 2009. By tracking both old and new media—everything from blogs and tweets to broadcast news and newspapers—researchers found much of the news that people received contained little original reporting. The study showed that 80 percent of the news stories were derived from previously published information, and more than 95 percent of original news stories were generated by old media, especially the *Baltimore Sun* newspaper.[182] Other studies have identified a similar dependency on stories originating with newspapers.[183]

These trends are troubling given the special importance that local news holds within the entire news media ecosystem. Studies, polls, and surveys have consistently shown that large majorities of readers trust their local news providers at much higher levels than they do national news outlets.[184] It is through local journalism that communities stay connected to and informed about what is happening in their backyards—especially in their schools, their governments, and other critical institutions and infrastructures. They rely on local news to find out about the quality of their environment—whether their air and water are safe—and who is running for local office and why. Yet it is precisely this kind of journalism that is quickly disappearing. If we as a society want to encourage this sort of reporting, we must find ways to support it.

Defining the Crisis in Discourse and Data

The studies discussed above suggest that the journalism crisis continues to worsen and is having a negative impact on democratic society—even as the entire US media ecosystem continues to depend on traditional journalism. Nonetheless, any sense of urgency for structural reform of our news media gradually tapered off with no policy response following the 2009 crisis. Meanwhile, as this chapter has shown, the situation has only deteriorated. Late-stage afflictions—from unscrupulous advertisers to the predations of private equity firms—are like opportunistic parasites feeding off a dying beast. The lack of a policy response in the face of a collapsing press system is inexcusable. With historic economic inequality and impending environmental catastrophe, our political moment desperately needs a fearless press that can uncover the roots of social problems and provide a space for vigorous debate about how to solve them.

Before we design a media system that encourages that kind of journalism, we have to recognize the structural constraints that are preventing us from doing so. Thus far, I have discussed the various commercial pressures and attendant discursive capture that afflict for-profit news media in the United States. I now turn to some of the policy failures and structural threats—especially monopoly control over digital infrastructures—that undermine journalism today.

4

Monopoly Control
over Digital Infrastructures

In early 2018, millions of Americans witnessed the rare spectacle of corporate power being brought to account. After months of damning revelations about Facebook's role in enabling disinformation and foreign interference in the 2016 US elections—including an enormous breach of users' privacy by the political consulting firm Cambridge Analytica—Congress subjected Facebook's CEO Mark Zuckerberg to a two-day grilling broadcast on national television.[1] Zuckerberg remained evasive during the hearings, and the questions posed to him by technologically inept politicians were sometimes laughable. Nonetheless, public exposure of the scandal triggered a long overdue conversation about monopoly power, its pernicious effects on society, and government's role in stopping it.

These ongoing debates have brought certain facts, long known among internet critics, to public attention: Facebook's business model relies on a massive surveillance machine, the company routinely pursues profit over democratic principles, and its CEO, Mark Zuckerberg, is not unlike a late-nineteenth-century robber baron. The company had flouted transparency and accountability for far too long. Americans had finally come to realize that a new Gilded Age of monopoly power had been visited upon them, forcing policymakers to give new currency to old ideas, like "antitrust."

While users may have once regarded Facebook as a positive force in society, the US public increasingly sees the company for what it is: an unaccountable monopoly. And, like all monopolies, Facebook will do whatever it takes to preserve its dominant market position and reap as much money as legally (and sometimes illegally) possible. In November 2018, a *New York Times* exposé revealed how Facebook hired a disreputable public relations firm to smear its political adversaries with anti-Semitic conspiracy theories.[2] Amid continuous damning reports, the company remains in damage-control mode, doing everything from apology tours to defensively accusing the *New York Times* of anti-Facebook bias.[3]

Democracy Without Journalism?. Victor Pickard, Oxford University Press (2020). © Victor Pickard
DOI: 10.1093/oso/9780190946753.001.0001

Meanwhile, a growing awareness that Facebook's unregulated power imperils democracy has fostered a growing—and exceedingly rare—bipartisan consensus that government must rein in platform monopolies. Until recently, the concept of regulating technology firms seemed unfathomable, but now even many Republican policymakers believe they have become so powerful that government must intervene. This growing public scrutiny of digital monopolies has implications far beyond Facebook. Extended to the broader media landscape, this moment offers a rare opportunity for structural reform. Even Zuckerberg—notoriously reluctant to take responsibility for the social problems caused by his company—now concedes that perhaps, after all, Facebook should be regulated.[4] But *what kind* of regulation can address these issues? What can we as a society do to incentivize—nay, *demand*—that powerful information monopolies act in the public interest and serve democracy, not merely their own profit imperatives? Is this objective even attainable when anti-democratic behavior is baked into Facebook's DNA?

Answering these questions requires us to directly confront the impact of platform monopolies on journalism. Monopoly ownership is a broad structural threat to a healthy news media system, affecting everything from control of internet access to the range of voices in our news media. This chapter looks at the monopoly problem for our news and information systems and shows why media ownership still matters. It also examines how several media policy failures, such as approving media mergers and repealing net neutrality protections, have contributed to the problem. Finally, it considers Facebook's central role in the misinformation ecology and potential regulatory approaches to stopping it. The chapter concludes with a brief discussion of what policies could help democratize news media institutions.

Why Media Ownership Matters

In the early days of digital media, technological utopians argued that the affordances of digital media and the rise of "network societies" and the like would flatten power hierarchies throughout the world. Recent developments in US and global politics, combined with a growing number of empirical studies, have shown that this was wishful thinking. Material and structural factors—including how media institutions and information systems are owned and organized—dramatically impact a media system's openness and diversity, whether that media system operates in print, over the airwaves, or online. This pattern is especially true in the United States, where corporate duopolies and oligopolies dominate most media sectors. Media monopolies—whether new digital giants like Facebook or conglomerates of older media like Comcast—hold tremendous power over political culture and communication infrastructures, both within the United States and globally.

Media ownership structures fall into several general categories.[5] These include horizontal (the ownership of similar media products), vertical (the ownership of different stages of production and distribution of media), and diagonal (the cross-ownership of diverse media businesses) integration. As we saw in the previous chapter, different ownership structures rely on specific systems of control. Whether firms are owned by families, stockholders, private equity, or the public, these structures affect key issues ranging from informational diversity to media effects. Furthermore, scholarship increasingly shows that differences in media ownership and control (e.g., whether it is concentrated, commercialized, or publicly owned) lead to differences in media content, with important implications for democracy.[6]

Three general types of information/communication monopolies loom large within our media systems: news and entertainment media, telecommunications, and platforms.[7] Each type of monopoly carries with it specific hazards, harms, and vulnerabilities for journalism in particular and democratic society in general. Over the years, a number of scholars have documented how a handful of corporations dominate the US media landscape, especially news and entertainment media. Ben Bagdikian began drawing attention to media monopolies in the 1980s when he discovered that a mere fifty companies controlled most of the US media system. By the 2000s, this number had dropped to six.[8] Similarly, in 2018 *Fortune* magazine identified six large media conglomerates that dominate much of the US media system: Comcast, AT&T, CBS, Viacom, 21st Century Fox, and Disney.[9] After the Disney-Fox merger, this list has become the "Big Five," and CBS and Viacom are in serious discussions about recombining. These eye-catching metrics, of course, deserve scrutiny because they can omit important distinctions and sometimes rely on slippery criteria. Moreover, even as old media firms continue to dominate media markets, newer firms such as Facebook, Google, Microsoft, Netflix, Amazon, and Apple are also ascending in this space as they acquire content companies. Netflix and Amazon, in particular, are becoming entertainment media powerhouses.[10]

Nonetheless, many old ownership patterns have transferred to new digital media as traditional news media giants with name recognition and massive resources continue to dominate online traffic. In a book published a decade ago, media scholar Matthew Hindman found that a small number of news media sites commanded the digital content market and received the vast majority of users' attention. Hindman moreover found a "long tail" of numerous sites receiving little or no traffic, with surprisingly few websites occupying the middle ground.[11] Recent research continues to show that legacy institutions dominate the media landscape, with only a few significant independent news websites emerging.[12] As of 2018, most online traffic to news and political sites was highly concentrated among mainstream news organizations, or aggregators that relied on them for their content.[13] A key takeaway from this research, one that has remained more or less constant for the past decade, is that in some respects online news media are becoming *more* concentrated than traditional media.

Despite what may seem like an explosion of media sources from social media, innumerable websites, and cable television channels, a few media outlets capture most Americans' attention. As part of his broader argument that the US media system's commercial nature has a corrosive impact in shaping our news and politics, the political scientist Matthew Guardino synthesizes recent research showing that a handful of corporations command individual-level news attention in the United States. These data indicate that the firms with the greatest reach and largest share of news consumers' attention are Facebook, Time Warner (now owned by AT&T), and News Corp. According to one study, the United States leads industrialized nations in "information inequality," a situation in which "exposure to news sources owned by multiple firms is concentrated in a small share of the population." This research also shows that Americans suffer from a very high level of "information poverty," which the authors of this study define as "the percentage of the population that relies on just one news source, or is exposed to no news at all."[14]

Under Republican and Democratic administrations alike, news media have become progressively more concentrated, but the Trump administration has ushered in a merger mania of historic proportions (though Trump's Justice Department did unsuccessfully oppose the Time Warner-AT&T merger). Even as his administration facilitates this concentration, President Trump has played to the public's distrust of media monopolies by attacking the "AmazonWashingtonPost" on Twitter and threatening antitrust investigations.[15] Although Trump's motives are suspect—likely in response to the *Washington Post*'s negative coverage of his administration—he points to a legitimate concern: As Amazon gains sizeable market share in multiple industries, the *Washington Post*'s potential for serious conflicts of interest increases significantly. At the very least, the newspaper has an incentive to protect its publisher's economic interests. Indeed, some critics writing from the other end of the ideological spectrum have suggested that this power relationship helps explain why the *Washington Post* so aggressively criticized then-presidential candidate Bernie Sanders' policy proposals.[16]

The dangerous power of monopolies to push ideology becomes increasingly evident when we consider a cluster of right-wing media outlets and their role in purveying misinformation to an insulated audience. A trailblazing study by Yochai Benkler and his coauthors found that media organizations such as Fox News, Newsmax, Daily Caller, Breitbart, and other outlets comprise a right-wing echo chamber sealed off from the rest of the news media system. A symbiosis between conspiracy theories fueled by online communities and social media platforms, and conservative news outlets such as Fox (which consistently has the highest levels of engagement on Facebook among news publishers), creates a "propaganda feedback loop" that amplifies even the most outlandish far-right conspiracies.[17]

On any given night, even casual observers will notice Fox News programs breathlessly covering imaginary threats posed by undocumented immigrants and a manufactured "border crisis" instead of reporting on social problems that actually exist but might reflect negatively on President Trump and other powerful interests. Such fearmongering diverts attention from a myriad of inequalities, pollutes the nation's political discourse, and renders a democratic public sphere almost impossible. This toxic media ecology helped advance far-right discourses that redounded to Trump's advantage. A healthy news and information system must find a way to contain and contest the corrosive spread of misinformation. These measures must go beyond fact-checking after the damage has occurred.

Key sectors of the traditional news media deserve special scrutiny because people are singularly dependent on them for information. For example, tens of millions of Americans rely on local television broadcasting for their news—37 percent of adults, according to the Pew Research Center.[18] Even as broadcast television audiences have steadily declined in recent years, and trust has plummeted in media institutions overall, people still have relatively high levels of trust in their local news outlets. One survey by the Poynter Institute found that 76 percent of Americans across the political spectrum have "a great deal" or "a fair amount" of trust in their local television news.[19] Over the past two decades, however, the ownership of local television stations has become increasingly concentrated among a few players. This consolidation has further eroded local programming and constricted the range of views and voices people see and hear in their local news media.

One notorious example is the largest owner of local TV stations in the United States: the overtly right-wing Sinclair Broadcast Group. With many of its stations clustered in swing states, the company has stealthily accumulated tremendous political power. In 2004, Sinclair aired footage from the propagandistic documentary "Stolen Honor," which falsely attacked the Democratic presidential nominee John Kerry's Vietnam War record. Well known for promoting the Bush administration's policies, Sinclair's Executive Chairman David Smith is also a close ally of the Trump administration. Smith reportedly met with Trump during his presidential campaign, telling him: "We are here to deliver your message."[20] According to various reports, Trump's son-in-law Jared Kushner brokered a private agreement with Sinclair executives to conduct a series of exclusive interviews with Trump and other campaign officials. In exchange for access, Sinclair agreed to broadcast the interviews without any critical commentary.[21] Sinclair also has gained negative attention for forcing its local affiliates to air conservative commentaries, called "must-runs," as part of their news broadcasts. This practice continues unabated, even following scandals such as when former Trump staffer and frequent Sinclair political commentator Boris Epshteyn defended the use of tear gas against immigrant women and children at the US-Mexico border to repel an "attempted invasion."[22]

While force-feeding news outlets to air must-runs flies in the face of editorial independence and is deeply problematic for democracy, Sinclair has resorted to even more insidious practices. In April 2018, the sports news website Deadspin produced a video that compiled dozens of segments with news anchors all parroting the same script: "Some members of the media use their platforms to push their own personal bias and agenda to control exactly what people think. This is extremely dangerous to our democracy." The video went viral and elicited a public uproar, prompting the comedian John Oliver to quip: "Nothing says, 'We value independent media' like dozens of reporters forced to repeat the same message over and over again like members of a brainwashed cult."[23]

This practice of forcing local outlets to reproduce political messages is especially insidious because the script never identifies the content's original source. Most casual viewers who see right-wing talking points voiced by their local news anchor have no reason to assume such opinions are actually dictated from afar by an unseen broadcasting monopoly with particular political interests and allegiances. The local personalities are not wearing t-shirts with the name Sinclair emblazoned upon them, and there is no indication that this prepackaged content is being scripted by corporate headquarters. As the media critic Jay Rosen astutely notes: "These are local stations that advertise themselves as affiliates of ABC, CBS, NBC, and draw off the credibility of local anchors to present themselves as part of the community, with Sinclair HQ in Baltimore forcing delivery of these Trump-a-grams."[24]

Sinclair's willingness to play the ideological apparatchik paid off—at least at first. Its desire to merge with Tribune Media Company was an open secret, but many analysts were skeptical Sinclair would ever acquire regulatory approval. Immediately after the appointment of Trump's FCC Chairman, Ajit Pai, the FCC began making policy changes that seemed tailor-made to benefit Sinclair. In the first months of the Trump administration, the FCC pursued an aggressive regimen of regulatory rollbacks. For example, Pai reportedly granted an earlier request by Sinclair executives to relax some oversight on shell companies, and it abandoned its policy of closely scrutinizing "sidecar" or "joint sales agreements" that allow broadcasters to run the news operations of competing stations. These seemingly subtle policy alterations enable media giants like Sinclair to maintain control of multiple newsrooms and stations in the same market.[25]

In another dramatic reversal, the FCC repealed long-standing cross-ownership regulations that prevented one company from owning television and radio stations and a newspaper in one town. It also tossed out local TV ownerships limits that prevented a media firm from owning two of the top four stations (sometimes referred to as the duopoly rule) in the same city.[26] The FCC also did away with the so-called main-studio rule, which required local stations in a community to maintain a physical presence in or near that location. Without this protection, big corporate media giants like Sinclair can operate an entire station from a different part of the country, far removed from local voices and concerns.[27] Pai has indicated that he also wishes to jettison the media ownership cap that ensured that one company cannot own stations that collectively reach more than 39 percent of the country, but this would require an act of Congress.

The FCC's most egregious pandering, however, was in reinstating the UHF (Ultra-High Frequency) discount. This policy counts a UHF station's viewership as only half that of other stations because of its weak signal. The rule had become clearly obsolete after the country's broadcast frequencies transitioned to a digital system, which is why the previous FCC Chairman Tom Wheeler retired it. No persuasive argument or technological rationale existed for reinstating it—especially since the vast majority of Americans receive television channels through cable services where UHF has no meaning—but Sinclair could never merge with Tribune under existing ownership caps. Chairman Pai reintroduced the rule, thereby allowing Sinclair to obscure its actual market share and appear to stay within acceptable limits.

Had the merger gone through, it would have given Sinclair access to over 70 percent of US households (it now has access to 39 percent). To everyone's surprise, however, Chairman Pai suddenly reversed course and pulled his support late in the process, derailing Sinclair's attempt to dominate the US broadcast market. By most accounts, the deal almost certainly would have gone through had Sinclair not repeatedly misled the FCC regarding its efforts to divest itself of stations in particular markets, even after the FCC had relaxed key ownership restrictions.[28] Despite this anomalous move, the FCC's green-lighting of megamergers and repealing of cross-ownership bans in local news markets will likely hasten the rise of one-newsroom towns, leading to fewer local journalists and less diversity in voices and viewpoints represented in local media.

The Politics of Regulation and Regulatory Capture

How we regulate communication systems, including their ownership structures, has profound implications for news media and journalism. From early debates over the postal system to the founding of each new communication medium—including telegraphy, telephony, and broadcasting— government policy has always been central to media institutions and journalistic practices. That government is an unwanted interloper is, in reality, a libertarian fantasy: From spectrum management to copyright protections to internet governance, government is *always* involved—albeit often to the benefit of large media corporations.

The real question is *how* the government should be involved. Although it defies market fundamentalist mythology, the internet was in fact itself largely a government creation. While the predominant Silicon Valley narrative tends to portray the internet's birth as the product of tinkerers in garages, boy geniuses, and bold entrepreneurs, in actuality the internet largely grew out of massive public subsidies via military expenditures, the National Science Foundation, and public research institutions. This source of funding should not be surprising: Government has the advantage of taking on long-term, capital-intensive technological projects that the private sector typically avoids given the inherent short-term financial risks.

Erasing government's crucial role in developing our news media system implicitly positions the market as the sole driver of technological innovation and democratic progress. This common historical fallacy miscasts the state as either an impediment to good journalism or entirely absent from the field. For issues as diverse as public interest regulations, the enforcement (or lack thereof) of media ownership restrictions, and antitrust laws—to give just a few examples—policy plays a key role in how media systems are designed, owned, and operated. To pretend otherwise positions the architecture of our media systems as something that lies outside human agency.

Market libertarians typically describe the sorts of interventions being conducted by Chairman Pai's FCC as "deregulation." A more accurate term for this pro-industry agenda, however, is *regulation*. The current FCC is actively restructuring media systems to benefit corporate interests instead of the public. Accordingly, Chairman Pai has sought to satisfy cable and phone companies' long-standing policy wish lists. These moves signal a textbook definition of regulatory capture, a situation in which a government agency loses its independence by internalizing the commercial logics and value systems of the industries it is supposed to regulate.[29]

A key contributing factor to regulatory capture is the oft-lamented revolving door between the FCC and major media industries. For decades, FCC personnel have shuffled directly from the agency to the very corporations they once oversaw.[30] One analysis by the media reform organization Free Press found that of the twenty-seven commissioners and chairs who served on the FCC between 1980 and 2018, at least twenty-three had gone to work for companies and lobbying groups for the industries that they previously regulated.[31] Former FCC Commissioner Michael Copps, a committed public interest activist involved with several media reform organizations, is one of the exceptions. More typical is the career trajectory of former FCC Chairman Michael Powell.[32] Since leaving the FCC, Powell has been an outspoken advocate for pro-telecom policies as president and CEO of NCTA, the top lobbying group for the cable industry. In another egregious case, former FCC commissioner Meredith Atwell Baker left her post to become a top Comcast lobbyist several months after voting to approve the company's mega-merger with NBC.[33] Baker now heads the CTIA, a leading wireless trade association.

Regulatory capture is the norm throughout much of US government. Writing in the *American Conservative*, Jonathan Tepper, author of the book, *The Myth of Capitalism*, decries regulatory capture at the FTC and the DOJ, the leading agencies that oversee mergers and acquisitions. Tepper notes that these bodies are now "revolving doors for highly paid economists and lawyers whose only goal is to look after their corporate clients rather than voters, consumers, workers, suppliers, and competition."[34] Although many see deference to corporate power as a predominantly Republican position, the revolving door has been truly bipartisan. Many of President Obama's former FTC and DOJ officials now lobby for the firms they only recently regulated.[35]

Congress has also succumbed to similar dynamics—especially since congressional members rely on campaign donations, leaving them particularly susceptible to the direct effects of federal lobbying, a $3.37 billion industry in 2017.[36] The *New York Times* columnist Thomas Edsall aptly described this influence machine when he wrote: "The upper stratum of the Washington lobbying community often exercises de facto veto power over the legislative process, dominating congressional policymaking, funneling campaign money to both parties, and offering lucrative employment to retiring and defeated members of the House and Senate."[37] During my brief time as a congressional staffer, I witnessed firsthand the constant throngs of corporate proxies patrolling the halls of Congress, crowding into key offices, and lining up outside of important hearings. These often affable emissaries typically did not bring suitcases of money to bribe lawmakers, but they reinforced their subtle influence with phone calls, emails, and office visits.[38] Their communications were backed with the unspoken power of political donations and retributions.

Meanwhile, Congress's revolving door has become increasingly active. The *Washington Post* reports that a decade after the financial crisis brought the US economy near the abyss, about 30 percent of the lawmakers and 40 percent of the senior staff who wrote the Dodd-Frank Act—a key set of economic regulations—have gone to work for or on behalf of the financial industry.[39] Policymakers and citizens in other countries rightly see this extreme coziness between industry and government regulators as corruption, but it is standard procedure in the United States. While criticism of these unseemly political practices is rising, it will take major reforms to change them.[40] In the meantime, press reports that Facebook and Google spent tens of millions of dollars each on government lobbying in 2018 occasioned little public discussion.[41]

These power relationships matter for media policy because, over time, corporate influence over key regulatory agencies and other areas of government contributes to the broader ideological and discursive capture that I discussed in chapter 2. Backed up by a phalanx of right-wing think tanks and quasi-academic institutions, this corporate libertarian framework treats market forces as inviolable and deems aggressive regulation and public governance of media institutions as "off limits."[42] It creates what the media scholar Des Freedman terms "media policy silences"—the subtle turns of discourse "by which alternative options are marginalized, conflicting values delegitimized and rival interests de-recognized."[43] How we define key policy principles such as the "public interest"—and the government's role in upholding them—translates to policy and therefore shapes the fundamental design of our media system. These policy discourses—and the power structures behind them—helped lead us to where we are today: at the mercy of media monopolies.

Media Monopoly Power

With nearly every major sector of the economy now dominated by monopolies and oligopolies, Americans are slowly realizing they now inhabit a new Gilded Age.[44] The rise of monopoly power has dramatically restructured media and telecommunications markets. For example, two massive corporations, Comcast and Charter (which bought Time Warner Cable), dominate the cable television market. Comcast and Time Warner Cable actually tried to merge in early 2014—many commentators at the time thought the merger would sail through—but the deal fell apart in the face of a huge public backlash. The cell phone market is dominated by four (soon to be three) providers: together Verizon and AT&T command nearly 70 percent of the market, while the remaining two companies, T-Mobile and Sprint, are in the process of merging. Together these firms control 98 percent of the cell phone service market.[45] These firms often act in concert, forming oligopolies that do not compete with each other but rather function as cartels, with each member carving out a particular market for itself to maintain regional monopolies.[46]

While telecommunications monopolies are beginning to receive more scrutiny from regulators—especially as they buy up content companies—this skepticism has yet to translate to meaningful regulations. AT&T, following its merger with Time Warner, now owns HBO, Warner Bros, CNN, and has a stake in Hulu; Comcast owns NBC Universal (which includes the presumably liberal cable news channel, MSNBC) and DreamWorks Pictures; and Verizon owns Yahoo!, AOL, Tumblr, and the *Huffington Post*. Whereas horizontal integration allowed a small number of firms to gain control over the physical conduits for information, vertical integration allows these same companies to gain control over different stages in the supply chain of producing and disseminating that information.[47]

Vertical media ownership structures pose a particular threat to democracy. When the same company that owns the pipes also produces and controls the content flowing through them, a number of potential hazards arise that can harm consumers and the quality of our information system. Vertical integration creates structural vulnerabilities and perverse incentives for anti-competitive and anti-consumer behavior. For example, AT&T can privilege its own programs and content—a portfolio which has greatly expanded since the merger with Time Warner—over its competitors' and prevent other internet and cable companies from having access to them.[48] As internet service providers (ISPs) move into providing internet content and applications, they have increasing incentives to engage in such traffic discrimination. Vertical integration creates a significant conflict of interest, as these providers serve as both conduits of data, information, and content and owners and producers of much of this content.

In what antitrust reporter Sally Hubbard terms "platform privilege," monopolies such as Google and Amazon are similarly incentivized to prioritize their content and services over those of their competitors.[49] Hubbard offers the example of Google exploiting its monopoly position among mobile operating systems to exclude competition in mobile apps. As she notes, in 2018 the European Commission fined Google $5 billion for requiring phone makers that use Android to preinstall only Google's apps. Because over 80 percent of smartphones run on the Android system, this requirement effectively ensured Google's continued monopoly in mobile search.[50] The previous year, the commission had fined Google $2.7 billion for suppressing competitors' information in Google search results.[51] In recent years, Google has been charged with prioritizing its own reviews, maps, images, and travel-booking services in its search results while excluding its competitors in those markets.[52] These infractions fit a recurring pattern in which Google exploits its monopoly power to the detriment of consumers.

Despite the obvious and predictable problems that result from vertical mergers, they often get a free pass in the United States. Whereas horizontal ownership concentration typically faces intense regulatory scrutiny, courts often wave vertical integration through, putting only weak merger conditions in place. This has greatly facilitated the growth of media conglomerates such as Comcast, which merged with NBC Universal in 2011.[53] The conventional thinking in these cases is that vertical integration preserves competition while increasing efficiencies, which benefits consumers by providing them with better, more innovative, and affordable products and services. In the case of vertical integration between ISPs and content producers, however, mergers reduce competition and have not typically resulted in lower prices (in fact, companies can use their expanded content offerings to argue for hikes in their cable prices).

Monopolies harm consumers by stifling innovation (by purchasing competitors), raising prices (by extracting more wealth from consumers who have nowhere else to go), and tilting policy toward the firm's interests (by influencing politics through campaign donations). To give just one stark example of this latter problem, Rupert Murdoch built up his global media empire over decades by directly shaping media policy to his economic advantage—especially regarding ownership limits—in democratic nations around the world.[54] These machinations have had tremendously detrimental effects on culture, politics, and democratic prospects in a number of countries, including the United States, United Kingdom, and Australia.

Monopolistic behavior also undermines democratic ideals by favoring prepackaged, formulaic programming over locally produced content that resonates with specific communities. Such anti-competitive behavior harms consumers by leading to fewer content providers, higher prices, reduced information flow, and poorer service in general. When only a handful of corporations wield such tremendous cultural and political authority, this arrangement also obviously presents a political problem.[55] Concentrated media power—whether vertical or horizontal—makes it easier for oppressive political forces and oligarchs to dominate a media system.[56]

Neoclassical economics generally accepts that markets require competition to operate efficiently.[57] But without regulatory protections in place, dominant market players can abuse their control over output and price to prevent new competitors from entering the market. For this reason and others, governments typically prevent monopolies from forming via two general methods: restraining anti-competitive behavior through regulations and/or blocking mergers and acquisitions through antitrust laws. In the United States, however, decades of neoliberal policymaking have stripped these laws and regulations of their power. Aside from the quest for profit and political power, various economic factors encourage media markets to tend toward concentration, including—as discussed in chapter 2—high first-copy costs in producing original content (with near zero marginal costs for additional production). Moreover, the high fixed costs of telecommunications push the industry toward economies of scale, creating incentives for companies to covet large markets. Furthermore, the positive externalities that come with "network effects" of an always-expanding communications network—whether telephone systems or social media—also promote bigger firms. Finally, the fact that commercial media sells services to both audiences and advertisers incentivizes consolidation for one simple reason: The larger the audience, the greater the advertising revenue.[58] The presence of these tremendous financial incentives makes it extremely unlikely that media market concentration can be prevented through competition laws alone. Moreover, public interest protections are difficult to maintain when communication firms, whose first loyalty is to shareholders and profit imperatives, have few incentives to uphold them. It is nonetheless the role of media policy to mandate that communication firms honor public service principles such as universal and affordable access, transparency, and other democratic concerns.

Ultimately, the question of media ownership comes down to power. Des Freedman reminds us that media ownership confers various kinds of "media power" beyond profit margins. These range from the overt, such as when media magnates like Rupert Murdoch exploit editorial control to set policy agendas and parlay media ownership into political influence, to more subtle forms of "power elite" processes that reinforce alliances among the upper class and gently steer discourse in ways that "reproduce and legitimize the narratives of vested interests in society."[59] For these reasons and more, media ownership debates are typically among the most contentious policy battles within democratic societies. How these conflicts are resolved has profound implications for the health of journalism.[60]

Policy Battles over Media Ownership

Media ownership patterns are neither natural nor inevitable, but rather stem from explicit media ownership policies that typically received little public input or consent. Many policy battles over media ownership in the United States have focused on FCC regulations during which, more often than not, government intervened to advance corporate rather than public interests. With notable exceptions, the FCC has since the 1940s allowed the US news media system to become more commercialized and concentrated.[61] Potential alternatives to concentrated broadcast media such as cable television and satellite communications fell under the control of similar commercial interests. Making matters worse, the Reagan-era FCC jettisoned a number of public interest protections that sought to buffer media from undue commercial pressures, including the Fairness Doctrine. The deregulatory zeal that characterized 1980s media policy largely continued under subsequent Republican and Democratic administrations, as exemplified by the FCC's 2003 move to relax media ownership restrictions.[62]

The FCC has not been the only part of government that has facilitated merger sprees; Congress has also helped. Exhibit A was the 1996 Telecommunications Act, the first major overhaul of the landmark 1934 Communications Act. Purportedly an attempt to reform US media policy for the digital era, the bill passed Congress with significant bipartisan support, and President Bill Clinton signed it into law. This legislation replaced structural regulations with market incentives, deregulated cable rates, and removed key broadcast ownership limits, leading to massive consolidation and increased ownership concentration, particularly in broadcast media.[63] The Telecom Act eliminated the forty-radio-station national ownership cap, which allowed the media behemoth Clear Channel to acquire more than one 1,200 stations nationwide, dominating most major markets and limiting the diversity of voices on the public airwaves.[64]

As media ownership becomes more concentrated, commercial pressures intensify, often leading to cost-cutting and disinvestment in newsgathering operations. While difficult to substantiate specific causal links between media ownership structure and media content, scholars have long argued that ownership concentration and lack of competition leads to less local, investigative, and international news; less fact-based, critical reporting; and more homogeneous formats, trivial content, and slanted coverage.[65] Many also assume that media ownership concentration limits the diversity of voices in the news media, and research continues to bear this out. For example, Edda Humprecht and Frank Esser found in their comparative analysis of online news media across six countries that, while the relationships were not always straightforward, media ownership impacted diversity, with the presence of strong public service media having a significant positive influence.[66] Another important study on media ownership found that increased concentration of media ownership substantially increased coverage of national instead of local politics.[67] It is noteworthy that this ownership change also led to a significant rightward shift in the ideological slant of news coverage, but only small decreases in viewership. This suggests a substantial *supply-side* role in the trends toward nationalization and polarization of politics news, with negative implications for accountability of local elected officials and mass polarization. In other words, changes at the top were driving shifts in the audience, not the other way around.

Although the proliferation of digital media systems suggests a surface-level appearance of decentralization and a "high-choice media environment," in reality the root sources of this content are typically limited to a small number of large media conglomerates generating most of the available online content. While digital media technologies complicate media ownership patterns over time and obscure sector-specific concentration, the bigger picture has remained relatively stable, and concerns about extreme media concentration remain. One major concern among reformers has been that, even if further media consolidation and syndication might cut costs, create efficiencies, and pay short-term dividends (mostly to owners and shareholders), in the long term it leads to less original, in-depth news and information, as well as less creative entertainment media.

Unlike many other democratic nations, the United States does not have strong media diversity protections in place to maintain pluralistic systems, despite having a long anti-monopoly tradition going back to the dawn of the republic. Democracies typically assume that pluralistic and diverse societies require similar characteristics in their media systems. A wide range of media sources helps guarantee free-flowing information, commentary, and cultural content—all conducive for an informed citizenry, democratic participation, and consumer choice.[68] However, providing diverse cultural, political, and informational content is often commercially unviable and therefore such content remains under-produced. Since the market often fails in this regard, it is the role of policy to ensure heterogeneous media systems.

In a report where we outline essential media policy principles, Robert Picard and I argue that a healthy media system requires content defined by three overlapping characteristics: pluralism, variety, and diversity.[69] Pluralism refers to the range of ideas and views available in a media system, variety to the mix of genres and types of media content, and diversity to difference in characteristics and form. Media ownership concentration threatens all three. Most democratic nations promote media diversity in all its forms to ensure access to a wide variety of information sources.[70] Recall from chapter 1 the Supreme Court's famous AP decision declaring that democratic societies have a unique need to maintain a media system based on "diverse and antagonistic sources."[71] A commitment to this principle requires that all members of society have access to different ideas, form their own opinions, create their own media, and see and hear their voices and views represented. Therefore, media diversity necessitates multiple independent and autonomous media outlets that represent diverse political and ideological positions and cultural and ethnic perspectives specific to regions and municipalities beyond a country's capital and largest cities.[72] Employing either structural- or content-based approaches, democratic societies can ensure media representations of different regions, cultures, and social groups, especially minorities and other marginalized people regardless of gender, sexuality, age, ability, ethnicity, race, nationality, language, or income.[73]

Many democratic countries encourage pluralism and diversity through policies designed to foster competition, including ownership caps, direct and indirect subsidies for weaker firms, and other redistributive measures.[74] Unfortunately, US media policy rarely lives up to these principles, with considerable evidence showing that the FCC's media ownership policies have disproportionately harmed minority media ownership, especially in broadcast media.[75] Regulators can instead use a number of policy instruments to encourage new entrants into media markets. Picard and I lay out several options, such as facilitating more independent local, regional, and national media providers; placing domestic content requirements on foreign firms operating in the country; and deploying intellectual property laws and taxes to encourage diverse content.

Ultimately, however, market-based incentives for private investments in communication systems can only go so far. A healthy mixed media system also requires "structural diversity" that includes noncommercial elements—an idea I discuss more in the book's conclusion. And while ownership and content regulations are central concerns for maintaining a diverse media system, control over the underlying necessary infrastructure—such as broadband access—is also important.

The Broadband Problem for Journalism

Too often, questions about the future of journalism ignore the necessary underlying infrastructures that enable news media production and access. Journalism's digital turn has created new potentials—and new problems. While it has in some cases lowered barriers of entry and increased user choice for those with internet access, it has also created new forms of discrimination and censorship, high levels of dis/misinformation, and widespread corporate and state surveillance, among other hazards. These structural vulnerabilities have profound implications for digital journalism's future. Questions about the politics of digital infrastructures—namely digital media policies like net neutrality that relate to ownership, control, and inequality—should be central to discussions about the future of news.

Poor internet access, for example, is an infrastructure problem with serious implications for digital news media. According to 2015 FCC data, nearly a fifth of all US households still lack broadband internet. More recently, the FCC has tried to gloss over this problem by claiming that 92 percent of Americans have broadband access, but there is good reason to be skeptical of these claims.[76] For example, a 2018 Microsoft study has roundly refuted the FCC report, showing that an incredible 50 percent of Americans lack broadband access.[77] There are important debates over what exactly qualifies as "broadband" and important distinctions between access vs. adoption and availability vs. affordability. Nonetheless, state-level data continue to bear out troubling patterns, showing that the digital divide remains a serious social problem in the US, and one that has dire implications for the future of journalism.[78] Moreover, these divides are part of a broader systemic racism that disproportionately hurts communities of color.[79]

Prohibitive costs and lack of access are major contributors to the ongoing digital divide in the United States. These problems stem from the fact that most Americans are at the mercy of local monopoly markets with little choice in selecting an ISP, and therefore little recourse in dealing with costly and subpar service.[80] According to FCC estimates—which are notorious for overstating the amount of competition in the residential broadband market—42 percent of Americans have access to no more than one broadband provider. Susan Crawford refers to these scenarios as "captive markets" that disempower customers who are unable to switch providers despite being dissatisfied with their ISP.[81] Of the remaining internet users outside of captive markets, most are limited to just two ISPs in their communities.[82]

For these reasons and more, US broadband is notoriously shoddy compared to that in other advanced economies. Only 15 percent of the United States would be counted as having broadband access to more than one provider according to global standards for high-speed internet of 100 Megabits per second (Mbps) instead of the current 25 Mbps standard.[83] By sanctifying such low standards, the FCC allows ISPs to withhold investments in their aging infrastructure, for example by refusing to upgrade their lines from copper to fiber. In many cases, actual measures of these networks' speeds show that they fall short of even this paltry 25 Mbps standard, which can barely sustain today's levels of data usage. With more data-intensive applications on the horizon, and media outlets increasingly turning to video, these infrastructure-level policy failures will increasingly hinder Americans' ability to access news media—as well as journalists' ability to produce the news.

While the broadband market has disadvantaged consumers and democratic participation, it has handsomely rewarded internet service monopolies with enormous profits.[84] Most Americans pay more for slower connections compared to internet users around the world. The average monthly price for an internet plan ranging in speed from 25 to 50 Mbps in major US cities ranges from $64.95 (New York City) to $69.98 (Los Angeles). Meanwhile, an internet user in London pays an average of $24.77 per month to enjoy the same internet speed.[85] Swedish and Norwegian internet users have access to some of the world's highest average speeds while paying a monthly fee of up to 30 percent less than the average US internet user.[86] Most residents in South Korea can choose between three major high-speed ISPs and pay less than $30 a month for some of the world's fastest broadband services.[87] These disparities result from different competition policies in broadband markets. Without policy protections, ranging from public interest regulations to anti-monopoly measures, internet service monopolies like Comcast and Verizon are free to extract monopoly rents from their customers far beyond what competitive markets would normally command.[88] Firms such as AT&T, Charter, Comcast, and Verizon dominate the broadband access market by acquiring and merging with potential rivals and by avoiding direct competition with each other—comprising what David Berman and I term a "broadband cartel."

US broadband policy differs from that of much of the democratic world in another key area: lack of net neutrality protections. Net neutrality refers to the safeguards that prevent ISPs from interfering with access to online communications or unreasonably discriminating against certain kinds of content. In our book on the history and politics of net neutrality, Berman and I note that since 2001—in stark contrast to the United States—the European Union (EU) has mandated that incumbents share their network infrastructure with competitors.[89] Many OECD countries outside the EU also enjoy open access policies, an approach that maintains healthy broadband markets. The United States is, yet again, a global outlier among democracies after the Trump FCC jettisoned net neutrality protections in 2017.

One obvious hazard with losing net neutrality is that ISPs can privilege specific kinds of internet traffic over others (recall the earlier discussion of vertical integration), allowing them to extract even more money from internet users and content providers alike. While they can now legally charge their customers more for accessing specific types of content such as high-quality video streaming, a more probable future scenario would have ISPs seeking to coerce payments directly from content creators. In a world without net neutrality, this "pay-to-play" digital landscape will see the costs of "paid prioritization" absorbed by those websites willing and able to pay for the privilege of fast lanes. Ultimately, however, internet users will probably suffer the costs in the form of fewer choices and higher fees.

Losing net neutrality when monopolies dominate internet markets is the worst of multiple worlds, giving the broadband cartel enormous advantages over both consumers and content providers. These conditions render internet users powerless to discipline their ISP for blocking or degrading access to their preferred websites and applications. Vertical integration is particularly concerning in this scenario because ISPs' increasing control over internet access incentivizes them to discriminate against content and applications in ways that benefit their bottom line. As noted earlier, a major conflict of interest emerges when media conglomerates own the conduits of data and information as well as much of the content that flows through their channels and wires in a given market. Such vertical combines can undermine rival content producers by deprioritizing competitors' traffic while privileging their own. For example, AT&T can now prioritize the traffic of content it owns, like streaming HBO movies, at the expense of other, competing media that flow through its pipes.

The degree to which ISPs can exploit their monopoly power by restricting the flow of content through their networks and setting expensive terms of access for consumers has profound implications for digital news media. Anyone involved in media production—especially journalists who are likely to upset powerful interests—should be concerned about a post-net-neutrality regime that legally sanctions corporate censorship online. Trump's FCC rendered the internet less hospitable for all media makers, but those most at risk range from professional print reporters to independent journalists—particularly those using video—who cannot afford to pay exorbitant fees to ensure that ISPs do not relegate their content to digital "slow lanes." These policy issues should be a key concern within conversations about the future of news media.

The battle to restore net neutrality continues in the courts, in Congress, in the states, and on the streets. But even with net neutrality protections— a necessary but insufficient safeguard—the future of a healthy news media system is imperiled by corporate capture of the internet. Instead, we need *public* broadband services owned and controlled by people—at the community, municipal, state, and national levels—not by a few massive corporations. Providing internet subsidies to low-income Americans while allowing communities to offer their own broadband services would likely expand access to online news media.[90] A number of exciting local broadband initiatives already exist in some 750 communities across the United States, but corporate-inspired state laws prevent widespread experimentation in 26 states by hindering or outright banning municipal internet services.[91]

If we are serious about preserving the future of journalism, we must consider the policy interventions necessary to sustain a free-flowing and reliable news media system. This will require ensuring a national "baseline connectivity" of sufficient speed and affordability that is universally accessible across the country. Before we take on this project, however, we must first address the larger threat of unregulated corporate power, especially that of the new platform monopolies.

Confronting the New Digital Monopolies

I started this chapter with a reference to Facebook. Before moving on to potential solutions, it is worth dwelling for a moment on this new kind of communication firm, the platform monopoly.[92] In some ways, it is not new at all. From the beginning, digital monopolies like Google and Facebook encouraged consumers and regulators to think of them as a new breed, the kind of companies that would "do no evil" and "move fast and break things." During these firms' early ascendance, too many commentators were seduced by Silicon Valley's ethos. Too many stood silent or joined the chorus when Mark Zuckerberg and his cohort told us that the internet was beyond the realm of regulation, that it was inherently democratic, and that benevolent corporations were the best arbiters of this vital communication system. Instead of transcending the laws of political economics, however, Facebook and its ilk act like any old monopoly, willing to do whatever it takes to maintain tremendous profits. By not applying antitrust laws and regulatory protections, we have permitted Facebook to abuse its power, and now we reap the consequences.

In other ways, the power wielded by platform monopolies is unprecedented.[93] For millions of users, especially in the global South, Facebook *is* the internet, in some cases even acting as a free ISP (limiting access to Facebook's "Free Basics" program).[94] As Facebook extracts profound wealth across the globe, it has generated tremendous negative externalities. Not only has it mishandled users' data, abused its market power, proliferated dangerous misinformation and propaganda, enabled foreign interference, and even abetted and embedded with the Trump campaign in the run-up to the 2016 elections.[95] It has also played a key role in destabilizing elections in places like the Philippines and facilitated ethnic cleansing in Myanmar.[96] Considering the accumulating damage Facebook wreaks around the world and the skewed power asymmetry between the platform monopoly and its billions of users, we need a new social contract. Despite the lack of silver-bullet policy solutions, this moment of increased scrutiny and public awareness offers a rare—and most likely fleeting—opportunity to hold a national (and international) debate about what interventions are best suited to address the problem. Ultimately, misinformation is a structural problem; it will take structural reforms to fix it.

It is difficult to overstate the social harms of Facebook's monopoly power, especially to the integrity of our news and information systems. As an algorithm-driven global editor and news gatekeeper for over two billion users, Facebook wields unprecedented power over much of the world's information system. In the United States, where Americans increasingly access news through the platform, Facebook's role in the 2016 presidential election has drawn well-deserved scrutiny. Moreover, along with Google, Facebook is devouring the lion's share of digital advertising revenue and

starving the institutions that provide quality news and information—
the same struggling news organizations that it expects to help fact-check
against misinformation. Journalism in general, and local news in particular,
are increasingly threatened by the Facebook-Google duopoly, which in recent years took a combined 85 percent of all new US digital advertising revenue growth, leaving only scraps for news publishers.[97] According to one
study, these two companies control 73 percent of the total online advertising
market.[98] Meanwhile, these same companies play an outsized role in proliferating misinformation.

Various forms of misinformation and propaganda have plagued societies
for centuries, but the profound media power now residing in one monopolistic platform arguably presents a unique challenge to democratic governance.[99] Critiques about Facebook's technology and design are growing
amid increased public scrutiny for the misinformation it purveys and from
which it profits, but a core problem of this business model deserves more
scrutiny.[100] The proliferation of dis/misinformation is symptomatic of
an unregulated media monopoly governed solely by profit imperatives.
Facebook is not evil; it is merely the natural outgrowth of an information
system governed by an unaccountable, commercial logic. Despite fines and
threats, especially in Europe, Facebook has taken few meaningful actions to
address hate speech and misinformation. In the United States, technocratic
discourses have dominated discussions, with suggested remedies typically
involving a combination of media literacy and user responsibility. This emphasis, of course, places the onus on users instead of Facebook. By avoiding
structural reforms that would require revising its business model, Facebook
deflects responsibility while pretending to be proactive, for instance by intro-
ducing new algorithms and policing specific ad networks. The company has
also crowd-sourced and outsourced fact-checking by off-loading the responsibility of flagging fake news to the public and to third parties, such as Snopes
(which has since terminated the partnership), the Associated Press, and even
partisan sites, including the now-defunct *Weekly Standard* and the far-right
Daily Caller.[101]

Despite compelling arguments that Facebook should be held accountable
to the legal requirements and norms of social responsibility associated with
media companies, Mark Zuckerberg has long refused to acknowledge that
Facebook is anything more than a technology company—except in courts
when Facebook tries to have it both ways by claiming First Amendment
rights normally reserved for media publishers. In public, however, Facebook

representatives maintain that the company is not a publisher, thereby avoiding responsibilities that normally accompany this distinction.[102] Facebook's devastating effects on journalism and its violations of our privacy are untenable. But until we as a society diagnose the structural roots of the misinformation problem, potential solutions will remain elusive.[103] History shows us that expecting good corporate behavior simply by shaming monopolies is a dubious proposition, at best.

Historically, the US government has deployed various laws and policies to contain monopoly power, particularly in industry sectors that tend toward "natural monopolies."[104] This arrangement acknowledges that specific industries, especially networks such as communication systems, tend toward one large centralized entity, partly due to the considerable high fixed costs of building such systems and partly due to greater efficiencies. Similar to that of a public utility, such firms often offer core services or infrastructures—such as electricity, transportation systems, and water. Because they are expensive to maintain but essential for the public good, many societies shield these services from unmitigated market forces. Instead of breaking up such monopolies, governments might use regulatory incentives and penalties to prevent them from exploiting their market power.[105] But Facebook has managed to escape this arrangement. It is not under close government regulation or oversight. Nor do regulators expect Facebook to provide the kind of deliverables that would normally be expected from a state-sanctioned monopoly.

A counter-example is the government's treatment of AT&T (also called the Bell System), whose phone network attained a similarly dominant position in the early twentieth century. To forestall government regulation (including a threatened government takeover of its network), AT&T agreed to exit from a related market (telegraphy), interconnect with most non-AT&T systems, invest heavily in research and development (Bell Labs), maintain reasonable rates (especially for local calls), and help promote universal service. These interventions did not solve all problems related to AT&T's monopoly, but they did create a number of tangible benefits for society. In addition to preventing AT&T from entering the newly emergent computer industry, part of a 1956 consent decree reached with the US government forced the telephone monopoly to share all of its patents free of charge. Some historians have credited this coerced generosity with major technological innovations; for example, the transistor was among AT&T's vast portfolio of patents. Freely licensable patents helped create the necessary conditions for developing the semiconductor and other major advances in computing, data communications, and software industries.[106]

The historical parallel is not perfect—AT&T was a common carrier that controlled the actual telephone wires—but it is instructive to consider what concessions a looming threat of antitrust litigation might bring. Before it was ultimately broken up in the 1980s, AT&T at various points agreed to divest key components of its portfolio, radically change its business practices, and offset social costs and negative externalities. Nor is AT&T the only example of the government using its antitrust powers to spur innovation. To give another stark example: If the DOJ had not intervened against Microsoft in the 1990s to halt its anti-competitive behavior in (among other areas) the internet browser market, Microsoft could have forced computer makers to only use its own search engine, and Google might not exist today.[107]

Antitrust and pro-competition laws have long protected competition and encouraged innovation, but the approach requires reframing key policy debates and broadening the political imagination of what is possible. In recent years, anti-monopoly protections have grown anemic, with antitrust authorities giving "a green light to merger after merger," in the words of the writer Jonathan Tepper. He continues, "The guardians who were meant to protect competition have become the principal cheerleaders of monopolies . . . Antitrust law is not so much dormant as it is actively sabotaged by the very people who should enforce it."[108] But after years of quiescence, there is now a growing clamor to reinvigorate antitrust laws to take on the new platform monopolies. For example, the government could force Facebook to divest specific components such as WhatsApp, Messenger, and Instagram. For its part, Google could be forced to divest DoubleClick, YouTube, and AdMob.

Antitrust measures should always be on the table as a credible threat, but they represent only one of several potential policy interventions against Facebook's monopoly powers. In Europe, regulators are trying to compensate for earlier policy failures that allowed Facebook to set its own terms by implementing new policies designed to protect users' privacy. The European Union's new General Data Protection Regulation (GDPR) ensures that internet users in the twenty-eight EU countries understand and consent to the data collected about them regardless of where that data is stored and processed. The GDPR also guarantees a "right to be forgotten" that allows EU citizens to permanently remove online personal data, as well as a right to "data portability" that allows users to download their data and move it elsewhere.[109]

Other European interventions have attempted to hold social media platforms accountable for the content posted on their sites and for their business practices. Germany, for example, passed a "Facebook law" that allows for fines against large social media platforms that fail to police against hate speech. Platform companies could face fines of €50 million for failing to remove identified hate speech within twenty-four hours.[110] The European Union has fined Google three times for various kinds of malfeasance since 2017, most recently $1.7 billion for unfair advertising practices.[111] Facebook, too, has repeatedly faced fines and threats from European countries for antitrust, hate speech, and data protection violations.[112]

The United States lags behind Europe in confronting digital monopolies, but more punitive measures are on the rise. Although it delivered a relatively light penalty in the eyes of many critics, the FTC charged Facebook $5 billion for privacy violations.[113] Other potential regulatory interventions being discussed in the United States include Federal Election Commission rules banning political advertising by dark money groups and foreign governments; reforming Section 230 of the Communications Decency Act of 1996 that shields interactive computer services from legal liability for user-generated content (and the removal of such content); mandating complete transparency of algorithms and data collection; and requiring data portability and interoperability. Many of these potential interventions are unlikely to ever be enacted—and some may create problems of their own—but they attest to an entire toolbox of regulatory instruments at policymakers' disposal to rein in unruly monopolies.

Earlier policy failures have had dire consequences, but it is not too late to fix things. Facebook's power does not stem from magical technology or the market's genius. Rather, all societies face political decisions over how they will govern their communication infrastructures, and, for most of the world, Facebook has become a critical communication infrastructure. Facebook's technology is not inviolable; humans create its algorithms. Facebook proved this point when it suddenly adjusted its algorithms in 2018 to privilege friends and family posts over those from news publishers.[114] Facebook is not beyond regulation. Moreover, given its massive profits, Facebook could commit money to journalism (an idea to which I return in the conclusion) and hire legions of human screeners and editors (and provide better working conditions for those they already employ).[115]

Facebook's defenders have countered that Facebook's content-related problems are too vast to fix. It is not reasonable, these commentators say, to ask a corporation to police the posts of 2.3 billion users around the globe.

While it is true that this problem is not simply Facebook's to solve, we cannot let the company that created the problem off the hook. Democratic societies must determine Facebook's social responsibilities and how to enforce them. International grassroots groups, watchdog institutions made up of independent experts, an independent council of journalists, technologists, and public advocates, should devise means of oversight and help monitor and audit Facebook's actions, all while pressuring Facebook to be more transparent and accountable. These bottom-up discussions should be held openly and internationally, with the participation of diverse constituencies. Public governance should be the ultimate objective.

Social media is never "free." We pay for it dearly in our content, data, labor, and attention. As the old saw goes: if you are getting something for free, most likely *you* are the product. But even today, many users do not understand the true nature of this exchange and the egregious lack of privacy protections online. Survey data show that when people understand the extent to which Facebook shares their personal information with advertisers, the majority of users are uncomfortable with such a relationship.[116] At the same time, other studies show, they feel a sense of resignation about these terms because they feel disempowered to change the power relationship.[117]

In response to the growing awareness of Facebook's many infractions, a #DeleteFacebook movement has emerged, especially in the United States. While it is tempting to simply quit Facebook and delete one's account, such an individualistic, consumer-based reaction does not encourage institutional change, which generally requires collective action. Given the social media company's tremendous network effects (the network's increasing size makes it more valuable to users and more costly to leave), it is unreasonable to expect a mass exit from Facebook. Rather, continued expansion is the more likely outcome, especially since many groups of people around the world depend on Facebook for basic communications. Containing corporate power at this scale requires systemic reform—not individual action—and such a massive project in turn requires a commitment to collective action and meaningful policy interventions.

What Is to Be Done: Break-up, Regulate, or Remove from the Market?

Facebook and other platform monopolies such as Amazon, Google, and Apple simply have too much power over the world's media and politics.

Checking their power requires a combination of trustbusting, regulation, and creating public alternatives. The US political imaginary is too often limited to individual freedoms and consumer rights, but we can rise above this impoverished vision to draw from a social democratic tradition that conceptualizes news and information as public goods that should not be left solely to the corrosive commercialism of unregulated monopolies—a theme I return to in the next chapter.

A new social contract for digital media must assert public control over communication systems and provide funding for the public infrastructure that sustains democratic society. We especially need journalism that can focus on local issues and hold the powerful to account. Any new arrangement should protect content creators and individual users (i.e., those who actually produce the labor from which Facebook profits). Most importantly, this new contract must privilege society's democratic needs over platform monopolies' sole objective of maximizing profit. Doing so is a necessary step toward restructuring our global media system and preventing unaccountable information monopolies from ever arising again. But how do we get there? Do we repeat old mistakes and impose self-regulation requirements that are weakly enforced and likely to erode over time? Or do we subject Facebook's monopolistic power to real public oversight and implement redistributive measures?

Fortunately, a growing anti-monopoly movement has coalesced over the last several years, channeled by politicians such as Senator Elizabeth Warren and advocacy groups such as the Open Markets Institute.[118] At the intellectual level, this movement benefits from a growing consensus that something must be done to confront concentrated corporate power in general and the new tech monopolies in particular. It also coincides with a growing "techlash" against Silicon Valley-based internet firms. A lively debate has emerged in recent years with two major camps—mostly on the Left, but including people from across the political spectrum—crystallizing around what sometimes are referred to as the Jeffersonian or neo-Brandeisian approach, which emphasizes breaking up monopolies, and the Hamiltonian approach, which favors regulated monopolies.[119]

The neo-Brandeisian approach (named after Supreme Court Justice Louis Brandeis) focuses on breaking up concentrated market power and encouraging competition, especially through antitrust measures. This framework guides much of the growing US anti-monopoly movement, whose main objective is to break up monopolies into smaller units along structural lines, thus creating a much more decentralized economic environment in which numerous firms compete for consumers.[120] Anti-monopoly activists rightly identify the Chicago School of antitrust analysis, especially that associated with conservative economists and legal scholars such as Robert Bork, as the intellectual paradigm that led us down the path to excessive monopolization. More than anyone else, Bork helped reorient antitrust law toward what is known as the "consumer welfare standard," which supposedly seeks to maximize consumer benefits, but is less concerned with public interest considerations such as unemployment and protecting small businesses.[121] During the Reagan administration, this approach became the dominant paradigm, with the government willing to approve mergers so long as companies promised to keep prices low. Regulatory bodies exhibited less concern toward other well-known problems related to concentrated economic and political power, which led to highly concentrated industries exacting terrible social costs.[122] Future historians will puzzle over how this paradigm ever became so prevalent.

The neo-Brandeisian intervention, therefore, is a timely and necessary corrective. US antitrust enforcement has been on the wrong path for decades—with disastrous consequences. But while the ideal of maintaining robust competition among many small producers is an appealing one, one limitation of the anti-monopoly model is that it fails to directly challenge the commercial basis of US communication systems. Many anti-monopoly activists tend to scrutinize the size of monopolies and the lack of competition, rather than the commercial values and relationships that underpin them. This critique tends to sideline critical questions about whether media systems should be governed by market relationships in the first place—or whether they should be, as much as possible, entirely removed from the market. After all, it is reasonable to assume that all of our media-related problems cannot be solved simply by reducing the size and multiplying the number of commercial outlets that depend on surveillance advertising, disseminating low-quality content, and undervaluing democratic concerns. In other words, Facebook is also a capitalism problem, not just a monopoly problem.[123]

Neo-Brandeisians may see their mirror opposite as the Hamiltonian approach, which favors centralization. Part of this position rests on the notion that greater efficiencies stemming from scale and scope may create benefits for workers and consumers. According to this view, progressive Hamiltonians are comfortable with large producers because they are easier to unionize and regulate. Within this regulated monopoly paradigm, big government can serve as a countervailing force against the excesses of big capital. The neo-Brandeisians, for their part, criticize the Hamiltonian position as naïve and accommodationist. Their understandable concern is that regulating monopolies instead of smashing them risks locking in and legitimating concentrated corporate power. The neo-Brandeisian notion that "big is bad"—or, as Brandeis himself referred to it, "the curse of bigness"— benefits from a kind of intuitive resonance of justice. Moreover, the desire to trust-bust monopolies has a populist appeal, connects with a rich history, and often presents itself as the radical—or at least the more progressive—option in policy debates. But in fact, the neo-Brandeisian approach is, in some ways, a conservative position; it sees a fair and orderly market as the proper regulator of news media. In other words, it assumes that commercial systems can serve democracy well, if only we manage them appropriately.

Some analysts have begun arguing that antitrust is necessary but insufficient in designing a media system that serves democratic aims.[124] These critics argue that it should not be an either/or but rather a both/and. Even leading analysts who fall squarely within the neo-Brandeisian camp argue that the plan should be "break-up and regulate."[125] But there is also a third way. What both of these approaches lack is a systemic critique of the market's failure to support public goods. Unaccountable monopoly power is both a contributing factor to and symptom of this structural problem. We need to search for structural alternatives to the "surveillance capitalism" that drives so much of our digital news and information systems.[126] We need public options.

The Search for Structural Alternatives

A clear-eyed view of the structural problems facing journalism entails understanding not only that questions of media ownership and control are central to journalism's future, but also that government will have to take a more active role. It has been particularly challenging to have this conversation in the United States, where for many years a corporate libertarian paradigm has dominated policy debates and First Amendment absolutism impeded government intervention on behalf of news institutions. Nonetheless, we can advance the debate if we clarify what is at stake and what policy interventions are necessary to guarantee a viable system for public service journalism. Many threats facing journalism—from the spread of monopoly power to the regulatory capture of our entire policy-making apparatus— are structural problems that require structural remedies. These remedies must include containing monopolies and, as much as possible, minimizing commercialism's effects on journalism.

The run-amok concentration of media ownership underscores the structural nature of US media's failures. Irresponsible journalism results from commercial pressures that privilege particular types of news coverage over others, not the malfeasance of a few bad journalists or news organizations. For example, Facebook designs its algorithms to encourage its users to engage with content on the platform, because this is the action that sells targeted ads and drives corporate profits. As users, we are more likely to engage with material that has an emotional pull—if something makes us angry or scares us or entertains us. Hence, Facebook's algorithms reward content that fuels outrage—which mainstream news media produces by emphasizing political conflict. Consumer tracking and profiling encourages advertisers and news outlets to focus their efforts on narrowly tailored clickbait, regardless of a story's veracity. In the end, commercial logics and, specifically, the need to maximize profits via advertising revenue over all other concerns, drives contemporary digital journalism. Ultimately, the commercial nature of our media system enables and amplifies misinformation.

A clickbait-riddled news media system is obviously a suboptimal way to design a core global information system. To return to an observation I made earlier in this chapter, perhaps the real question is why we ever expected anything different to emerge from such a commercialized, profit-driven system? Why did we ever assume that Facebook would behave differently from any other monopoly throughout history? This recurring blindspot is just one more reminder that if we do not understand the logics of a commercial media system—or, put differently, if we do not understand the effects of capitalism on a media system—we will always be taken by surprise by the behavior of bad actors.

Des Freedman put it plainly when he challenged the notion that social media offered a radical redistribution of power. Given the now overwhelming evidence that earlier utopian aspirations for the internet have not transpired, Freedman observes, "the digital economy, just like the 'analogue' one . . . is marked by the same tendencies towards concentration and consolidation, towards enclosing and protecting private property."[127] The thought that digital media somehow transcended these capitalistic imperatives was always an ideological assumption, not an empirical one. We are now reaping the consequences of this magical thinking.

Must we merely repeat these same mistakes and patterns? Must we watch, yet again, commercial interests squander the democratic potentials of new media technologies? Is there a way out of this paradigm? Can we imagine a communication system guided by a democratic logic? In the next chapter, I draw on historical and international examples to discuss what alternative infrastructures to our current monopoly-dominated commercial system might look like. One alternative model—and a very old one at that—is the public media option.

5

American Media Exceptionalism and the Public Option

Imagine trying to describe the US news media system to a visitor from another dimension. After noting how vital the press is for our democratic way of life, you would have to explain that this system is primarily financed by selling advertising to often-unwitting media consumers. Then you would have to describe how our major media institutions are owned and controlled by a few people—mostly white, rich men—who accumulate wealth by informing and entertaining audiences. Finally, you would have to explain how the overall value of our news media system is largely determined by ratings, clicks, and profitability for these owners and investors.

If we were to design a media system from scratch—a media system based on serving democratic needs, not private profits—the US model would not be our first choice. In fact, as my previous work shows, the current system reflects the policy victories of media corporations more than the desires of US citizens.[1] Much of what we now take for granted about the shape of our media is the direct result from previous struggles in which at key moments commercial interests triumphed over democratic concerns. The lasting legacy of this commercial consensus has had dramatic consequences. The system we have inherited in the United States differs remarkably from most others throughout the democratic world. In what follows, I unpack this "US media exceptionalism" and discuss its implications for journalism's future. The rest of the chapter explores what is arguably the most viable alternative to a commercialized system: public media.

US Media Exceptionalism

The US media system occupies a special category according to three indices.[2] First, a handful of corporations—essentially oligopolies or duopolies—dominate the US media system. As we saw in chapter 4,

Democracy Without Journalism?. Victor Pickard, Oxford University Press (2020). © Victor Pickard
DOI: 10.1093/oso/9780190946753.001.0001

this pattern holds steady across many sectors, including social media, search engines, internet access, cable television, digital advertising, cell phone services, and many sectors of the news media. Second, the US media system is only lightly regulated by public interest protections. Earlier regulations such as the Fairness Doctrine, which mandated that broadcasters present diverse views on important issues in a balanced manner, were jettisoned decades ago.[3] Third, the US media system is largely commercial with underfunded public alternatives. In most cases, this commercialism has depended on advertising revenue. As mentioned earlier, unlike many of their counterparts around the world, US newspapers relied heavily on advertising for the past century. Until only recently, advertising still comprised, on average, more than 80 percent of overall revenue.[4]

Democratic countries often face one or two of these problems in their media system, but the perfect trifecta is rare. The US system is an outlier among democracies, providing a case study by which scholars can observe the effects of largely unmitigated commercial pressures on journalistic practices. Professional ethics (such as adherence to truth-based reporting and separating advertising from news), unionization (such as The Newspaper Guild's efforts discussed in Chapter 1), and a few public interest regulations (such as the aforementioned Fairness Doctrine for broadcast media) have long sought to protect news media from undue commercialism. But these buffers have been entirely dismantled or significantly weakened in recent years. The resulting unchecked commercialism sets US media apart from other systems.[5] The most significant difference, however, is the lack of a strong public media system. Public media can provide a baseline for reliable information and act as a safety net when the market fails to support adequate levels of news production. In its paltry support of public media, the United States is in a league of its own.

Comparisons with several industrialized nations show the extent of US exceptionalism.[6] Whereas Japan, Britain, and Northern European countries spend anywhere from $50 to well over $100 per capita on public media, the United States government allocates about $1.40 per person per year. Even if you add in the meager funding from local and state governments, the total still amounts to less than $4. The United States is a global outlier among leading democracies, as illustrated in Figure 5.1, which shows how the country is almost literally off the chart for how little it spends on its public media system.

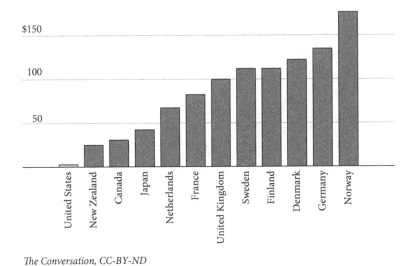

Figure 5.1 Amount Spent on Public Media on a Per Capita Basis (in US dollars)

In recent years, US public media have been threatened with further im-
poverishment by Republican attempts to defund public media altogether.[7]
The United States' ongoing failure to properly fund such a crucial system is
especially disheartening considering that research, which I discuss later in
this chapter, shows considerable social benefits associated with strong public
media systems. The US public media system never lived up to its democratic
potential, but its democratic promise remains. Given the various challenges
facing US journalism, now is an opportune time to reassess the merits of
public media. Before we design a new system, we must glean lessons from
mistakes and best practices—both from our past and from around the world.
Therefore, it is necessary to briefly recount the history of US public media
and revisit the original justifications for creating a noncommercial media
system. I begin by providing a general overview of how Americans came to
inherit a media system that is so commercialized and a public media system
that is so anemic.

A Social Democratic Vision of Broadcast Media

The US commercial model could not have triumphed without first
delegitimating a social democratic alternative.[8] In many ways, US public

broadcasting is a vestige of this lost alternative. Few Americans are familiar with the term "social democracy," and fewer still know the long history of social democratic challenges to the corporate libertarianism underpinning the US commercial media system. Tracing these ideological roots to their foundational debates in the postwar decades is instructive for how specific political battles over early radio shaped the entire US media system.

I use the term "social democracy" to refer to a specific ideological project, one that privileges a media system's public service mission over its profit-making objectives.[9] Emphasizing social benefits over property rights, this perspective assesses a media system according to whether it benefits all of society rather than how it enhances individual freedoms and profits for a privileged minority. As discussed in earlier chapters, two normative premises feature prominently within most versions of social democracy: positive freedoms (freedom for) are valued as much as negative freedoms (freedom from), and universal rights are championed as much as individual property rights. In other words, social democracy elevates a positive liberty that values *collective* rights—pertaining to publics, audiences, and communities—at least as much as the individual freedoms most cherished within libertarianism and classical liberalism. To countervail against unregulated capitalism's oligarchic tendencies, this ideology legitimates an activist state that redistributes resources in an egalitarian fashion. Social democracy begins with the question of whether a policy is good or just, as opposed to whether it is profitable or efficient.[10]

Moreover, social democracy assumes that some services and infrastructures are especially susceptible to various kinds of market failure and are too vital to be pegged to market fluctuations. Therefore, social democracy promotes a mixed system and treats fundamental services like education as public goods that require subsidies and special protections from commercial pressures—sometimes removing them from the market altogether. A social democratic project seeks to bolster civil society by investing in critical infrastructures and institutions like health care, libraries, and schools.[11]

While many of the US media system's commercial foundations had already been established by the 1930s, the social contract defining media's role within a democracy remained in flux. In particular, the question of what commercial media owed the public—and how the government should enforce those obligations—was left unresolved until the 1940s. Ultimately, policymakers pivoted away from a social democratic model of media governance, instead encouraging a lightly regulated, oligopolistic system increasingly defined by profit imperatives. This model viewed news media not as public goods but primarily as private properties and business commodities—a commercial logic that paved the way for our current journalism crisis. The corporate capture of the First Amendment further shielded media firms from regulatory interventions.[12] Crystallized in the postwar 1940s, this logic continues to straitjacket much of the discourse about potential reforms for supporting journalism. It was only in the past several decades, however, that this corporate-friendly view of the US media system came to be commonsensical.

But while a social democratic approach to media was the "road not taken," the vision never entirely vanished. Despite vicious red-baiting, corporate lobbying, and other forms of political coercion, the notion that a different media system was possible lived on. Although much of their agenda had failed by the end of the 1940s, reformers continued advocating for structural change. Their efforts eventually led to what became the United States' only major institutional alternative to the commercial media system.

The Rise and Fall of US Public Broadcasting

A history of how the United States' strange media system came to be might begin with the three-plus decades leading up to the 1967 Public Broadcasting Act.[13] Fleshing out the ideological battles throughout the prehistory of public broadcasting—what was then usually referred to as "educational broadcasting"—brings into focus the original aspirations for public media, particularly the more radical strands that sought to create a structural alternative to the corporate-dominated, commercial model. Looking back and recovering some of the arguments for establishing an alternative to the prevailing commercial media model suggests a largely forgotten social democratic ideal, one that clearly recognized that a market-driven media system could not provide for all of democratic society's communication needs.

Scholarship on its early political history shows competing visions for public broadcasting, including fundamental differences over how the "public" was imagined.[14] A related critique that emerges is the perennial charge of cultural elitism—as well as a lack of focus on issues pertaining to low-income households—in public radio and television programming.[15] A recurring theme in many of these histories show there was a lost promise to public broadcasting's original ideal.[16] While some of these accounts illuminate the rationales for investing in a strong public media system, the implicit ideological project—that public broadcasting stemmed from a social democratic vision directly at odds with commercial values—has not been made explicit enough in the existing historiography.[17] In what follows, I tease out some of the tacit ideological aims behind these early attempts to establish a public broadcasting system. Doing so reveals what was lost—and what still might be gained.

Missed Opportunities of the 1930s and 1940s

In US radio's early days, a serious discussion unfolded regarding the fundamental nature and normative foundations of broadcast media in a democratic society. Formidable coalitions of educators and activists began to sway members of Congress to support a broadcast system that devoted significant swaths of the radio spectrum to noncommercial, educational purposes. However, these discussions began to taper off after the early 1930s. At the time, commercial broadcasters and their allies in Congress successfully dismantled radio reform efforts like the 1934 Wagner-Hatfield Act, which would have reserved 25 percent of all radio frequencies for nonprofit broadcasting.[18] Instead, with the Communications Act of 1934, Congress largely sanctioned a commercial model over alternatives championed by educators and other reformers.

A strong public broadcasting system, therefore, did not take root during US radio's early days as it did in most other democratic nations. The US media landscape was instead dominated by an oligopoly of large networks, including CBS and NBC. These same commercial interests came to monopolize FM radio and later television. This now seemingly inevitable outcome was not uncontested. Grassroots organizing for educational broadcasting and other noncommercial alternatives continued well into the 1940s. Groups like the Institute for Education by Radio, for example, remained committed to media reform, holding annual conferences on educational broadcasting at Ohio State University from 1930 to 1953. A key figure in radio reform efforts was Morris Novik, the former director of WNYC, New York City's municipal radio station.[19] Novik helped form the National Association of Educational Broadcasters (NAEB) and is sometimes credited with coining the term "public broadcasting"; he continued as an advocate into the 1980s.[20] Another particularly active group of educators was based at the University of Wisconsin and affiliated with the radio station WHA, which claimed the status of "oldest station in America."[21] In partnership with the US Office of Education, this group created the FM Educational Radio Institute, which every summer held a two-week conference to focus on developing educational programming, which FCC staffers would sometimes attend.

Even as radio increasingly commercialized in the 1940s, media reformers continued to advocate for noncommercial alternatives. Seeing this history through the lens of key players helps illuminate the social democratic vision that had begun to emerge in the 1940s. This idealism toward the educational potential of broadcast media—and an overarching skepticism toward commercial radio—was perhaps best articulated by Charles Siepmann, a British-born, US-naturalized policy advocate. As the BBC programming director in the 1930s, he played an instrumental role in pushing British radio to broaden its appeal beyond London by paying attention to other regions and dialects, by experimenting with new formats, and by promoting lively public service–oriented radio fare. Siepmann's BBC-inspired, social democratic assumptions about media's educational role was also reflected in the controversial FCC "Blue Book" report that he wrote in the mid-1940s. Because Siepmann's report called for devoting specific amounts of time to local, experimental, and advertising-free programming, commercial broadcasters aggressively fought against it, calling it the "pink book" and accusing Siepmann and his allies at the FCC of being secret socialists who were trying to "BBC-ize" US radio.[22]

Despite this red-baiting, Siepmann continued to push for noncommercial, educational broadcasting for decades. Siepmann's 1946 book *Radio's Second Chance* inspired postwar media reform efforts by arguing that FM radio offered a new opportunity to establish a more public interest-oriented medium. (AM radio had by this time been thoroughly commercialized by several large media corporations.) Emphasizing that radio should be primarily a public service and not simply a profit-accumulation system for broadcasters and advertisers, the book lamented that business interests had convinced Americans they were indebted to commercial broadcasters for offering entertaining programming.[23]

Siepmann frequently reiterated his critique of commercial broadcasting and the need for public alternatives. In a speech at the first of two famous Allerton House seminars—convenings that the radio historian Josh Shepperd describes as representing "the first stable articulation for how a 'public broadcasting' infrastructure would be organized in the U.S."—Siepmann defined educational broadcasters as being in opposition to commercial operators.[24]

He argued that "we must presume that there is a distinction between our function and that of the commercial broadcasters." In illustrating the many differences between the two types of broadcasting, Siepmann cited the film and novel *The Hucksters* (a scathing critique of advertisers and the commercial broadcast industry) to identify commercial broadcasting's inherent exploitation of audiences. In Siepmann's view, these failures of commercial radio provided "a signal opportunity for winning listeners to noncommercial broadcasting." Namely, he believed it was the role of educational broadcasting to expose listeners to a broader scope of programming, and in doing so, to broaden listeners' imagination of what radio could be.[25]

Another key policy figure in the 1940s struggle for educational broadcasting was Clifford Durr, a progressive FCC commissioner from Montgomery, Alabama.[26] Durr passionately supported educational broadcasting throughout his tenure at the FCC in the 1940s. He often enthused about the "educational potentialities of radio," though he was also painfully aware of its unmet promises.[27] Durr remained convinced that educational radio, with programming superior to commercial outlets, would eventually become the dominant model for US broadcasting. He predicted that, "if a few good ones get started, many others will follow along and in the course of five or six years there will be enough of them on the air to make a significant impression on our general broadcasting picture." Durr's plan was to gradually ease in a handful of successful FM stations at post-secondary institutions since the average college or university could presumably afford their operation costs.[28]

Durr and fellow media reformers working at the FCC had a three-pronged approach to establishing a public alternative to commercial radio. First, they tried to set aside frequencies specifically for noncommercial and educational use. In 1945, Durr and other progressive FCC commissioners—with the strong backing of educators—succeeded in setting aside a twenty-channel band on FM radio for educational programming. Second, they tried to carve out space within the commercial system by designating swaths of time dedicated to "sustaining" (noncommercial) programming instead of "sponsored" programming, which was one of the central aims of the FCC's Blue Book.[29] Although ultimately unsuccessful, the FCC's maneuvering arguably pushed broadcasters into providing more public service programming.[30]

A third method was to build a dialectical relationship between progressive policymakers and grassroots activists. The FCC tried to organize educators while educators, in turn, lobbied and cultivated the FCC, often inviting FCC staffers to university conferences and workshops.[31] As part of this relationship, the FCC also brought in educators to testify at public hearings. For one particular hearing that lasted a day and a half in front of all of the commissioners, the National Educational Association (NEA) worked with the FCC and the US Office of Education to mobilize nearly thirty representatives from educational institutions and associations. As one historian of this activism describes it: "Resolutions were drafted; testimony was planned; witnesses were lined up and questionnaires circulated."[32] Armed with exhibits and evidence, the educators pleaded for additional frequencies. FCC staffers even helped coach the educators on what to say during their testimony.

As these efforts suggest, educators comprised a passionate contingent within the 1940s media reform movement. Largely based at big land-grant institutions in the Midwest, these reformers were relentless in their demands that a significant portion of the airwaves be allotted for educational purposes since commercial broadcasters clearly were not committed to educational fare. By the mid-1940s, commercial broadcasters had crowded out most noncommercial radio, with the number of educational stations dropping dramatically from the 1920s.[33] Nonetheless, reform efforts eventually panned out as educational broadcasters secured a foothold in FM radio by the late 1940s. Durr described how his pessimism regarding radio's future was lifting because educators "seem to be waking up to the opportunities of radio and some of the university stations already on the air are doing a first-rate job." As Durr wrote, "A few dozen—or preferably a hundred—good university stations operating on FM might not solve all of our problems [with commercialism], but they certainly would be a tremendous help."[34]

However, the fight for noncommercial radio suffered a major blow when Durr's FCC tenure ended in 1948. As an anti-communist hysteria gripped Washington, Durr took a principled stance against President Truman's loyalty oath program and turned down his reappointment. Before leaving, Durr credited educational broadcasters with making him realize "that good radio was worth fighting for." His parting advice was to subject other FCC commissioners to the same lobbying and to "get a strong organization and an angel or angels to put up some money." He warned, however, that reformers would also need an inside strategy with someone in Washington "who can keep his hand on the Commission's pulse all of the time and let you know whenever it gets a little weak. You can't hold back the commercial boys with nothing but good will and good intentions."[35] Educational broadcasters begged him to stay and fight, helping "people try to think of radio as it might be instead of as it is."[36] But Durr left Washington amid the rising tide of red-baiting and blacklisting, as did most of the remaining New Dealers.[37] One progressive at the time said to Dallas Smythe, the FCC's chief economist who was also fleeing DC, that it felt like an "exodus."[38]

The lasting imprint that this period of political repression had on the US media system—as it did on many of the United States' core systems— is generally under-appreciated. Left-wing activists were purged from so-cial movements across the country, and progressive policymakers were removed from power.[39] With this dramatic shift in the political landscape, many of the reformists' aspirations for creating a less-commercialized media system came to naught. Instead what emerged was a "postwar settlement" for US media marked by three overlapping assumptions that news media should: remain only lightly regulated; adhere to a negative conception of the First Amendment (a freedom of the press privileging media producers' and owners' individual rights over the broader public's collective rights); and practice a mostly industry-defined version of social responsibility.[40] Nonetheless, reformers and educators continued to push for noncommer-cial alternatives and never completely gave up their vision of what media could be.

One exception to the commercial sway of the US media system came in the form of Durr's replacement, Frieda Hennock, the first woman to serve as a FCC commissioner. A stalwart advocate for educational broad-casting, Hennock was instrumental in reserving 242 channels for educa-tional television as part of the FCC's 1952 "Sixth Report and Order"—a truly significant public interest victory.[41] Educational radio also saw some small but notable gains during this time period: By 1952, there were more than ninety FM educational stations. Many of these, how-ever, were low-power stations broadcasting to campus communities that remained under continual threat of commercial takeover. Furthermore, such allocations were for educational but not necessarily noncommercial programming.[42] Nonetheless, these stations kept an alternative model alive until the 1960s, when a national broadcasting system finally came to fruition.

Establishing a Public Broadcasting System

Despite setbacks in the 1940s, media reform efforts against the commercially-dominated media system persisted. As Allison Perlman notes, the 1950s was a highly pivotal era for educational broadcasting. It was a period of uncertainty and experimentation that saw a diverse range of stations and programming emerge, setting the stage for what would become public broadcasting. As educators and grassroots activists continued to push for alternatives, a number of foundations had joined the cause by the 1960s (the Ford Foundation had begun even earlier in the 1950s). Ford commissioned Charles Siepmann—who since authoring the ill-fated FCC Blue Book report had become the chair of a new communication department at New York University—to direct a large study on the effectiveness of in-school TV.[43] He also advised the National Educational Television Center (NET) during its struggle to define a progressive vision for educational and public broadcasting in the United States, and he left a lasting imprint on its mission. As the media historian Michele Hilmes narrates, Siepmann made a dramatic intervention that called for better programming instead of a "poor replica of a commercial program."[44]

Based on Siepmann's advice, NET became a centralized national program production center. For NET, Siepmann also authored a report titled "Educational Television: Blueprint for a Network" that called for daily broadcasts of children's programs, news, and criticism, as well as weekly broadcasts of various international media, multicultural shows, and science and cultural documentaries. In addition to these themes, Siepmann proposed a weekly, year-round show, called "The Unfinished Business of Democracy," that would feature documentaries inspired by the earlier work of the famous CBS producer Fred Friendly.[45]

The most influential call for public broadcasting came from the Carnegie Commission on Educational Television. Established in 1965 by the Carnegie Corporation of New York, the commission investigated the state of educational broadcasting and popularized the idea of *public* television. It took up themes similar to earlier calls for public broadcasting and in 1967 published the report *Public Television: A Program for Action*.[46] This report stated upfront that its proposed programs for public broadcasting "are in general not economic for commercial sponsorship" and should be part of a "comprehensive system that will ultimately bring public television to all the people of the United States." Local stations that in their "totality will become a new and fundamental institution in American culture" would provide programming that "should reach all parts of the country and be individually responsive to the needs of the local communities." Among other things, the report encouraged experimentation and hailed public broadcasting as "an instrument for the free communication of ideas in a free society."

The Public Broadcasting Act (PBA) of 1967 largely embraced these social democratic themes and heralded a new system that would "constitute a source of alternative telecommunication services for all the citizens of the nation." The text declared that "it is in the public interest to encourage the development of programming that involves creative risks and that addresses the needs of unserved and underserved audiences, particularly children and minorities." Emphasized throughout the report was a commitment to diversity—both in types of content and regarding the people consuming and producing that content. The report also underscored the need for all Americans having access to this programming.[47] When signing it into law, President Johnson delivered a speech with soaring rhetoric, stating that despite "support from our Government" public broadcasting "will be carefully guarded from Government or from party control. It will be free, and it will be independent—and it will belong to all of our people." He likened the PBA to the 1862 Morrill Act that "set aside lands in every State—lands which belonged to the people—and it set them aside in order to build the land-grant colleges of the Nation. So today we rededicate a part of the airwaves—which belong to all the people—and we dedicate them for the enlightenment of all the people."[48]

Despite these noble ideals, the story of public broadcasting in the United States has largely been one of decline, primarily owing to a fatal flaw in its fundamental design. For as much as the PBA replicated the social democratic vision of the Carnegie Commission's original blueprint, one key detail was different: the funding model. The Carnegie report was clear that success depended on adequate funding, which the commission recommended should come from a trust fund supported by up to a 5 percent manufacturer's excise tax on television sets—essentially a significant guaranteed subsidy that bore some similarities to the BBC's funding model (which derives from a license fee that everyone who watches television programs must pay). Instead, the PBA determined that public broadcasting's funding would depend on congressional appropriations, rendering it vulnerable to constant budget fights and political attacks.

Broadcast historian Robert Avery argues that despite being the most significant piece of communication legislation in the latter half of the twentieth
century, the fatal flaw of having an inadequate funding structure—along
with lacking an insulated and autonomous board of directors—prevented
public broadcasting from ever achieving its democratic potential.[49] Indeed,
without a permanent and secure source of federal funding sheltering
public broadcasting from political attacks—which is what an independent
trust fund could have guaranteed—PBS has been subjected to congressional squabbling. This dependency has kept it impoverished and politically constrained, especially in how it reflects and serves diverse publics.[50]
Predictably enough, public broadcasting has struggled to create programming appealing to viewers across racial and class lines.[51]

Even under these considerable limitations, however, as work by historians
Laurie Oullette and Allison Perlman shows, the possibilities for an alternative progressive trajectory was evident, at least during a relatively brief moment in the late 1960s and early 1970s. In those early days, public television
(much of it still produced by NET) did produce and broadcast hard-hitting,
even radical, programming on topics such as poverty and civil rights.[52] The
show "The Great American Dream Machine" regularly satirized members of
congress and featured left-wing figures such as Studs Terkel. Another show,
"The Nader Report," featured Ralph Nader and focused on consumer rights
and shady corporate practices. Some shows questioned US intervention in
Cuba and other regions and were seemingly sympathetic toward communist
leaders. Documentaries aired on public television examined social problems,
such as the plight of poor people, and took on powerful institutions such as
banks. Even the children's educational show "Sesame Street" was more radical and activist back then, tackling thorny issues related to class and race,
and frequently hosting progressive guests like Pete Seeger.[53] This more visible commitment to radical politics (with many inherent tensions) did not
mesh well with a funding model dependent on foundations and weak public
subsidies—a model that the radio historian Josh Shepperd aptly notes, "did
not fund dissent."[54] Such radical programming unsurprisingly invited a conservative backlash, one that would never fully relent.

Another significant tension hindering the early US public broadcasting
system was a power struggle within the network itself. Somewhat paradoxically, the more top-down and centralized NET, the national hub of educational television based in New York City, produced more progressive and
overtly political programming.[55] NET was sometimes accused by more

conservative local stations, especially in the South, as having a left-wing bias and being culturally elitist.[56] Because it was supplanted by PBS, which took on the main role of national planning and program distribution, NET's influence gradually waned. However, with the Ford Foundation's support, it continued to produce programming into the 1970s. For many progressive activists who were initially optimistic about public broadcasting's radical potential, NET was the high-water mark—the exemplar of what could have been. Veteran broadcaster and former NET president James Day described what became of PBS as a "hobbled" medium "whose place in American television broadcasting has been purposefully marginalized by public policy" and "effectively neutered" by Congress.[57]

With public radio (which was added into the Public Broadcasting Act at the last minute), the struggles were perhaps not as stark, but we see a similar legacy of social democratic hopes deferred. The big land-grant universities and smaller community radio stations had significantly different understandings of educational radio's pedagogical and ideological purposes.[58] The smaller stations—the network that eventually coalesced into the National Federation of Community Broadcasters (NFCB)— were initially left out of the Corporation for Public Broadcasting's (CPB) funding criteria. This created considerable friction within the movement for noncommercial radio, especially since the smaller stations were often rooted in local communities. These often more activist stations saw the larger educational stations benefitting from the existing public radio structures.[59]

Although the more established educational stations won out within the public broadcasting system, the progressive legacy of radical and community radio persists today. An important alternative public model is the Pacifica radio network that first emerged from the media reform struggles of the 1940s. In 1949, the pacifist Lewis Hill, inspired by reformers like Charles Siepmann, launched Pacifica Radio (KPFA-FM) in Berkeley, California, as an ad-free, nonprofit, listener-supported station. Eventually, Pacifica Radio would expand to a small network of stations. Still broadcasting today—though often under intense economic pressures—Pacifica stations represent a more independent and overtly political model of community radio.[60] Another exemplar is low power FM broadcasting (LPFM), which emerged in the early 2000s to establish hundreds of hyper-local, noncommercial radio stations that reflect diverse cultures and voices of underserved communities.[61]

Ongoing Political and Economic Challenges

Public broadcasting came under increasing political attack in the 1970s, especially from the Nixon administration, which threatened to cut off all funding.[62] Nixon treated those involved as political subversives producing "far-left" programming (especially the kind coming from the NET studios) and he devised various schemes to hinder their operations.[63] Newt Gingrich and other conservative politicos would carry on this tradition of targeting public broadcasting for having a presumably liberal bias. During the Bush administration in the early 2000s, Kenneth Tomlinson, the Republican CPB chairman, closely monitored Bill Moyers's show for political leanings and pressured PBS to air more conservative content.

With its funding perpetually uncertain, public broadcasting has come to depend on other sources—including corporate sponsors. From native advertising to the reliance on "enhanced underwriting"—essentially full-blown advertisements—public broadcasters increasingly have blurred the distinction between commercial and noncommercial media. For example, national NPR platforms as well as regional NPR and public television stations work closely with the "sponsorship sales team" National Public Media (NPM) to promote various kinds of native advertising made available to sponsors.[64] On its website, NPM boasts "custom native integrations" of their products with NPR's content, promising that sponsors "can amplify their brand alignment." They guarantee clients: "From custom websites to award-winning 360 experiences, we can extend your sponsorship across NPR's most unique digital experiences."[65]

This growing economic dependence on corporate sponsorship becomes a vicious cycle: As public media outlets increasingly become indistinguishable from commercial media, it becomes harder for PBS to justify its federal funding. Yet financial pressures force public media to become more entrepreneurial in their search for corporate funding. The plight of Sesame Street, one of public television's most-celebrated shows for over four decades, is indicative of this trend. As of 2015, the program's new episodes are being shown first on the premium cable channel HBO.[66] The familiar alternative—relying on listener and viewer support—forces public broadcasters to maximize their audiences in a manner similar to that of commercial broadcasting, which can encourage a move away from local programming and toward more homogenous formats.[67]

Placing yet more economic and political stress on public broadcasters, President Trump has repeatedly introduced budgets that (unsuccessfully) proposed eliminating their federal funding.[68] Despite these challenges, survey data consistently show high levels of enthusiasm for public broadcasting, suggesting that the American people might actually accept arguments for *increased* support.[69] The threats facing public broadcasting today are generating public concern, but whether it is enough to save it for the long term remains unclear.[70] Ideally, advocates would move beyond defensive postures to articulate a vision for strengthening and reinventing public media for the digital age. We can even hope our public media system might still actualize its original ideals.

Public Media Subsidies Around the World

A common reaction against proposals for expanding public media is to point out public broadcasting's significant shortcomings as proof that the model can never succeed. Such arguments conflate what is (in this case, a poorly funded system) with what must always be. They assume that (as Margaret Thatcher once said in a different context) "there is no alternative" to the commercial system. But we know from both our own history and from many examples around the world that public alternatives are indeed available. Democratic societies have long invested in publicly subsidized media systems. Beyond maintaining vibrant public broadcast systems, many countries, especially in Western and Northern Europe, also directly and indirectly subsidize newspapers. For example, Norway relies on state subsidies for newspapers to lessen commercial pressures, counteract the effects of competition, and prevent newspaper monopolies.[71] Many other kinds of state-supported journalism exist around the world, and a wide range of international media policies mandate proactive government engagement to ensure diverse media.[72] These international comparisons offer potential lessons for US policymakers, especially as the journalism crisis worsens and the lack of a social safety net for news becomes glaringly apparent.

A prime example of a media system *with* a safety net can be found in the United Kingdom. In 2016, the BBC began leveraging its considerable resources to shore up the United Kingdom's struggling news industry. It assigned nearly one hundred and fifty "local democracy reporters" at news organizations across the country to help compensate for the loss of jobs and to focus specifically on local politics while sharing coverage with other media outlets.[73] The BBC is also bolstering the British news industry by funding accessible digital content for media organizations' local journalism and sharing coverage with various news providers. These collaborative projects include a massive "local news partnership," a "local democracy reporting service," and a "news hub" giving news partners access to a vast trove of BBC video and audio footage.[74]

More recently, the BBC has proposed a new charity, the Local Democracy Foundation, that will take over and expand the earlier democracy reporting program. In conjunction with tech companies and other potential contributors, the BBC foundation will fund regional public interest journalism to cover council meetings and other events that otherwise would likely go unreported. With over fifty thousand stories published through this collaborative model so far, many media observers hope the programs will continue to expand. However, the project has also faced accusations that its model reinforces market concentration since it placed the vast majority of its reporters with local newspapers owned by only three major regional publishers.[75] Smaller publishers have charged that the BBC program allows large, debt-laden publishers to take advantage of taxpayer support to compensate for earlier profit-seeking measures—actions that contributed to the very crisis in journalism the program seeks to address.[76] Nonetheless, the program offers a potentially useful measure at a time when the market is woefully incapable of supporting the journalism that democracy requires.

With their leading newspaper—the *Guardian*—owned by the Scott Trust, the British are no strangers to nonmarket-based support for newspapers.[77] In a high-profile speech, Labour Party leader Jeremy Corbyn argued that, in addition to expanding and reforming the BBC, the British government should institute redistributive measures to support journalism. Noting that French and Belgian news publishers had negotiated a settlement with Google, he argued that the United Kingdom should compel "the digital monopolies that profit from every search, share, and like we make" to pay into an independent "public interest media fund."[78] Six months later, the Cairncross Review, a detailed report on the future of British news media, similarly called for a new institute to oversee "direct funding for public-interest news outlets, with public funds used to support the reporting of local democracy."[79]

Canada is also pursuing significant journalism subsidies, reflected in three important reforms included in its budget. First, it changed the Canadian tax code to allow for nonprofit journalism organizations—the equivalent of 501(c)(3) journalism businesses—and tax-deductible contributions to these institutions, neither of which were previously permissible in Canada. Second, the Canadian government earmarked money for a refundable tax credit for news organizations (both for-profit and nonprofit) to offset news labor costs. What organizations can qualify and what percentage of the fees will be credited will be determined by an independent commission of journalists. Third, it established a 15 percent tax credit for individuals' subscriptions to qualifying digital news media, with media eligibility to be determined by an independent commission. The government allocated a total of $595 million CAD over 5 years, or approximately US$90 million per year.[80] This generous subsidy is in addition to a pledge by the Canadian government of $50 million CAD (US$38 million) to local journalism made earlier in the year.[81] These proposals have been met with a fair amount of legitimate criticism— especially from smaller publishers who feel that these subsidies favor undeserving incumbents—but despite such flaws they have started an important and ongoing conversation about public policy interventions to support journalism.

Australia, too, is considering press subsidies. In 2012, the government's "Finkelstein Report" looked at the state of Australian media and media regulation.[82] The report surveyed a broad range of media subsidies and other regulatory interventions that governments around the world have deployed to bolster public service journalism. While this report eventually faded from view, more recently Australians both in and outside government have begun to call for a tax on digital intermediaries and other forms of subsidy to help support journalism.[83] Rupert Murdoch, for less-than-noble reasons, has come out in support of these interventions. But they are also beginning to gain more public support as Australia's journalism crisis worsens.

While a number of other countries—in Europe as well as Malaysia and South Korea—are considering similar new proposals for subsidizing struggling news outlets, a more long-standing model for funding local journalism exists in Sweden.[84] When faced with a newspaper crisis over forty years ago, the Swedish government drew from the Norwegian model of press subsidies to begin taxing newspaper ads. It created a fund that was administered by an independent agency that supported struggling papers and staved off bankruptcies. The government used these subsidies to support smaller newspapers and broaden the bounds of news discourse. Today, an administrative governmental body called the Press Subsidies Council allocates funds based on circulation and revenue to newspapers other than the dominant paper in a particular municipality or region.[85] Even though these subsidies account for a relatively small percent of the papers' total revenue, they have successfully kept smaller, provincial newspapers in business and prevented one-newspaper towns from proliferating.[86] Reduced taxes and distribution subsidies also financially aid Swedish newspapers.[87] While these programs initially stirred controversy by making newspapers more dependent on the state, over time Swedish citizens have come to accept their necessity in preserving media pluralism.

In 2009, conservative French President Nicolas Sarkozy proposed giving every eighteen year old a one-year subscription to one of the country's major newspapers and free subscriptions to all high school students. In a request for a $780 million package for France's ailing newspaper industry, Sarkozy asserted that it is the state's responsibility "to make sure an independent, free, and pluralistic press exists."[88] The government implemented a nine-fold increase in its support for newspaper deliveries and doubled its annual print advertising expenditures. After a three-month study, Sarkozy announced that the state would increase its annual support for newspaper and magazine deliveries from $10.5 million to $90 million, spend an additional $26.5 million more per year for its advertisements in print publications, and suspend some publication fees.[89]

In other European countries, different cultural and ownership patterns have left their newspaper industries in better stead. For example, the German Newspaper Publishers' Association attributed the healthier state of journalism in that country (with a readership of 70 percent) to structural differences and also noted that most German newspapers are owned by families or small businesses with strong ties to local communities.[90] This is representative of many European press systems. Even if they are not thriving economically, the sense of crisis is somewhat reduced because of lower expectations of profitability and fewer commercial pressures. European press institutions have been less likely than their US counterparts to be traded on the stock market. While newspaper industries in these countries are also suffering from the shift to the internet, they did not have as far to fall because they were never commercialized to the same extent as US newspapers.[91] And yet, even though their journalism crisis has been more severe, the United States continues to trail other democracies in responding via public policy. The many models for public media subsidies that exist around the world could help broaden the social imaginary for what is possible in the US. Meanwhile, a number of experiments are beginning to take root.

Potential Funding Models for a New Public
Media System

Slowly but surely, even the United States is beginning to entertain non-market experiments, including public media subsidies. For example, in 2018 the New Jersey legislature passed a bill dedicating $5 million to the "Civic Information Consortium," an innovative nonprofit with a mandate to help revitalize local media. The consortium was first proposed by the media reform organization Free Press and further developed during two years of grassroots advocacy and community engagement. Its primary objective is to fund news projects designed to meet New Jersey residents' information needs, especially in underserved, low-income areas and communities of color. The consortium aims to increase the quantity and quality of both legacy and start-up news outlets, as well as support media literacy and civic engagement programs.[92] The initial $5 million was later reduced to $2 million, a mere drop in the bucket in light of the news industry's catastrophic losses over the last decade. Nonetheless, it serves as a significant proof-of-concept that state governments can financially support local journalism.

Another interesting case—this one a scenario where public media stepped directly into the breach to shore up suffering journalistic institutions—occurred in 2018 when New York City's public radio station WNYC helped resuscitate a local news site. With funding from anonymous donors, the station acquired the defunct *Gothamist* and will also integrate *Gothamist*'s satellite sites in Washington and Los Angeles with local public radio stations.[93] WNYC is not alone; public media stations around the country are increasingly collaborating with local news institutions and civil society groups to become multimedia hubs. These collaborations often produce various kinds of digital print media—from transcripts to stand-alone reports—in addition to traditional radio and television broadcast media. Increasingly, public media outlets are outright buying digital print start-ups. Examples of this phenomenon include the Philadelphia public broadcast station WHYY buying Billy Penn, Colorado Public Radio buying Denverite, KPCC buying LAist, WAMU buying DCist, and WNET buying New Jersey Spotlight.[94] This model—where local public media outlets serve as a kind of "anchor institution"—promises to expand in the coming years.[95]

A former Alaska public radio reporter reminds us that the Public Broadcasting Act of 1967 stated clearly that local public TV and radio stations are "valuable local community resources" that should be used "to address national concerns and solve local problems through community programs and outreach programs."[96] This public media system now includes more than a thousand local stations, each licensed to a nonprofit, community group, or educational organization such as a college or university. These stations are embedded within local communities and maintain strong connections with those whom they serve. For example, the public broadcast station WILL in Urbana, Illinois, where I used to work as a radio show producer, has long branded itself as "public media" and maintains strong ties to local citizens.

Such public media experiments will no doubt continue, but for them to be universally accessible and scale up to the national level, we must first resolve the age-old question of how we might pay for their expansion. A number of options exist. The most obvious one is that the United States could simply reverse course and join the rest of the democratic world by funding a strong public media system. The United States could rectify earlier mistakes by guaranteeing long-term financial support and removing public media's budget from the congressional appropriation process. A permanent trust for public media would shield the system from political pressures and provide enough stability for long-term planning (I return to this argument in the book's conclusion).

A larger budget also would allow the US public media system to experiment with new formats and increase its capacity, diversity, and reach. With a bigger funding base, we could broaden the definition of public media to include not just PBS and NPR, but also LPFM and other community stations, public-access cable television, independent community news sites, and other local outlets. By transitioning them into multimedia centers, these established institutions could combine their collective resources (as some already are doing) to collaborate on the local and investigative reporting that is no longer covered by collapsing commercial newspapers.

Other creative proposals could jumpstart innovative forms of public media without direct government subsidies. Policymakers in other countries are already proposing some of these plans, such as tax vouchers that people can put toward their choice of media.[97] Others draw inspiration from existing US institutions, such as a proposal to establish an AmeriCorps-style, government-subsidized journalism jobs program or to create a government research-and-development fund to encourage innovative, multi-platform models of journalism.[98] Yet others would create subsidies without increasing government outlays, for instance by repurposing funds for international broadcasting, charging commercial broadcasters fees for their use of the public spectrum, implementing an equivalent to the universal service charge added to monthly phone bills; or placing a small consumer tax on cellphones, computers, and other devices.[99]

An even more ambitious plan would transform existing public infrastructure, such as post offices and public libraries, into local community media centers. In addition to providing public internet access—perhaps as part of a municipal broadband network—these spaces could help facilitate local reporting through various print, digital, and audio media.[100] The Indymedia experiment of the early 2000s could serve as a potential model, allowing for the condition that these community media centers would be publicly funded as well as receive various forms of support from local communities instead of relying on all-volunteer labor, which was always a major challenge to this model's efficacy.[101]

Strong public institutions benefit the entire media system by competing with commercial outlets and pressuring them to be more responsible, diverse, and informative. To advance such arguments requires an ideological narrative, one that stresses democratic values while unequivocally criticizing commercial media's limitations in providing society with adequate news and information. Yet significant barriers remain. Even many Americans who believe something must be done to save journalism—especially journalists themselves—fear that government involvement means government *control*. Therefore, it bears underscoring that government supporting the necessary structures for a healthy media system is *not* tantamount to government control of media content. Indeed, public policies that support journalism should be ideologically and viewpoint neutral.

The current journalism crisis presents a rare opportunity to revitalize and repurpose US public broadcasting as a new media system dedicated to local newsgathering and public service reporting across multiple platforms. The first step toward creating the necessary politics for this new system is to reframe discussions around public media subsidies.

Public Media Subsidies: As American as Apple Pie

A central tenet within US political discourse holds that state-funded media subsidies are deeply antithetical to American values. As discussed earlier in this book, however, historical evidence belies this assumption. Not only have various media subsidies been firmly established within US traditions, the historical record shows that press subsidies are completely compatible with democratic society in both the United States and around the globe—in fact, they positively correlate with stronger democracies. Nonetheless, misconceptions about subsidies continue to abound in the United States, impeding rational policy debates on their merits in light of the implosion of the older subsidy model—namely, advertising revenue.

As a case in point, consider postal subsidies. Scholars have calculated that if contemporary postal subsidies were applied at the same level as in the Post Office Act of 1792, they would amount to billions of dollars.[102] According to a calculation by the late legal scholar Ed Baker, postal subsidies still amounted to $80 million even in the early twentieth century, which in today's dollars would equal approximately $6 billion.[103] These subsidies have steadily declined since the Postal Reorganization Act of 1970; indeed, the entire postal system has come under attack from conservatives who reject the traditional consensus that it need not be self-funding. Nonetheless, these subsidies persist, and leading political magazines ranging from the liberal *Nation* to the conservative *National Review* still depend on them. In popular discourse, however, these government allocations are rarely understood as media subsidies.

The large US international broadcasting apparatus is another subsidy that usually goes unmentioned in policy discussions. In recent years, the Broadcasting Board of Governors (BBG, now called the US Agency for Global Media) received nearly $800 million to run programs such as Voice of America (VOA) and Radio Free Europe (the annual budget is now closer to $700 million).[104] Because of concerns about government propaganda, the 1948 Smith-Mundt Act forbade international broadcasting services such as the VOA from being broadcasted directly to US audiences.[105] However, in 2013 Congress amended the original law so that these broadcasts could air within US borders.[106] While potential capture by government warrants caution, and we must always vigilantly maintain proper safeguards, the United States could redirect such large media subsidies toward supporting local public service media.[107]

The most well-known media subsidy in the United States is, of course, its public broadcasting system. At present levels, the federal governments funds PBS at a rate of approximately $445 million a year. For comparison, the government spends, on average, $626 million annually and employs around two thousand media workers on the Pentagon's public relations budget.[108] Historically, the United States also has been quick to subsidize the creation of media systems in other countries.[109] At the precise moment that reactionaries were red-baiting media reformers who were advocating for a more public-oriented media system in the United States, US occupying forces were building strong public media in Japan and in Germany— what would become, respectively, the public broadcasting systems of NHK and ARD.

Despite this long history of media subsidies, calls for rebuilding the US news system with public monies are often met with howls of alarm. Over the past decade, however, proposals for press subsidies have slowly bubbled up into mainstream discourse. In 2010, for example, Columbia University President Lee Bollinger authored a *Wall Street Journal* op-ed titled "Journalism Needs Government's Help."[110] Around the same time, other legal scholars argued that press subsidies pass constitutional muster and are consistent with US history and international standards.[111] James Curran described this early response as "public reformism," which calls for strengthening public media to sustain the journalism that the private sector can no longer support.[112] Accumulating evidence that public media systems provide significant social benefits further justifies this approach to the journalism crisis.

A growing body of academic research shows that public media tend to present a wider range of voices and perspectives than commercial media. This scholarship demonstrates that publicly owned media and government-subsidized private media are no less critical of government than nonsubsidized, privately owned media.[113] Counterintuitively, some of this research suggests that the state actually can play a bigger role in shaping the news in liberal democracies with predominantly commercial media systems than it does in democracies with publicly subsidized media systems. For example, Daniel Hallin notes that comparative analyses show "very strong evidence that press subsidies don't lead journalists to be timid" and even suggests that the Swedish press became *more* adversarial after public subsidies were introduced.[114]

Another comparative analysis demonstrates that public television in other democratic nations devotes more attention than does the US market-driven model to public affairs and international news, which fosters greater public knowledge in these areas, encourages higher levels of news consumption, and shrinks the knowledge gap between economically advantaged and disadvantaged citizens.[115] Other research shows that strong public media systems correlate with higher political knowledge and other social benefits, including higher levels of voting and democratic engagement.[116] Research also shows that public media tend to be more independent, ideologically diverse, and critical of dominant policy positions compared to commercial news organizations.[117] Research suggests that the popular BBC, an unrivaled source for international news, demonstrates an independence that compares favorably with the US system.[118] Another group of scholars continues to document the benefits of the Nordic public media model—what some have called a "media welfare state."[119]

In general, these studies illustrate that public media tend to produce higher-quality international reporting, as well as programming that serves communities of color, women, linguistic and ethnic minorities, and other groups and regions that for-profit media often neglect.[120] Research finds that people exposed to public television news have higher levels of social trust, a more realistic view of their own society, and less extremist views.[121] For example, one study on attitudes toward immigrants found that commercial news contains more sensationalized coverage on immigration than public news and that those who consumed more commercial news held more negative and less balanced views toward immigrants.[122] Other scholarship shows that public broadcasters produce higher-quality public affairs coverage and hard news compared to their commercial counterparts. One study concluded that, free from both market forces and government interference, publicly subsidized broadcasting is "markedly 'better' than its commercial rivals."[123]

The concept of "market failure," discussed in chapter 2, is central to understanding the need for public media subsidies. To legitimize public policy intervention, especially among US policymakers where market fundamentalism still reigns, articulating the case for market failure is key. Because commercial media favor entertainment-focused programming of low-quality information that reaches broad audiences with non-controversial, often-unimaginative content, the resultant media product disadvantages minority representation and arguably avoids riskier, more innovative fare. Scholars such as Ed Baker have gone even further to argue that advertising-based media systems contribute to inequality, skewed content, market censorship, concentrated media ownership, and other deleterious outcomes.[124] Based on similar assumptions, democratic societies have long relied on a market-failure rationale to invest in public broadcasting systems.[125]

If commercial media's systemic market failures were better understood in the United States, there might be a stronger push for public media to step into the vacuum created by the collapsing newspaper industry. Absent ideological constraints, the current historical juncture could create an opening for establishing a new autonomous public media system devoted to public service. Such a plan may be presumed dead on arrival, especially among Republicans. We may recall that in a presidential debate against President Obama, then-candidate Mitt Romney famously said he would cut subsidies to PBS even though he loves Big Bird.[126] But despite the rhetoric of Republican elites, polling data from across the political spectrum consistently show high levels of support for public broadcasting, especially from liberals, but even a surprising level among conservatives.[127] We need to harness this popularity to expand public media—before it is too late.

Toward a New Public Media System

Sustaining US democracy requires that we fund an alternative media infrastructure, one insulated from the commercial pressures that ushered in the current journalism crisis. A media system can accommodate both commercial and noncommercial models; what is ideal is a *mixed* media system that subordinates profit-making to democratic imperatives and is better able to withstand market oscillations. A wholly commercial system—one focused on optimizing advertising revenue and maximizing profits—is structurally vulnerable and inadequate for serving democratic needs. Combined with policy failures in addressing market concentration and extreme commercialism, these structural flaws have produced a news media system in the US uniquely susceptible to a full-blown journalism crisis. The aim of any reform project should be to salvage public service journalism from the ravages of a dying commercial media system.

Subsidizing US journalism requires a paradigm shift in our thinking about the fundamental nature of media. Because US journalism has depended for so long on advertising revenue (with news a by-product of the main transaction), this funding model is often taken for granted and constrains our imagination about what could or should be done. For example, a number of recently proposed reforms focus on ensuring that news organizations receive a fair share of the advertising revenue produced by social media platforms and search engines.[128] Not only are these reforms paltry, they miss addressing the underlying problem of extreme commercialism entirely. Publishers should have never been so reliant on advertising revenue in the first place. It is long past time to champion noncommercial methods for nurturing a free and adversarial press in the United States. Without public service journalism, democracy itself becomes dangerously vulnerable to a debased media culture of misinformation.

Increasing evidence suggests that private capital alone can no longer fully support professional journalism, but new tax laws could help transition commercial news organizations into new low- and nonprofit ownership structures (discussed in chapter 3). The incentive structures of these nonprofit outlets are fundamentally different—typically more focused on producing public service journalism—from those driving the commercial press. Nonetheless, while these private, nonprofit models should be embraced, tax-status changes alone will not make these outlets viable. Many must still rely on subscriptions, donations, advertising, and other revenue sources to pay the bills. They are still at the mercy of market forces, even if they do not face the same commercial pressures.

In the final analysis, increasing public funding for public media is the surest systemic approach to the journalism crisis. Given the spate of recent newspaper closures and bankruptcies, as well as the vast wasteland of commercial radio and television journalism, the crisis calls for democratically determined public policy interventions. Now is the time to carve out a permanent public news media system shielded from the market. The current crisis offers opportunities for reasserting the public service mission of the press. Removing profit pressures could liberate newsrooms from absentee corporate owners and return them to the communities they purportedly serve. Media conglomerates and private equity firms should not be permitted to treat news organizations as mere commodities. Those unwilling to invest in quality journalism over the long term would do the public a service as well as protect their own bottom line if they withdraw from the media business in an orderly fashion. In short, we must rescue good assets from bad owners. Public policy can help facilitate this transition.

To be sure, a social democratic approach cannot solve all of media's problems. A well-funded public media system that fails to address structural reform would likely reproduce the same problems of racism, classism, and elitism that have bedeviled public radio and television in the United States. Solving these problems would require more than simply shoring up support for incumbent media organizations or replicating elitist journalistic practices, such as an overreliance on official sources. Even the BBC, the most famous of all public media systems, has been fraught with elitist tendencies and deep-seated structural problems.[129] Many ongoing cultural issues of professionalism would take time to recalibrate in a truly public media system.

A new public media system must actively seek out and include historically marginalized groups, voices, and ideas. As we saw in chapter 1, traditional liberalism has often championed a marketplace of ideas without recognizing preexisting structural inequities, particularly along class, gender, sexual orientation, and racial lines. Ideally, this new system would be more radical than liberal; it would penetrate to the roots of power and ruthlessly scrutinize dominant assumptions and institutions. With a strong firewall between newsgathering and the state as a precondition for its existence, this public media system must remain antagonistic toward powerful interests regardless of political regime.

Ultimately, revitalizing US media requires a national approach driven by federal policy. If we confront the ever-evolving relationship between government and media without ideological blinders, the social democratic approach to media policy seems eminently reasonable. Too many people take it as an article of faith that such a model could never flourish in the United States. The fact that a more robust public media system did not take root is a testament to the political victories of US broadcasters and publishers in the 1930s and 1940s. The commercial system that emerged represented the triumph of a corporate elite consensus, not the public interest.

Of course, all public media subsidies should be based on principles of complete transparency, systems of accountability, and numerous safeguards and firewalls to ensure they do not become instruments of state influence. But as the historical record shows, many leading democracies—including the United States at various points in its history—have successfully employed press subsidies without sliding toward totalitarianism. As we assess the current journalism crisis, we must look to history and revisit the roads not taken—and consider taking them. Persuading a critical mass of Americans to embrace a social democratic approach to the journalism crisis today poses a difficult political struggle. But we simply do not have the luxury of retreating to ideological comfort zones when facing a crisis of this magnitude.

Conclusion

The Media We Need

Commercial journalism's collapse is now indisputable. But as a society we have yet to face up to what this means. No new business model that can save journalism is waiting to be discovered. No purely profit-driven model can address the growing news deserts that are sprouting up all over the United States. It is questionable whether commercial news media ever fully aligned with society's democratic needs, but now it is abundantly clear the market cannot support the level of journalism—especially local, international, policy, and investigative reporting—that democracy requires.

The past decade has witnessed a precipitous decline in newspaper revenue and readership, reducing the number of the nation's newsroom employees by nearly half. Actual journalism is vanishing, misinformation is proliferating, and our public media system—which ideally could provide a safety net for when the market fails to support the press—remains impoverished compared to its global counterparts. The economic threats facing journalism—from the collapse of its advertising-dependent business model to the dominance of platform monopolies like Facebook and Google—comprise a structural crisis for our news media system. But this crisis is also an opportunity to entirely reinvent journalism.

If we acknowledge that no entrepreneurial solution lies just around the bend—if we stop grasping for a magical technological fix or a market panacea—we can begin to look more aggressively for non-market-based alternatives. In doing so, we can dare to imagine a new public media system for the digital age, one that privileges democracy over profits. A journalism that goes to where the silences are in society and ruthlessly confronts those in power. An information system that keeps a laser-like focus on climate change, hyper-inequality, mass incarceration, and other pressing social problems. How would we design such a system?

History offers fleeting glimpses of this alternative journalism—investigative reporting that exposes corruption, changes policy, and benefits

Democracy Without Journalism?. Victor Pickard, Oxford University Press (2020). © Victor Pickard
DOI: 10.1093/oso/9780190946753.001.0001

all of society. Every now and then, we encounter media coverage that tells stories and introduces voices we otherwise would never hear. But for far too long, these moments have been the exception. The history of the US media system is a history of misrepresentation, exclusion, and ongoing market failure. But it did not—and does not—have to be this way. Another media system is possible, one that is more democratically governed and accessible to all. The biggest obstacle to this vision is a constricted view of what can be. We must broaden our political imaginary.

If we are willing to recognize the root of the problem facing journalism's future—namely, the relentless pursuit of increasingly unattainable profits— we can begin to address the crisis. If we find ways to minimize structural threats caused by rampant commercialism, we may actually achieve this new kind of journalism. But we must first consider the strategic frameworks and policies needed to realize this vision. Above all else, we must see journalism as an essential public service—a core infrastructure—that democracy needs to survive.[1]

Infrastructures of Democracy

We learn in school that an informed society—a bedrock of self-governing society—requires a free press. However, we as a society rarely reflect on the infrastructures and policies that are required to maintain a healthy press system. Today, as we look to journalism to protect us against misinformation and corruption, the press is in a structural crisis. Journalism's institutional support is collapsing, leaving entire regions and issues uncovered at a time when reliable information and robust reporting is desperately needed. The crisis is disproportionately harming specific communities and vulnerable groups.

A growing body of scholarship documents the negative social effects caused by information scarcity, the proliferation of misinformation, and the rise of news deserts. As we saw in chapter 3, studies show that those lacking access to reliable sources of news are less informed about politics, less civically engaged, and less likely to vote. Moreover, these communities are more polarized and face rising levels of corruption in their local governments. Much evidence suggests that many of these problems will only worsen in the coming years. The loss of journalism and rampant misinformation are structural problems that require structural solutions. More to the point, they are social problems that require policy interventions.

With increasing public attention focused on threats to the integrity of our news and information systems, now is an opportune moment to consider reforms that reorient US journalism for the digital age. While a public media system is not the perfect panacea for all that ails our communications, it can provide a strong base for a healthy information ecosystem. Accumulating evidence attests that public media are beneficial for strengthening political knowledge and democratic engagement as well as for encouraging diversity and independence in news coverage. Furthermore, public media systems are guided by a normative commitment to ensure that *all* members of society have access to information and communication systems.

True inclusion means that communities are not only receiving high-quality news, but are also deeply engaged in the news-making process itself. Community members should be involved in the governing process and empowered to organize their own newsrooms and collaborate in participatory journalism. Community engagement in the news-making process is the best way to create a new kind of journalism, one that is accountable and trustworthy.

With these concerns and emphases in mind, we must address the following questions: What might a new public media system look like? What policies, discourses, and politics are required to establish such a system in the United States? In some key respects, we have been here before, and historical knowledge about what worked and what failed in the past is instructive. Lessons gleaned from previous policy battles and media crises—including the decades-long campaign to establish a public broadcasting system in the United States—have much to tell us about charting a way forward.

A Policy Approach to the Journalism Crisis

The road to the misinformation society has been paved with policy failures. Many of the media-related challenges facing us today—misinformation, unaccountable monopolies, insufficient journalism—are actually old problems. Donald Trump's election was a symptom, not a cause, of a deeper institutional rot within the United States' core systems, especially its media system. These long-standing structural pathologies, I argue, are the direct result of media policy failures over time—a long history of policy actions and inactions that led to contemporary crises in our information systems. The failure to sustain public service journalism created a fertile environment through which misinformation and low-quality news coverage proliferated. The failure to maintain open and democratically operated communication infrastructures limited access to reliable information and democratic participation. The failure over time to prevent monopolistic control of key sectors of US information systems created a wide range of harms, including news gatekeeping, lack of media diversity, and extreme commercialism. These overlapping policy failures maintain a "systemic market failure" arising from commercial imperatives that have debased the US media experiment for much of its existence.

Any society that aspires to be a democracy must ensure the existence of reliable news and information systems. This necessitates approaching the journalism crisis as a major social problem and, therefore, a public policy problem. Transforming the US media system into a democratic force requires a robust policy program of regulating or breaking up information monopolies, creating public alternatives to commercial news media, and empowering media workers, consumers, and communities to engage with and create their own media.

The Path Forward: De-Commercializing Journalism

Beyond the politics and policies required to actualize these alternatives, establishing a noncommercial vision as a long-term normative goal is in itself a worthwhile project. Of course, removing commercial imperatives will not solve all journalism-related problems. Deeply embedded cultural orientations, hierarchies, and routines—both within newsrooms and throughout society—will persist after removing journalism from the market. Nonetheless, de-commercialization is an important first step toward democratization. Removing commercial values (an emphasis on sensational, conflict-driven, trivial news that attracts attention to advertising) and adding public values (an emphasis on high-quality information, diverse voices and views, and reporting that confronts concentrated power and social problems) could foster a journalism that is universally accessible but attentive to diverse cultures and social contexts.

Salvaging a nonprofit model from the ashes of market-driven journalism goes far beyond nostalgia for a golden age that never existed. This project is not about finding the right business model to preserve the status quo or to resuscitate a past that was steeped in inequality and discrimination. Any path toward reinventing journalism must acknowledge that the market is its destructor, not savior. Commercialism lies at the heart of this crisis, and removing it could be transformative. The ravages of the market escape the same level of alarm compared to other risks facing news media today. While journalism's external threats range from oppressive state governments to changes in audiences and technologies, the market poses an existential challenge. We should therefore either remove news production from the market entirely or, at the very least, minimize commercial pressures.[2]

The late sociologist Eric Olin Wright left us a useful schematic that can help society think through the possibilities for de-commercializing journalism and creating a truly public media system. Wright was a key thinker in envisioning "real utopias" and he provided a vocabulary for imagining a different social world. He proposed four general models for creating alternatives to capitalism, each one based on a different logic of resistance: smashing, taming, escaping, or eroding.[3] After assessing these four approaches, Wright suggested that the strategies of eroding and taming capitalist relationships over time offered the best chance for change. On the one hand, we can push for reforms to the existing system that greatly improve the everyday lives of people (taming), and on the other hand, we can create alternative structures that will gradually replace commercial models (eroding).

We can apply this strategic vision of taming and eroding capitalistic relationships to free our media system from commercial logics. There are five general approaches conducive to such a project:

- Establishing "public options" (i.e., noncommercial/nonprofit, supported by public subsidies), such as well-funded public media institutions and municipal broadband networks.
- Breaking up/preventing media monopolies and oligopolies to encourage diversity and to curtail profit-maximizing behavior.
- Regulating news outlets via public interest protections and public service obligations such as ascertainment of society's information needs.
- Enabling worker control by unionizing newsrooms, facilitating employee-owned institutions and cooperatives, and maintaining professional codes that shield journalism from business operations.

- Fostering community ownership, oversight, and governance of newsrooms, and mandating accountability to diverse constituencies.

While society should pursue all of these approaches simultaneously, the most surefire way to tame and erode commercial media is to create a truly public system, one that can pressure for-profit outlets to be more responsible and provide a structural alternative to systemic market failure.

Creating a New Public Media System

If we agree that nonprofit outlets alone are beneficial but insufficient, then a public media system is vitally necessary. We should be clear up front that any such national network for providing news would require tremendous resources. In the United States, proposing the idea of massive public subsidies for news media usually elicits two immediate objections. One is the concern that a publicly subsidized system would create a mouthpiece for the state. The other objection is its cost.

I have been arguing throughout this book that media subsidies are not a slippery slope toward totalitarianism. Indeed, democratic nations around the globe have somehow figured out how to create strong public media systems while enjoying democratic benefits that put the United States to shame. Nonetheless, independence from government capture is certainly a legitimate concern. An ironclad prerequisite for any public media system is that it must be firewalled from government (as well as from other powerful influences). Regardless of the funding source, a key requirement is severing all previous ties once money enters the trust. All donations must be cleansed of any institutional or personal attachments to ensure that journalism retains complete independence from any funder or government entity. These donations should follow the "double-blind" process mentioned earlier: No one will know exactly what kind of journalism their money is funding, and no grantee will know from whence their funding came. This political autonomy must be tethered to economic independence—in other words, adequate funding and resources—otherwise this new system would simply reenact the earlier errors of public broadcasting and create another weak system susceptible to political and economic pressures.

Creating a solid foundation for a new public media system will require tens of billions of dollars. This may seem large, but relative to the scale and type of problem—a first order need on par with public health, a standing military, and other non-negotiable expenses—it is actually a modest proposal. This is especially true if we consider the enormous opportunity costs to society if we proceed without a functioning news media system. Americans rarely question the cost of government actions deemed necessary for the country's survival, such as public education and other core systems and infrastructures. A functioning press system is arguably as essential as these other imperatives, and we therefore should not require its funding to be budget neutral, which is an ideologically-loaded position passed off as hard-headed realism. A viable press system is not a luxury; it is a necessity. Similar to a classic merit good discussed in chapter 2, journalism is not a "want," but a "need." We should treat it accordingly and draw a budget of $30 billion from the treasury on an annual basis—a miniscule amount compared to massive tax cuts and military budgets passed in recent decades.[4]

While a guaranteed annual budget derived directly from the US Treasury is the ideal means of supporting a new public media system, a second option would be a large public media trust fund supported by multiple revenue streams. As discussed in chapter 5, there are many possible means of funding this trust. Most importantly, this financial support should not be a political football left to the mercy of the congressional appropriations process. Instead, it might rely on charitable contributions from foundations and philanthropists, already-existing subsidies, and other sources. Protected from powerful interests, this trust should be publicly operated and remain autonomous from government. While individuals could also contribute to the trust, a project of this scope requires large funders. Other possible sources of funding (all mentioned in chapter 5) might include consumer taxes on electronics and devices, tax vouchers, repurposing international broadcasting subsidies (worth hundreds of millions), and proceeds from spectrum sales (worth tens of billions of dollars). Two other major methods of funding a public media system are taxing platform monopolies and having foundations pool their resources to serve as "incubators" for what can later become a public media system.

Platform monopolies are not solely responsible for the systemic market failure undermining digital journalism, but Facebook and Google are certainly exacerbating the crisis. It is tragically ironic that this duopoly starves the very institutions they expect to fact-check the misinformation proliferating through their platforms. To offset some of the damage they are causing, these firms could help fund local news, investigative journalism, policy reporting, and other kinds of coverage that democracy requires regardless of whether its profitable for monopolistic firms. Thus far, Google and Facebook have supported journalism at a level that amounts to a public relations initiative. Google has pledged $300 million over three years for its News Initiative (less than 1 percent of Google's 2017 profits). For its part, Facebook has launched a $3 million journalism "accelerator" (representing about 0.007 percent of the company's 2017 revenues) to help ten to fifteen news organizations build their digital subscriptions using Facebook's platform. It also launched a program "Today In" to aggregate local news in communities across the United States, but ran into problems when it found many areas were already entirely bereft of local news.[5] These efforts are woefully insufficient.

Redistributing revenue as part of a new regulatory approach could address the twin problems of unaccountable monopoly power and the loss of public service journalism. Facebook and Google (which owns YouTube) should help fund the very industry that they simultaneously profit from and eviscerate. These firms could pay a nominal "public media tax" of 1 percent on their earnings, which would generate significant revenue for a journalism trust fund. Based on their 2017 net incomes, such a tax would yield $159.34 million from Facebook and $126.62 million from Google/Alphabet. Combined, this $285.96 million would go a long way toward seeding an endowment for independent journalism, especially if combined with other philanthropic contributions that accumulate over time. A similar, but more ambitious, plan proposed by the media reform organization Free Press calls for a tax on digital advertising more broadly, potentially yielding $2 billion dollars per year for public service journalism.[6]

These firms could certainly afford such expenditures, since they currently pay preciously little in taxes.[7] In recent years, the European Commission has suggested instituting a new tax of between 1 and 5 percent on digital companies' revenues. The British Media Reform Coalition and the National Union of Journalists have both proposed allocating the money from such taxes specifically for public service journalism. These campaigns have thus far been unsuccessful, but they reflect rising awareness about the connections between digital monopolies' illegitimate wealth accumulation, the continuing degradation of journalism, and the rise of misinformation.[8] If we are to grant platform monopolies such incredible power over our vital communication infrastructures, a new social contract must protect democratic society from such harms.

Another possibility for supporting public media—an idea I touch on throughout this book—is for foundations to serve their historic role of incubating new media models. As we saw in chapter 5, foundations such as Ford, Carnegie, MacArthur, and many others played a key role in shaping what became US public broadcasting. They could play a similarly important role in creating the next public media system, especially in its early stages of development. Once a new public media system becomes established and demonstrates its utility, public monies could be increased as reliance on private foundations decreases. This would be similar to US public broadcasting's development in the late 1960s, but a key distinction between then and now is that major foundations—especially Carnegie—encouraged government to step in and fund these infrastructures. Regardless, this time we should forbid the new public media system from taking voluntary corporate donations to avoid the quid pro quos that come with sponsorship and ensure that we do not repeat the same mistakes.

Given permanent support through a combination of private philanthropic contributions and public subsidies, a well-funded national journalism service could help guarantee universal access to quality news. This "public option" for journalism can address commercial media's endemic problems that render our information systems vulnerable to crisis.

What Would a Truly Public Media System Look like?

The fight for a truly independent public media system does not stop with funding. Once we have created the structural conditions for these new journalistic spaces, we have to make sure they remain truly public and democratic. Therefore, we must have structures in place that ensure these institutions are controlled by journalists and representative members of the public and operated in a bottom-up, transparent fashion in constant dialogue with engaged local communities. In short, these newsrooms must look like the communities they serve.

We might envision this project constituted in layers: the funding layer (how will this public media system be financially sustained?); the governance layer (how will resources be allocated and how can these decisions be made democratically?); the ascertainment layer (how will information needs be determined?); the infrastructure layer (how can we ensure distribution of and access to information, including universal broadband service?); and the engagement layer (how can we ensure that local communities are involved in making their own news and contributing their own voices and stories?). While administrators can distribute resources via a centralized hub, local media bureaus that represent the communities in which they reside should make key governance decisions. Federal and state-level commissions can calculate how resources should be deployed to target news deserts, meet special communication needs, and focus on addressing gaps in news coverage (e.g., around elections, inequality, global warming, and other specific social needs and problems).

Actualizing this system will require a public media consortium comprised of policy experts, scholars, technologists, journalists, and public advocates that specialize in work relevant to each of these layers. Most importantly, each layer must engage local communities. Researcher Lindsay Green-Barber reminds us that "engaged journalism" must "respect and include the public in its processes and practices." Ultimately, she concludes, this journalism is about reflecting lived realities, meeting information needs, and "cultivating and listening to sources *throughout the community*, rather than in niche sectors or in the upper echelons of power" (her emphasis).[9] A related project is "solutions journalism," which focuses on addressing social problems while highlighting local voices and ground-level sourcing.[10]

In short, our goal should be to create a robust and well-funded media system that is truly public, designed for our digital age, and democracy-driven, not market-driven. Whatever form they ultimately take, building viable noncommercial models will be a long, hard slog. Many flowers will bloom and wither, but the experiments will continue. Starting with the premise that commercial journalism is a dead end allows us to reorient tired conversations about the future of news. It frees us to think more boldly and creatively. Liberating journalists from commercial constraints would allow them to practice the craft that led them to the profession in the first place. In other words, it would *let journalists be journalists*. This means they should have a stake in the ownership and governance of media institutions. At the very least, journalists need strong unions to protect labor conditions and democratize newsrooms. Beyond that baseline, a truly public media system should include worker-run cooperatives and other forms of collective ownership. Journalists, in close conversations with local communities, should dictate what reporting they take on.

Ultimately, public media means *public ownership* of media institutions.[11] This requires a social democratic paradigm that sees the Fourth Estate as an indispensable countervailing force against concentrated power. Any progressive agenda worth the name must fight for an adversarial news media that provides accurate information about social problems, challenges powerful interests, and opens up a forum for underrepresented voices and alternative visions for society. The US media system is riven with stark inequalities— it reflects class and racial divides, just as it perpetuates them. But given the right structural conditions, journalism can instead be a force for social justice and radical change.

Unhooking media from profit imperatives and commercial pressures does not solve all of journalism's problems, but it is a necessary starting point. Absent subsidies for noncommercial media, it is impossible to support journalism that is expensive to produce but rarely profitable. Left entirely to the market, stories that do not attract advertisers and wealthy interests will go untold. Anything that captures our attention for advertisers—from shouting heads on cable television to clickbait online—is likely to be amplified. Commercial news values bolster the status quo; they rarely challenge it. Too often, market forces are treated as a guarantor of a free press and a free people. This faux-populist "give the people what they want" mythology naturalizes the powerful and profitable and treats oppositional journalism as a risky anomaly. The demise of local journalism should serve as the proverbial canary in the coalmine. It is a telltale sign that we need a radical media project that penetrates to the roots of market censorship. Otherwise, we face a future in which the market crushes actual journalism and a few corporations choose which stories we hear.

Reframing the Debate

The current crisis could fuel a period of bold experimentation with new journalistic models. If society treats news as only a commodity, then it is rational to maximize profits by any means possible. But if we see journalism as primarily a public service, then we should try to minimize market pressures, return news production to local communities, and sustain public media into perpetuity, just as we preserve permanent spaces in society for museums, parks, libraries, and schools. Commercial constraints have long created barriers for particular voices and views in the press. Journalism's public service mission and its profit motives have always been in tension. Indeed, the very project of developing ethical codes and professional standards was to prevent journalism from being overwhelmed by business priorities.

Unfortunately, these earlier lessons have been either ignored or forgotten. Today we are witnessing an apotheosis of those tensions, a culmination of long-standing structural contradictions in commercial journalism. Yet, there are positive signs that US society is slowly coming to realize that these flaws in commercial journalism—to use contemporary parlance—are not a bug in the system but a feature. However, our analyses of this crisis remain deeply impoverished. In the United States, we treat the market's effects on journalism—as we treat the market's effects on nearly everything—as an inevitable force of nature beyond our control or, at the very least, a public expression of democratic desires.

This "market ontology" simultaneously naturalizes the market's violence against journalism and forecloses on alternative models. Ultimately, this fealty to the market ensures that society will not attempt a serious public policy response to a major social problem. By this logic, if publics (or rather, advertisers, investors, and media owners) do not support certain kinds of journalism, we must let them wither. This position's inherent absurdity is cast into stark relief if we designed our public education according to a similar commercial logic. If students elect not to pay for civics class, then it is discontinued. Or consider academic labor: If scholars' journal articles do not receive enough clicks or likes, they must abandon their research agendas. While it seems preposterous when applied to other areas of society, this savage logic is snuffing out journalism in broad daylight.

All democratic theories and foundational principles—including the First Amendment itself—assume a thriving press system. The Fourth Estate's current collapse is a profound social problem that screams for public policy intervention. That no such intervention has occurred stems as much from discursive capture as it does from regulatory failure. Discourses about digital journalism's democratic potential often overlook the policy roots and normative foundations of our communication systems. An abiding faith in technological liberation discouraged public policies that could prevent corporate capture of our core information systems. This discursive orientation at least partly explains why US society ever allowed platform monopolies—driven by a ruthless "surveillance capitalism"—to obtain such tremendous and unaccountable power in the first place.[12] It also helps explain the meager policy responses to our ongoing journalism crisis. The degraded media system resulting from these policy failures created a fertile landscape for various kinds of misinformation to thrive.

The Road Ahead

Since the market cannot provide for all our information needs, a policy program based on a social democratic vision of public media would facilitate policies that do the following: reduce monopoly power; install public interest protections; remove commercial pressures; and build out public infrastructure. At the state and local levels, we can work to support programs to build community broadband services and local journalism initiatives. For inspiration, we can look to past experiments—from municipal newspapers to cooperative telephone networks—to imagine what these nonprofit experiments might look like.

Other elements of this program lend themselves to a long-term transformation at the federal level—driven by grassroots social movements from below—to create a new national public media system. Now is the time for creating counter-narratives and radical alternatives to the still-dominant libertarian paradigm. It is precisely during dark political moments such as ours that we should envision and plan for a more enlightened future. The journalism crisis—as well as the commercialization and corporate monopolization of our news and information systems—are significant social problems. They fall within the realm of policy, and therefore, politics.

For too long, US society has held the wrong debate over what new business model might support journalism. Too many otherwise smart people—conditioned not to see capitalism's corrosive impact on journalism—misdiagnosed the problem because they failed to see commercialism at its core. Instead, we must clarify the structural roots of the crisis, expand the political imaginary for potential futures, identify alternatives, and help chart a path toward actualizing them. Most importantly, we must look ahead rather than behind us. Waxing nostalgic about a golden era of newspaper reporting, or pining for the days of three major television networks when Walter Cronkite told us "and that's the way it is," brings us no closer to the type of public media system that democracy requires. Our goal must be to reinvent news media, not shore up old commercial models. Our focus should be on the future of journalism, not the plight of newspapers or any other specific medium. If we unhook journalism from commercial imperatives to create truly public alternatives, we just might design a media system that serves democracy.

Acknowledgments

Any book project is a collective endeavor, and that is especially true for one that spans a decade. It's impossible for me to thank everyone with whom I've had meaningful conversations over the years about the future of journalism and why it matters for democracy. I'll begin by thanking my friend and mentor Bob McChesney, who was the ideal scholar-activist to study under in graduate school. Bob always encouraged me to approach my interests in media and democracy from a structural and historical perspective. In the summer of 2007, as I was finishing my dissertation, Bob asked me to conduct research on a "Save Journalism" project for the media reform organization that he co-founded, Free Press. I have been working on this issue ever since.

Other key mentors I wish to thank are John Nerone and Dan Schiller, whose profound influence on my thinking are found throughout the book. My interest in understanding the structural failures of commercial media and the need for alternatives goes even further back to working with Lance Bennett at the University of Washington while studying for my master's degree. My work also follows in the tradition of the late Ed Baker, who was always generous in talking to me about media, markets, and democracy.

A number of friends and colleagues deserve special thanks for reading and commenting on early drafts of specific chapters or parts of chapters. These kind folks include Rod Benson, Mike Copps, Des Freedman, Aske Kammer, Mark Lloyd, Allison Perlman, Robert Picard, Lee Shaker, Josh Shepperd, Briar Smith, and Joe Turow. I am especially grateful to several folks who generously read the entire book and offered incredibly helpful feedback: Chris Ali, Jay Hamilton, Audra Wolfe, and Craig Aaron. Craig and I, along with Josh Stearns, co-authored a 2009 report titled "Saving the News" when I was a Research Fellow at Free Press (where I now sit on the Board of Directors) during the early days of our contemporary journalism crisis. I have continued to benefit from Josh's astute input on everything from journalism's benefits to democracy to new models for local news.

I also want to thank a strong intellectual community of friends and colleagues who encouraged me along the way, offering moral support, advice, and the occasional libation: Sarah Banet-Weiser, Jack Bratich, Kevin Coe, Jeff

Cohen, Christina Dunbar-Hester, Susan Douglas, Bob Entman, Brett Gary, Natalie Fenton, Oscar Gandy, John Gastil, Tom Glaisyer, Ted Glasser, Ellen Goodman, Larry Gross, Bob Hackett, Jayson Harsin, David Hesmondhalgh, Richard John, Marwan Kraidy, Chenjerai Kumanyika, Marie Leger, Yph Lelkes, Jessa Lingel, Steve Livingston, Robin Mansell, Carolyn Marvin, Rick Maxwell, Sascha Meinrath, Lee McGuigan, Mark Miller, Tony Nadler, Russ Newman, John Nichols, Kaarina Nikunen, Matt Powers, Monroe Price, Manuel Puppis, Craig Robertson, Ben Scott, Inger Stole, Tom Streeter, Sharon Strover, Siva Vaidhyanathan, Janet Wasko, Guobin Yang, and Barbie Zelizer. Dear friends Jonathan Evans, Joe McCombs, and Noah Rahm helped keep me grounded. A number of friends from our Ithaca community deserve special gratitude, especially Jenny Mann and Guy Ortolano. I also thank Aaron Sachs for asking me to help coach our sons' fourth grade basketball team, which was the perfect therapy during final book writing.

I am grateful for my wonderful colleagues and the amazing staff at the University of Pennsylvania's Annenberg School for Communication who provide a supportive environment for critical research. I especially would like to thank our former dean, Michael Delli Carpini, and our current dean, John Jackson, for being strong supporters of social justice work. It has been a special privilege to work with my good friend Todd Wolfson, who co-directs with me the new Media, Inequality and Change (MIC) Center. Along with our stellar program manager Briar Smith, we officially launched the center during the final stages of book-writing, and I relish the opportunity to commit our research to various kinds of activism in the coming years.

I could not have finished this book without top-notch research assistance from a number of highly talented graduate students at Annenberg over the years: Doug Allen, David Berman, Lauren Bridges, Zane Cooper, Nick Gilewicz, Antoine Haywood, Jenn Henrichsen, Sanjay Jolly, Tim Libert, Chloé Nurik, Paul Popiel, and Alex Williams. Chloé deserves special recognition for proofing the entire book, editing all of my footnotes, and offering sharp feedback. Paul also gave the entire book a close and careful read and helped me out with innumerable research tasks. I have co-authored various writing projects with Alex, Paul, Tim, and David—for example, David Berman and I co-authored a book on net neutrality that came out in the fall of 2019—and I draw from some of the research in those writings. My political economy graduate seminar deserves much appreciation for reading early drafts of a couple chapters in class.

I hashed out bits and slices of this book in earlier articles, chapters, and essays, which I indicate in my notes. I am especially thankful to Katrina vanden Heuvel for inviting me to write several essays on the politics of media policy and journalism for the *Nation*, which allowed me to work out some arguments that I develop further in this book. I also was fortunate to participate in a SSRC working group on the history of disinformation in 2018–2019 that allowed me to air out some of the book's key arguments. I am deeply indebted to the good folks at Oxford University Press, especially my editor Angela Chnapko. Angela has been very supportive of this project since the moment I first reached out to her, and she calmly and assuredly guided me through the many stages of book production.

Every working parent knows how exceedingly difficult it can be to balance one's professional life with everything else, and I am blessed with a loving family that is tolerant toward my writing obligations, but also allows me to completely forget about work and focus on the important things. I want to thank my sister's family—Lara, Steve, Willow, and Ryan—and my wife's large family, especially Julilly Kohler, Chuck and Jean Hausmann, and Issa Kohler-Hausmann, who all have been incredibly supportive over these years, humoring me while I rant or geek out about the finer details of media policy. I thank my heroic mother, Kay Pickard, to whom I owe everything. And I thank my two precious children, Zaden and Lilia (who always make sure that their names are mentioned in my books), for reminding me every day why this world is worth fighting for.

I dedicate this book to my life partner and closest friend, Julilly Kohler-Hausmann. In addition to being an incredible mother and loving wife, Julilly possesses a keen intellect, and her spot-on comments on my book were invaluable. I have talked to her about this stuff for many years and her clear thinking has improved my own, and her companionship in this crazy world has made me a better person. I am so thankful to have her in my life.

Finally, I hope in some small way this book may honor and help the journalists and activists who continue to work every day against great odds to inform us, to empower us, to create the media we so desperately need. Their fight is our fight.

Notes

Introduction

1. Andrew Tyndall, "Campaign 2016 Coverage: Annual Totals for 2015," *Tyndall Report*, December 21, 2015, http://tyndallreport.com/comment/20/5773/.
2. Nicholas Confessore and Karen Yourish, "$2 Billion Worth of Free Media for Donald Trump," *New York Times*, March 15, 2016, https://www.nytimes.com/2016/03/16/upshot/measuring-donald-trumps-mammoth-advantage-in-free-media.html; Mary Harris, "A Media Post-Mortem on the 2016 Presidential Election," *MediaQuant*, November 14, 2016, https://www.mediaquant.net/2016/11/a-media-post-mortem-on-the-2016-presidential-election/; Robert Schroeder, "Trump Has Gotten Nearly $3 Billion in 'Free' Advertising," *MarketWatch*, May 6, 2016, http://www.marketwatch.com/story/trump-has-gotten-nearly-3-billion-in-free-advertising-2016-05-06.
3. Thomas Patterson, *News Coverage of the 2016 Presidential Primaries: Horse Race Reporting Has Consequences* (Cambridge: Shorenstein Center on Media, Politics and Public Policy, 2016), https://shorensteincenter.org/news-coverage-2016-presidential-primaries/; Thomas Patterson, "Harvard Study: Policy Issues Nearly Absent in Presidential Campaign Coverage," *The Conversation*, September 20, 2016, https://theconversation.com/harvard-study-policy-issues-nearly-absent-in-presidential-campaign-coverage-65731.
4. Duncan Watts and David Rothschild, "Don't Blame the Election on Fake News. Blame It on the Media," *Columbia Journalism Review*, December 5, 2017, https://www.cjr.org/analysis/fake-news-media-election-trump.php.
5. I have addressed some of these questions in previous writings. For example, see Victor Pickard, "Media and Politics in the Age of Trump," *Origins: Current Events in Historical Perspective* 10, no. 2 (2016), https://origins.osu.edu/article/media-and-politics-age-trump.
6. Victor Pickard, "Media Failures in the Age of Trump," *Political Economy of Communication* 4, no. 2 (2017): 118–122.
7. Jonathan Mahler, "CNN Had a Problem. Donald Trump Solved It," *New York Times*, April 4, 2017, https://www.nytimes.com/2017/04/04/magazine/cnn-had-a-problem-donald-trump-solved-it.html.
8. Eliza Collins, "Les Moonves: Trump's Run Is 'Damn Good for CBS,'" *Politico*, February 29, 2016, https://www.politico.com/blogs/on-media/2016/02/les-moonves-trump-cbs-220001.
9. Amy Chozick, "Why Trump Will Get a Second Term," *New York Times*, September 29, 2018, https://www.nytimes.com/2018/09/29/sunday-review/trump-2020-reality-tv.html.

10. Craig Silverman, "This Analysis Shows How Viral Fake Election News Stories Outperformed Real News on Facebook," *BuzzFeed News*, November 16, 2016, https://www.buzzfeed.com/craigsilverman/viral-fake-election-news-outperformed-real-news-on-facebook?utm_term=.kyNMQ7pa8#.uqEVNx5kd.

11. Jeffrey Gottfried and Elisa Shearer, "News Use across Social Medial Platforms 2016," Pew Research Center, May 26, 2016, http://www.journalism.org/2016/05/26/news-use-across-social-media-platforms-2016/.

12. Mathew Ingram, "Sorry Mark Zuckerberg, but Facebook Is Definitely a Media Company," *Fortune*, August 30, 2016, http://fortune.com/2016/08/30/facebook-media-company/.

13. Sally Hubbard, "Fake News Is a Real Antitrust Problem," *Competition Policy International*, December 19, 2017.

14. Ken Doctor, "Newsonomics: The Halving of America's Daily Newsrooms," *NiemanLab*, July 28, 2015, http://www.niemanlab.org/2015/07/newsonomics-the-halving-of-americas-daily-newsrooms/

15. Penelope Abernathy, *The Rise of a New Media Baron and the Emerging Threat of News Deserts* (Chapel Hill: UNC Center for Innovation and Sustainability in Local Media, 2016), http://newspaperownership.com/wp-content/uploads/2016/09/07.UNC_RiseOfNewMediaBaron_SinglePage_01Sep2016-REDUCED.pdf.

16. Victor Pickard, "Being Critical: Contesting Power within the Misinformation Society," *Communication and Critical/Cultural Studies* 10, no. 2–3 (2013): 306–311.

17. Michael Barthel, "State of the News Media 2016: 5 Key Takeaways," Pew Research Center, June 15, 2016, http://www.pewresearch.org/fact-tank/2016/06/15/state-of-the-news-media-2016-key-takeaways/#.

18. Anthony Nadler, "Nature's Economy and News Ecology: Scrutinizing the News Ecosystem Metaphor," *Journalism Studies* 20, no. 6 (2019): 823–839.

19. C.W. Anderson, Emily Bell, and Clay Shirky, *Post-Industrial Journalism: Adapting to the Present* (New York City: Tow Center for Digital Journalism, 2012), https://archives.cjr.org/behind_the_news/post_industrial_journalism_ada.php.

20. Recent works that focus on such normative concerns include the following: C. Edwin Baker, *Media, Markets, and Democracy* (New York: Cambridge University Press, 2002); Michael Schudson, *Why Democracies Need an Unlovable Press* (Cambridge: Polity, 2008); Clifford Christians et al., *Normative Theories of the Media: Journalism in Democratic Societies* (Champaign: University of Illinois Press, 2009); Mike Ananny, *Networked Press Freedom: Creating Infrastructures for a Public Right to Hear* (Cambridge: MIT Press, 2018). Daniel Kreiss and J.S. Brennen, "Normative Models of Digital Journalism," in *The SAGE Handbook of Digital Journalism*, ed. T. Witschge, C. W. Anderson, David Domingo, and A. Hermida (Los Angeles: Sage, 2016), 299–314; Barbie Zelizer, *What Journalism could be* (Malden, MA: Polity Press, 2017).

21. Dan Schiller, "The Legacy of Robert A. Brady: Antifascist Origins of the Political Economy of Communications," *Journal of Media Economics* 12, no. 2 (1999): 89–101.

22. For canonical interpretations of the political economic approach to media, see Vincent Mosco, *The Political Economy of Communication*, 2nd ed. (London: Sage,

2009); Robert McChesney, *Communication Revolution: Critical Junctures and the Future of Media* (New York: New Press, 2007); Oscar Gandy, "The Political Economy Approach: A Critical Challenge," *Journal of Media Economics* 5, no. 2 (Summer 1992): 23–42.

Chapter 1

1. I return to this "US media exceptionalism" in chapter 5.
2. John Locke, *The Second Treatise of Government: And a Letter Concerning Toleration* (Mineola: Courier Corporation, 1956).
3. David Held, *Models of Democracy*, 3rd ed. (Cambridge: Polity, 2006).
4. These freedoms often were assumed to apply primarily to white, propertied men of a particular class.
5. John Milton and John Hales, *Areopagitica* (Oxford: Clarendon Press, 1886).
6. John Stuart Mill, *On Liberty*, 4th ed. (London: Longmans, Green, Reader, and Dyer, 1869).
7. Mill, *On Liberty*, 101.
8. Abrams v. United States, 250 U.S. 616, 630 (1919).
9. Philip Napoli, "The Marketplace of Ideas Metaphor in Communications Regulation," *Journal of Communication* 49, no. 4 (1999): 151–169.
10. Sam Lebovic, *Free Speech and Unfree News: The Paradox of Press Freedom in America* (Cambridge: Harvard University Press, 2016), 17–25. John Durham Peters notes that the "marketplace of ideas" came into common usage at precisely the same moment as the term "mass communication" as a way of acknowledging and compensating for the shrinking media marketplace. See: John Durham Peters, "'The Marketplace of Ideas': A History of the Concept," in *Toward a Political Economy of Culture: Capitalism and Communication in the Twenty-First Century*, ed. Andrew Calabrese and Colin Sparks (Lanham: Rowman & Littlefield, 2004), 65–82.
11. Fred Siebert, Theodore Peterson, and Wilbur Schramm, *Four Theories of the Press: The Authoritarian, Libertarian, Social Responsibility and Soviet Communist Concepts of What the Press Should Be and Do* (Urbana: University of Illinois, 1956), 70.
12. For a critique of this liberal model, see, for example, Nancy Fraser, "Rethinking the Public Sphere: A Contribution to the Critique of Actually Existing Democracy," in *Habermas and the Public Sphere*, ed. Craig Calhoun (Cambridge: MIT Press, 1992), 109–142.
13. Sue Curry Jansen, "Market Censorship Revisited: Press Freedom, Journalistic Practices, and the Emerging World Order," *Annals of the International Communication Association* 17, no. 1 (1994): 481–504.
14. Thomas Jefferson, "Thomas Jefferson to Edward Carrington, 1787," in *The Writings of Thomas Jefferson: Containing his Autobiography, Notes on Virginia, Parliamentary Manual, Official Papers, Messages and Addresses, And Other Writings, Official and Private*, vol. 6, ed. Andrew A. Lipscomb and Albert Ellery Bergh (Washington, DC: The Thomas Jefferson Memorial Association, 1903), 57.

15. Thomas Jefferson, "Thomas Jefferson to Lafayette, 1823," in Lipscomb and Bergh, eds., *The Writings of Thomas Jefferson*, vol. 15, 491.

16. James Madison, "James Madison to W.T. Barry," in *The Founders' Constitution*, vol. 1, ed. Philip Kurland and Ralph Lerner (Chicago: University of Chicago Press, 1987), 103–109.

17. Potter Stewart, "Or of the Press," *Hastings Law Journal* 26 (1974): 631–638; Steven Shiffrin, *What's Wrong with the First Amendment?* (New York: Cambridge University Press, 2016), 126–127.

18. An excellent collection edited by Timothy Cook focuses on many of these questions. See especially: Charles Clark, "The Press the Founders Knew," in *Freeing the Presses: The First Amendment in Action*, ed. Timothy Cook (Baton Rouge: Louisiana State University Press, 2005), 33–50.

19. Benjamin Franklin expressed this view in "An Apology for Printers," in *The Political Thought of Benjamin Franklin*, ed. Ralph Ketcham (Indianapolis: Bobbs-Merrill, 1965). The essay and related arguments are discussed in Cook, *Freeing the Presses*, 8.

20. Robert Martin, *The Free and Open Press: The Founding of American Democratic Press Liberty, 1640–1800* (New York: NYU Press, 2001). See especially pp. 10–11, 163.

21. Cook, *Freeing the Presses*, 8. Similarly, the constitutional law professor Akhil Reed Amar has argued convincingly that the main original purpose of the First Amendment was to sustain a healthy majoritarian public sphere, not primarily to protect minority opinions from an overbearing government. See Akhil Reed Amar, *The Bill of Rights: Creation and Reconstruction* (New Haven: Yale University Press, 1998).

22. Richard John, *Spreading the News: The American Postal System from Franklin to Morse* (Cambridge: Harvard University Press, 1995), 38.

23. Ibid., 47–48.

24. Ibid., 30.

25. A stark counterexample was the confederacy postal system during the Civil War, whose fixation on a strict mandate to achieve fiscal self-sufficiency proved disastrous. John Anderson, "Money or Nothing: Confederate Postal System Collapse during the Civil War," *American Journalism* 30, no. 1 (2013): 65–86.

26. Geoff Cowan and David Westphal, "The Washington-Madison Solution," in *Will the Last Reporter Please Turn Out the Lights?: The Collapse of Journalism and What Can Be Done to Fix It*, ed. Robert McChesney and Victor Pickard (New York: The New Press, 2011), 133–137.

27. The historical significance of establishing the postal system is discussed in Robert McChesney and John Nichols, *The Death and Life of American Journalism: The Media Revolution That Will Begin the World Again* (New York: Nation Books, 2011), 121–126; Theda Skocpol, "The Tocqueville Problem: Civic Engagement in American Democracy," *Social Science History* 21, no. 4 (1997): 455–479; Richard Kielbowicz, *News in the Mail: The Press, Post Office, and Public Information, 1700–1860s* (Westport: Greenwood Press, 1989).

28. Winifred Gallagher, *How the Post Office Created America* (New York: Penguin Books, 2016).

29. Gerald Baldasty, *The Commercialization of News in the Nineteenth Century* (Madison: University of Wisconsin Press, 1992), 5.

30. John Nerone, *The Media and Public Life: A History* (Cambridge: Polity Press, 2015), 111. The new model is often referred to as the "penny press" but Nerone complicates the distinction.

31. Ibid. See also: Juan Gonzalez and Joseph Torres, *News For All The People: The Epic Story of Race and the American Media* (New York: Verso, 2011).

32. James Curran and Jane Seaton, *Power Without Responsibility: The Press and Broadcasting in Britain*, 2nd ed., London: Methuen, 1985, 34–39. See also: James Curran, *Media and Democracy* (New York: Routledge, 2011), 153–167.

33. C. Edwin Baker, *Advertising and a Democratic Press* (Princeton: Princeton University Press, 1994), 3. Because they skewed media coverage, he concluded that "Advertisers, not governments, are the primary censors of media content in the United States today," p. 99.

34. Randall Sumpter, "Think Journalism's a Tough Field Today? Try Being a Reporter in the Gilded Age," *The Conversation*, October 4, 2018, https://theconversation. com/think-journalisms-a-tough-field-today-try-being-a-reporter-in-the-gilded-age-103420. See also: Randall Sumpter, *Before Journalism Schools: How Gilded Age Reporters Learned the Rules* (Columbia: University of Missouri Press, 2018).

35. Louis Pérez, "The Meaning of the Maine: Causation and the Historiography of the Spanish-American War," *Pacific Historical Review* 58, no. 3 (1989): 293–322. For a strong refutation of this historical argument, see C.W. Anderson, Leonard Downie Jr., and Michael Schudson, *The News Media: What Everyone Needs to Know* (New York City: Oxford University Press, 2016).

36. W. Joseph Campbell, *Yellow Journalism: Puncturing the Myths, Defining the Legacies* (Westport: Praeger, 2001), 179.

37. Margaret Blanchard, "Press Criticism and National Reform Movements: The Progressive Era and the New Deal," *Journalism History* 5, no. 2 (1978): 33–37, 54–55; Marion Marzolf, *Civilizing Voices: American Press Criticism, 1880–1950* (New York: Longman, 1991); Robert McChesney, *The Problem of the Media: US Communication Politics in the Twenty-First Century* (New York: Monthly Review Press, 2004); Robert McChesney and Ben Scott, eds., *Our Unfree Press: 100 Years of Radical Media Criticism* (New York: The New Press, 2004); Amy Reynolds and Gary Hicks, *Prophets of the Fourth Estate: Broadsides by Press Critics of the Progressive Era* (Los Angeles, CA: Litwin Books, 2011).

38. James Weinstein, *The Decline of Socialism in America, 1912–1925* (New York: Vintage Books, 1969), 85.

39. Scholars such as W. Joseph Campbell argue against a neat division between yellow journalism and the establishment press, showing how the yellow press textured the content and form of elite newspapers even after the collapse of the yellow press itself.

40. This history has been discussed in Elliott Shore, *Talkin' Socialism: J.A. Wayland and the Role of the Press in American Radicalism, 1890–1912* (Lawrence: University Press of Kansas, 1988); John Nerone, *Violence Against the Press: Policing the Public Sphere in US History* (New York: Oxford University Press, 1994). For more general background on Los Angeles and the bombings, see: Marshall Berges, *The Life and Times of Los Angeles: A Newspaper, a Family, and a City* (New York: Atheneum Books, 1984).

41. Quoted in Robert Gottlieb and Irene Wolt, *Thinking Big: The Story of the Los Angeles Times, Its Publishers, and Their Influence on Southern California* (New York: Putnam Publishing Group, 1977), 51.

42. Louis Adamic, *Dynamite: The Story of Class Violence in America* (New York: Viking Press, 1931), 203.

43. Popular lore credits the origin of the term to Teddy Roosevelt, who in a famous speech likened these investigative reporters to a character in the Paul Bunyan stories who was known to "muck-rake." See Teddy Roosevelt, "The Man with the Muck-Rake," speech given in Washington, DC, April 14, 1906, *American Rhetoric*, https://www. americanrhetoric.com/speeches/teddyrooseveltmuckrake.htm.

44. See Nerone, *The Media and Public Life*, 136–141.

45. John Dewey, "Our Unfree Press," in *Common Sense*, vol. 4, 1935, 6–7.

46. All of the quotes in this paragraph are from Dewey, "Our Unfree Press," 6–7.

47. Walter Lippmann, *Liberty and the News* (New York: Harcourt, Brace and House, 1920), 75–76.

48. Ibid., 4–5. For a discussion of Lippmann's media criticism see Robert McChesney "That Was Now and This is Then," in McChesney and Pickard, *Will the Last Reporter Please Turn Out the Lights?* 151–161.

49. Upton Sinclair, *The Brass Check: A Study of American Journalism* (Pasadena: Upton Sinclair, 1919).

50. Ibid., 234.

51. Several of the quotes above are found in Margaret Blanchard, "Press Criticism and National Reform Movements: The Progressive Era and the New Deal," *Journalism History* 5, no. 2 (1978): 33–37. For other representative critics from this period, see: Henry George Jr., *The Menace of Privilege: A Study of the Dangers to the Republic from the Existence of a Favored Class* (New York: The Macmillan Company, 1906); James Edward Rogers, *The American Newspaper* (Chicago: University of Chicago Press, 1909); Charles Edward Russell, "These Days in American Journalism," *The International Socialist Review* 12, no. 4 (October 1911): 210–216; Edward Alsworth Ross, *Changing America: Studies in Contemporary Society* (New York: The Century Co., 1912).

52. Oswald Garrison Villard, "Press Tendencies and Dangers," *Atlantic Monthly*, January 1918, 63–64.

53. Hamilton Holt, *Commercialism and Journalism* (Boston: Riverside Press, 1909), 34.

54. Will Irwin, *The American Newspaper* (Ames: The Iowa State University Press, 1969), 30.

55. James Rorty, *Our Master's Voice: Advertising* (New York: The John Day Company, 1934).

56. Much of the press criticism is discussed in McChesney and Scott, *Our Unfree Press*. For other representative examples of 1930s press criticism not discussed here, see: Leo Rosten, *The Washington Correspondents* (New York: Harcourt, Brace and Company, 1937); Alfred McClung Lee, "Violations of Press Freedom in America," *Journalism Bulletin* 15, no. 1 (1938): 19–27; Silas Bent, *Newspaper Crusaders: A Neglected Story* (New York: McGraw-Hill Book Company, 1939).

57. Harold Ickes, *America's House of Lords: An Inquiry into the Freedom of the Press* (New York: Harcourt, Brace and Co., 1939), viii.
58. George Seldes, *Freedom of the Press* (Indianapolis: The Bobbs-Merrill Company, 1935); George Seldes, *Lords of the Press* (New York: J. Messner, Inc., 1938).
59. George Seldes, "To All Our Faithful Subscribers," *In Fact*, October 2, 1950. George Seldes Papers, Penn Libraries, University of Pennsylvania, Philadelphia, PA. I thank Chris Cimaglio for sharing these materials with me.
60. Randolph Holhut, "The Forgotten Man of American Journalism: A Brief Biography of George Seldes," Brasscheck.com Historical Archive, n.d., http://www.brasscheck.com/seldes/bio.html.
61. I.F. Stone talked about George Seldes's influence in Bryan Marquard and Robert Gershon's interview for their documentary "You Can't Print That," December 29, 1982, https://www.youtube.com/watch?v=yXAyitQ0Xsg
62. Stephen Ward, *The Invention of Journalism Ethics*, 2nd ed. (Montreal: McGill-Queen's University Press, 2004), 242–243; Gerald Baldasty, *E.W. Scripps and the Business of Newspapers* (Urbana: University of Illinois Press, 1999), 4–8. Interestingly, Scripps was also anti-advertising.
63. Marzolf, *Civilizing Voices*, 154.
64. George Marion, *The "Free Press": Portrait of a Monopoly* (New York: New Century Publishers, 1946), 20.
65. Another experiment considered at this time was the endowed newspaper. For an overview of this model, as well as non-profit and other structural alternatives, see: Denise DeLorme and Fred Fedler, "Endowed Newspapers: A Solution to the Industry's Problems?" *Journal of Humanities and Social Sciences* 2, no. 1 (2008): 1–14; Victor Pickard, "Can Government Support the Press? Historicizing and Internationalizing a Policy Approach to the Journalism Crisis," *Communication Review* 14, no. 2 (2011): 73–95; Victor Pickard and Josh Stearns, "New Models Emerge for Community Press," *Newspaper Research Journal* 32, no. 1 (2011): 46–62.
66. "'Adless' Newspaper Dies; Higher Cost of White Paper Causes End of Chicago Publication," *New York Times*, July 7, 1917; Duane Stoltzfus, *Freedom from Advertising: E.W. Scripps's Chicago Experiment* (Urbana: University of Illinois Press, 2007); Paul Milkman, *PM: A New Deal in Journalism, 1940–1948* (New Brunswick: Rutgers University Press, 1997).
67. George Dunlop, "A Municipal Newspaper," *National Municipal Review* 1, no. 3 (July 1, 1912): 441–443. See also: Mila Maynard, "A Municipal Paper," *Appeal to Reason*, December 23, 1911.
68. George Dunlop, "A Publicly Owned Newspaper," *Public* 15, no. 749 (1912): 758–762.
69. Robert Davenport, "Weird Note for the Vox Populi: The Los Angeles 'Municipal News,'" *California Historical Society Quarterly* 44, no. 1 (1965): 3–15.
70. James Melvin Lee, *History of American Journalism* (New York: Garden City Publishing, 1923), 410–412.
71. "A Newspaper Owned by the People," *La Follette's Magazine*, May 18, 1912, 7.
72. Ibid, 7.

73. "The Municipal Newspaper Idea Cannot Be Killed," *Los Angeles Municipal News*, April 9, 1913.
74. Ibid.
75. Bryan Lee Ellsworth, "Los Angeles 'Kills' City Newspaper," *Town Development*, Vol. 8–10, 20–21, May 1913.
76. Some versions of municipal newspapers exist today with government entities creating their own websites to disseminate information, but these sites generally do not include reporting or political commentary. See, for example, Detroit's outlet, *The Neighborhoods*, http://theneighborhoods.org/.
77. See especially Ben Scott, "Labor's New Deal for Journalism—The Newspaper Guild in the 1930s" (PhD diss., University of Illinois, 2009).
78. Nathan Godfried, *WCFL: Chicago's Voice of Labor, 1926–78* (Urbana: University of Illinois Press, 1997), 205–208.
79. The previous quotes are from Scott, "Labor's New Deal for Journalism," 4. See also McChesney and Scott, *Our Unfree Press*, 20–22. They quote a widely-discussed *Harper's* article alleging that "the romantic legend of the newspaper reporter's freedom . . . has been a sham." Isabelle Keating, "Reporters Become of Age," *Harper's*, April 1935.
80. Herbert Harris, *American Labor* (New Haven, CT: Yale University Press, 1938), 173, 185, cited in McChesney and Scott, *Our Unfree Press*, 20.
81. Scott, "Labor's New Deal for Journalism."
82. McChesney and Scott, *Our Unfree Press*, 20.
83. Sam Lebovic, "Fighting for Free Information: American Democracy and the Problem of Press Freedom in the Totalitarian Age, 1920–1950" (PhD diss., University of Chicago, 2010), 20; see also 477, 493–494
84. I discuss the ideas in the following section in more depth in Victor Pickard, *America's Battle for Media Democracy: The Triumph of Corporate Libertarianism and the Future of Media Reform* (New York: Cambridge University Press, 2015), 136–143. See also Victor Pickard, "Laying Low the Shibboleth of a Free Press: Regulatory Threats against the American Newspaper Industry, 1938–1947," *Journalism Studies* 15, no. 4 (2014): 464–480.
85. Nikki Usher, "Resurrecting the 1938 St. Louis Post-Dispatch Symposium on the Freedom of the Press: Examining Its Contributions and Their Implications for Today," *Journalism Studies* 11, no. 3 (2010): 311–326. See also Lebovic, *Free Speech and Unfree News*, 1–2.
86. Confidential Memorandum to Assistant Attorney General Arnold, "The Newspaper Industry," Hugh Baker Cox Papers, American Heritage Center, University of Wyoming, Laramie, WY. (prepared by Irene Till), #3128, Notebook 5, August 3, 1938.
87. McChesney, *The Problem of the Media*.
88. Confidential Memorandum to Assistant Attorney General Arnold, 1938.
89. The following quotes are from United States v. Associated Press, 52 F. Supp. 362, 372 (S.D.N.Y.1943).
90. Associated Press v. United States, 326 U.S. 1 (1945).
91. Ibid.

92. "Survival of a Free, Competitive Press: The Small Newspaper, Democracy's Grass Roots." Report of the Chairman to the Members of the Committee of the Special Committee to Study Problems of American Small Business, United States Senate, January 2, 1947. See also: "Monopoly Strangling Free Press, Senate Report Says," *Guild Reporter*, February 14, 1947, 5.

93. "Senate Body Probes Small Paper Newsprint Squeeze," *Guild Reporter*, November 8, 1946, 8.

94. Ward, *The Invention of Journalism Ethics*, 244.

95. Ibid., 243.

96. See, for example, Michael Schudson, *Discovering the News: A Social History of American Newspapers* (New York: Basic Books, 1978).

97. For example, historians such as Dan Schiller, Gerald Baldasty, and Richard Kaplan all underscore structural factors downplayed by Schudson. See, Dan Schiller, *Objectivity and the News: The Public and the Rise of Commercial Journalism* (Philadelphia: University of Pennsylvania Press, 1981); Gerald Baldasty, *The Commercialization of News in the Nineteenth Century* (Madison: University of Wisconsin Press, 1992); Richard Kaplan, *Politics and the American Press: The Rise of Objectivity, 1865-1920* (Cambridge: Cambridge University Press, 2002). For a critical review of Schudson's historical interpretation, see Dan Schiller, "Journalism and Society," *Communication Research* 7, no. 3 (1980): 377–386.

98. Nerone, *The Media and Public Life*, 180–183. The broader professionalization project also was connected to structural transformations with editorial, the wire, and city editors' organizational positioning. See John Nerone and Kevin Barnhurst, "US Newspaper Types, the Newsroom, and the Division of Labor, 1750-2000," *Journalism Studies* 4, no. 4 (2003): 435–449.

99. Curran, *Media and Democracy*, 1, 9.

100. I discuss the Hutchins Commission at length in Pickard, *America's Battle for Media Democracy*, 152–89. See also, Victor Pickard, "'Whether the Giants Should Be Slain or Persuaded to Be Good': Revisiting the Hutchins Commission and the Role of Media in a Democratic Society," *Critical Studies in Media Communication* 27, no. 4 (2010): 391–411.

101. C. Edwin Baker noted that the Commission's general report "provides the most influential modern account of the goals of journalistic performance," and stands as the "most important, semiofficial, policy-oriented study of the mass media in U.S. history." See, respectively, Baker, *Media, Markets, and Democracy*, 154; C. Edwin Baker, *Media Concentration and Democracy: Why Ownership Matters* (Cambridge: Cambridge University Press, 2007), 2.

102. Zechariah Chafee, Comment to chapter IV, (n.d.), Robert M. Hutchins Papers, Joseph Regenstein Library, University of Chicago, Chicago, IL, Box 8, Folder 1.

103. Siebert, Peterson, and Schramm, *Four Theories of the Press*. For a critical reassessment of this book, see John Nerone, ed., *Last Rights* (Urbana: University of Illinois Press, 1995).

104. Robert Horwitz, "Broadcast Reform Revisited: Reverend Everett C. Parker and the 'Standing' Case," *Communication Review* 2, no. 3 (1997): 312.

105. Robert Picard, *The Press and the Decline of Democracy: The Democratic Socialist Response in Public Policy* (Westport: Greenwood, 1985).
106. Victor Pickard, "Revisiting the Road Not Taken: A Social Democratic Vision of the Press," in *Will the Last Reporter Please Turn Out the Lights?*, ed. McChesney and Pickard, 174–184.
107. For example, see Lance Bennet, *News: The Politics of Illusion*, 10th ed. (Chicago: University of Chicago Press, 2014).
108. Norman Solomon, *War Made Easy: How Presidents and Pundits Keep Spinning Us to Death* (Hoboken: John Wiley & Sons, Inc., 2004).
109. For example, see Kevin Coe et al., "No Shades of Gray: The Binary Discourse of George W. Bush and an Echoing Press," *Journal of Communication* 54, no. 2 (2004): 234–252.
110. Lance Bennett, "Toward a Theory of Press-State Relations," *Journal of Communication* 40, no. 2 (1990): 103–125.
111. Quoted in Norman Solomon, "Announcing the P.U.-litzer Prizes for 2004," *Fair*, December 17, 2004, https://fair.org/media-beat-column/announcing-the-p-u-litzer-prizes-for-2004/. See also: Srinivas Melkote, "News Framing during a Time of Impending War: An Examination of Coverage in the *New York Times* Prior to the 2003 Iraq War," *International Communication Gazette* 71, no. 7 (2009): 547–559.
112. Jeff Cohen, *Cable News Confidential: My Misadventures in Corporate Media* (Sausalito: Polipoint Press, 2006).
113. Another example from the not-too-distant past includes the cancellation of Bill Maher's show *Politically Incorrect* by ABC in 2002.
114. Todd Gitlin, *The Whole World Is Watching: Mass Media in the Making and Unmaking of the New Left* (Berkeley: University of California Press, 1980), 7.
115. Robert Entman, "Framing: Toward a Clarification of a Fractured Paradigm," *Journal of Communication* 43, no. 4 (1993), 52.
116. See, for example, William Gamson, "News as Framing: Comments on Graber," *American Behavioral Scientist* 33, no. 2(1989): 157–161; Zhongdang Pan and Gerald Kosicki, "Framing Analysis: An Approach to News Discourse," *Political Communication* 10, no. 1 (1993): 55–75; Douglas M. McLeod and Benjamin H. Detenber, "Framing Effects of Television News Coverage of Social Protest," *Journal of Communication* 49, no. 3 (1999): 3–23; Gaye Tuchman, *Making News* (New York: The Free Press, 1978).
117. George Donohue, Phillip Tichenor, and Clarice Olien, "A Guard Dog Perspective on the Role of Media," *Journal of Communication* 45, no. 2 (1995): 115–132. See also: Dan Hallin, *The Uncensored War* (Berkeley: University of California Press, 1989).
118. Lance Bennett et al., "Managing the Public Sphere: Journalistic Construction of the Great Globalization Debate," *Journal of Communication* 54, no. 3 (2004): 437–455.
119. Todd Gitlin, "Prime Time Ideology: The Hegemonic Process in Television Entertainment," *Social Problems* 26, no. 3 (1979): 251–266. Des Freedman also highlights the contradictory nature of commercial media, which is often hegemonic but also at times opens up to progressive politics and reform. See Freedman, *The Contradictions of Media Power*.

120. Edward Herman and Noam Chomsky, *Manufacturing Consent: The Political Economy of the Mass Media* (New York: Random House, 2010), esp. xii, 1–2.

121. Edward Herman, "The Propaganda Model Revisited," *Monthly Review*, July 8, 1996, https://monthlyreview.org/2018/01/01/the-propaganda-model-revisited/.

122. Victor Pickard, "The Violence of the Market," *Journalism* 20, no. 1 (2019): 154–158.

123. Victor Pickard, "Rediscovering the News: Journalism Studies' Three Blind Spots," in *Remaking the News: Essays on the Future of Journalism Scholarship in the Digital Age*, ed. Pablo Boczkowski and C.W. Anderson (Boston: MIT Press, 2017), 47–60.

Chapter 2

1. US Congress, Senate Committee on Commerce, Science, and Transportation, *The Future of Journalism*, 111th Cong., 1st sess., 2009, 1–2.

2. Ibid., 28.

3. Ibid.

4. Ibid.

5. For a summary of this argument see Jeff Jarvis, "The Link Economy v. the Content Economy," *BuzzMachine*, June 18, 2008, https://buzzmachine.com/2008/06/18/the-link-economy-v-the-content-economy/.

6. Clayton Christensen, Michael Raynor, and Rory McDonald, "What is Disruptive Innovation," *Harvard Business Review* 93, no. 12 (2015): 44–53.

7. US Congress, House Judiciary Committee, Subcommittee on Courts and Competition Policy, *A New Age for Newspapers: Diversity of Voices, Competition, and the Internet* 111th Cong., 1st sess., 2009.

8. This testimony by C. Edwin Baker is reprinted in the book, Robert McChesney and Victor Pickard, eds., *Will the Last Reporter Please Turn Out the Lights? The Collapse of Journalism and What Can Be Done to Fix It* (New York: The New Press, 2011), 128–130.

9. Pickard, *America's Battle for Media Democracy,* 216–219.

10. David Davies, *The Postwar Decline of American Newspapers, 1945–1965* (Westport: Praeger, 2006); James Baughman, "'Wounded but Not Slain': The Orderly Retreat of the American Newspaper, 1945–2000," in *The History of the Book in America,* vol. 5, ed. David Paul Nord, Joan Shelley Rubin, and Michael Schudson (Chapel Hill: University of North Carolina Press, 2009), 119–134.

11. Laura Frank, "The Withering Watchdog" *Exposé: America's Investigative Reports,* 2009, https://www.thirteen.org/wnet/expose/2009/06/the-withering-watchdog.html

12. Christine Haughney, "New York Times Company Sells Boston Globe," *New York Times,* August 3, 2013, https://www.nytimes.com/2013/08/04/business/media/new-york-times-company-sells-boston-globe.html.

13. Anthony Ha, "Another Study Shows Craigslist is Killing Newspapers," *Venturebeat,* May 22, 2009, https://venturebeat.com/2009/05/22/another-study-shows-that-craigslist-is-killing-newspapers/.

14. Robert Seamans and Feng Zhu, "Responses to Entry in Multi-Sided Markets: The Impact of Craigslist on Local Newspapers," *Management Science*, 60, no. 2 (2013): 265–540.

15. Jack Shafer, "Don't Blame Craigslist for the Decline of Newspapers," *Politico*, December 13, 2016, https://www.politico.com/magazine/story/2016/12/craigslist-newspapers-decline-classifieds-214525.

16. New Orleans has since regained a daily newspaper, though it has lost many of its journalists: Keith Kelly, "Entire New Orleans Times-Picayune Staff Axed after Sale to Competitor," *New York Post*, May 3, 2019, https://nypost.com/2019/05/03/entire-new-orleans-times-picayune-staff-axed-after-sale-to-competitor/.

17. Edmund Andrews, "Greenspan Concedes Error on Regulation," *New York Times*, October 23, 2008, https://www.nytimes.com/2008/10/24/business/economy/24panel.html.

18. This section draws from Victor Pickard, "The Return of the Nervous Liberals: Market Fundamentalism, Policy Failure, and Recurring Journalism Crises," *Communication Review* 18, no. 2 (2015): 82–97.

19. The Newspaper Revitalization Act, Pub. L. No. S. 673 (2009), https://www.congress.gov/bill/111th-congress/senate-bill/673/text. See also Cardin's op-ed, "A Plan to Save Our Free Press," *Washington Post*, April 3, 2009, A33.

20. See, for example, The Knight Commission on the Information Needs of Communities, *Informing Communities: Sustaining Democracy in the Digital Age* (Washington, DC: The Aspen Institute, 2009), http://www.knightcomm.org/read-the-report-andcomment; Leonard Downie Jr. and Michael Schudson, "The Reconstruction of American Journalism," *Columbia Journalism Review*, 2009, https://archives.cjr.org/reconstruction/the_reconstruction_of_american.php.

21. Victor Pickard, Josh Stearns, and Craig Aaron, *Saving the News: Toward a National Journalism Strategy* (Washington, DC: Free Press, 2009), https://www.freepress.net/policy-library/saving-news-toward-national-journalism-strategy.

22. For a description of these events, see: https://www.ftc.gov/news-events/events-calendar/2009/12/how-will-journalism-survive-internet-age.

23. Federal Trade Commission, *Potential Policy Recommendations to Support the Reinvention of Journalism* (Discussion Draft) (Washington, DC: Federal Trade Commission, 2010), https://www.ftc.gov/sites/default/files/documents/public_events/how-will-journalism-survive-internet-age/new-staff-discussion.pdf.

24. For an overview and synopsis of press attacks against this report, see Adam Thierer, "FTC Draft Plan to 'Save Journalism' Drawing Scrutiny; Raising Concern," *Technology Liberation Front*, June 4, 2010, https://techliberation.com/2010/06/04/ftc-draft-plan-to-save-journalism-drawing-scrutiny-raising-concern/.

25. For an in-depth report on Michael Copps's policy principles (from which several of the following quotations are drawn) see Victor Pickard and Pawel Popiel, *The Media Democracy Agenda: The Strategy and Legacy of FCC Commissioner Michael J. Copps* (Evanston: Benton Foundation, 2018), https://www.benton.org/sites/default/files/Copps_legacy.pdf.

26. Michael Copps, "Remarks of FCC Commissioner Michael J. Copps Walter Cronkite Awards Luncheon" (Los Angeles: USC Annenberg School for Communication and Journalism, April 26, 2011).

27. Steven Waldman, *Information Needs of Communities: The Changing Media Landscape in a Broadband Age* (Washington, DC: Federal Communications Commission, 2011), https://transition.fcc.gov/osp/inc-report/The_Information_Needs_of_Communities.pdf. The report initially was called the "Future of Media Inquiry."

28. I attended one of these informal gatherings at New York University on December 8, 2009—coincidentally on the same day that C. Edwin Baker passed away.

29. Waldman, *Information Needs of Communities*, 362.

30. Ibid., 40.

31. Ibid., 57.

32. Ibid., 6.

33. Ibid., 397.

34. Ibid., 6.

35. Ibid., 9.

36. The quotes in the paragraph are all from Ibid., 9.

37. Ibid., 345.

38. Ibid., 125–26. See also: Christopher Ali, "Where Is Here? An Analysis of Localism in Media Policy in Three Western Democracies" (PhD. diss., University of Pennsylvania, 2013), 258.

39. Waldman, *Information Needs of Communities*, 347–348. For an account that covers the long history of the Fairness Doctrine, see Victor Pickard, "The Strange Life and Death of the Fairness Doctrine: Tracing the Decline of Positive Freedoms in American Policy Discourse," *International Journal of Communication* 12 (2018): 3434–3453.

40. Steven Waldman, personal conversation with the author, March 21, 2019.

41. Waldman, *Information Needs of Communities,* 290–293.

42. Steven Waldman, "New Rules on Political Ads: How to Mine Them," *Columbia Journalism Review*, May 4, 2012, https://archives.cjr.org/united_states_project/new_rules_on_political_ads_how.php. See also Steven Waldman, "Local TV Stations Rally to Oppose Media Transparency," *Columbia Journalism Review*, January 26, 2012, https://archives.cjr.org/behind_the_news/local_tv_stations_rally_to_opp_1.php.

43. Waldman, *Information Needs of Communities*, 345–346.

44. See, for example, Baker, *Media, Markets, and Democracy.*

45. Philip Napoli and Lewis Friedland, "US Communications Policy Research and the Integration of the Administrative and Critical Communication Research Traditions," *Journal of Information Policy* 6 (2016): 58.

46. Michael Copps, "Statement of Commissioner Michael J. Copps on Release of FCC Staff Report 'The Technology and Information Needs of Communities.'" (Washington, DC: Federal Communications Commission, June 9, 2011), https://www.fcc.gov/document/commissioner-copps-statement-release-staff-report.

47. Copps made the critical point that the commitment to positive freedoms, guaranteed by government-supported infrastructure, was well founded in jurisprudence. He cited the Supreme Court's 1969 *Red Lion* decision, which declared: "It is the purpose of the First Amendment to preserve an uninhibited marketplace of ideas." *Red Lion Broadcasting Co. v. Federal Communications Commission*, 395 U.S. 367 (1969). All quotes in this paragraph are from Michael Copps, "Commissioner Michael J. Copps's Remarks at New America Foundation a Conversation on The Future of The Media: Is

the Public Interest Bargain Dying?" (Washington, DC: New American Foundation, June 15, 2011). See also Pickard and Popiel, *The Media Democracy Agenda*.

48. Michael Copps, "What About the News? An Interest in the Public," in McChesney and Pickard, *Will the Last Reporter Please Turn out the Lights?* 289–298.

49. "FCC Report Falls Far Short of Real Solutions," Free Press, June 9, 2011, https://www.freepress.net/news/press-releases/free-press-fcc-report-falls-far-short-real-solutions?akid=2573.8753264.zonjD5&rd=1&t=4. They later issued a more detailed official response: "Bold Analysis, Weak Solutions: Rethinking the Recommendations in the Federal Communications Commission Report on the Information Needs of Communities," *Free Press*, June 2011, http://conference.freepress.net/sites/default/files/fp-legacy/Bold_Analysis_Weak_Solutions.pdf.

50. Ryan Blethen, "FCC's Timid Recommendations Won't Do Much to Boost Journalism," *Seattle Times*, June 17, 2011, http://old.seattletimes.com/html/opinion/2015352755_ryan19.html.

51. Rick Edmonds, "FCC Media Report Shows How Interest in Government Subsidies for Local Journalism Fizzled," *Poynter*, June 10, 2011, https://www.poynter.org/news/fcc-media-report-shows-how-interest-government-subsidies-local-journalism-fizzled.

52. Amy Schatz, "FCC Backs Away From Aiding Media," *Wall Street Journal*, June 8, 2011, https://www.wsj.com/articles/SB1000142405270230443230457637183298209 5722.

53. Eric Alterman, "The FCC's 'New' Local Focus: Too Little, Too Late?" *Huffington Post*, June 17, 2011, https://www.huffingtonpost.com/eric-alterman/the-fccs-new-local-focus-_b_878625.html.

54. Adam Thierer, "Initial Thoughts on the FCC 'Future of Media' Report," *Technology Liberation Front*, June 9, 2011, https://techliberation.com/2011/06/09/initial-thoughts-on-the-fcc-future-of-media-report/.

55. Robert McDowell, "Statement of Commissioner Robert McDowell. Re: Information Needs of Communities, GN Docket No. 10-25" (2011), https://apps.fcc.gov/edocs_public/attachmatch/DOC-307492A1.pdf. See also: Christopher Ali, *Media Localism: The Policies of Place* (Champaign: University of Illinois Press, 2017).

56. John Eggerton, "FCC Commissioning New Study on Information Needs of Public," *Broadcasting and Cable*, February 6, 2012, https://www.broadcastingcable.com/news/fcc-commissioning-new-study-information-needs-public-59785.

57. For some good context on how these scholars approached the project, see Napoli and Friedland, "US Communications Policy Research," 41–65. See also Ali, *Media Localism*, 120–121. My analysis also benefited from personal communication with Mark Lloyd on June 3, 2019.

58. Lewis Friedland et al., "Review of the Literature Regarding Critical Information Needs of the American Public," FCC, July 16, 2012, https://transition.fcc.gov/bureaus/ocbo/Final_Literature_Review.pdf. Lewis Friedland expands on this concept in Lewis Friedland, "America's Critical Community Information Needs," in *The Communications Crisis in America, and How to Fix It*, ed. Mark Lloyd and Lewis Friedland (New York: Palgrave Macmillan, 2016), 3–16.

59. For this detailed account, see Mark Lloyd, "The Battle Over Diversity at the FCC," in *Media Activism in the Digital Age*, ed. Victor Pickard and Guobin Yang (London: Routledge, 2017), 87–95.

60. Ibid., 87.

61. For an explanation of the study's objectives, see Lewis Friedland, "The Real Story Behind the FCC's Study of Newsrooms," *Washington Post*, February 28, 2014, https://www.washingtonpost.com/news/monkey-cage/wp/2014/02/28/the-real-story-behind-the-fccs-study-of-newsrooms/?noredirect=on&utm_term=.a5eeba7e20b7.

62. Tim Cavanaugh, "FCC to Police News Media, Question Reporters in Wide-Ranging Content Survey," *Daily Caller*, October 30, 2013, http://dailycaller.com/2013/10/30/fcc-to-police-news-media-question-reporters-in-wide-ranging-content-survey/.

63. Brendan Sasso, "Republicans Claim FCC Working on 'Fairness Doctrine 2.0,'" *Hill*, December 11, 2013, http://thehill.com/policy/technology/192774-republicans-claim-fcc-working-onfairness- doctrine-20; House of Representatives, "Committee Leaders Urge FCC to Suspend Work on 'Fairness Doctrine 2.0," December 10, 2013, https://www.benton.org/headlines/committee-leaders-urge-fcc-suspend-work-%E2%80%9Cfairness-doctrine-20%E2%80%9D.

64. Pickard, "The Strange Life and Death of the Fairness Doctrine."

65. Ajit Pai, "The FCC Wades Into the Newsroom," *Wall Street Journal*, February 10, 2014, https://www.wsj.com/articles/the-fcc-wades-into-the-newsroom-1392078376.

66. Lloyd, "The Battle Over Diversity at the FCC," 94. It also should be noted that these kinds of attacks had become all too common. Lloyd was viciously red-baited by Glenn Beck and other right-wingers during his time at the FCC.

67. Julian Hattem, "FCC Pulls Plug on Press Study," *Hill*, February 21, 2014, http://thehill.com/policy/technology/198943-fcc-kills-contested-press-study#ixzz2xhLPOeyQ.

68. Friedland, "The Real Story Behind the FCC's Study of Newsrooms," 2014.

69. Brett Gary, *The Nervous Liberals: Propaganda Anxieties from World War I to the Cold War* (New York: Columbia University Press, 1999).

70. Pickard, "The Return of the Nervous Liberals," 2015.

71. Des Freedman, *The Contradictions of Media Power* (London: Bloomsbury, 2014), 70.

72. I discuss the formation of this ideological project in Pickard, *America's Battle for Media Democracy*.

73. Núria Almiron, *Journalism in Crisis: Corporate Media and Financialization* (Cresskill: Hampton Press, 2010); Victor Pickard, "Can Government Support the Press? Historicizing and Internationalizing a Policy Approach to the Journalism Crisis," *Communication Review* 14, no. 2 (2011): 73–95; Hsiang Iris Chyi, Seth Lewis, and Nan Zheng, "A Matter of Life and Death? Examining How Newspapers Covered the Newspaper 'Crisis,'" *Journalism Studies* 13, no. 3 (2012): 305–324; Ignacio Siles and Pablo Boczkowski, "Making Sense of the Newspaper Crisis: A Critical Assessment of Existing Research and an Agenda for Future Work," *New Media and Society* 14, no. 8 (2012): 1375–1394; Barbie Zelizer, "Terms of Choice: Uncertainty, Journalism, and Crisis," *Journal of Communication* 65, no. 5 (2015): 888–908.

74. C.W. Anderson, Emily Bell, and Clay Shirky, *Post-Industrial Journalism: Adapting to the Present* (New York: The Tow Center for Digital Journalism at Columbia University, 2012).

75. Yochai Benkler, "A New Era of Corruption?" *New Republic*, March 4, 2009, https://newrepublic.com/article/61997/correspondence-new-era-corruption.

76. For the business perspective, see Alan Mutter, "Mission Possible? Charging for Web Content," *Reflections of a Newsosaur*, February 8, 2009, http://newsosaur.blogspot.com/2009/02/mission-possible-charging-for-content.html; for the technological perspective, see Jeff Jarvis, "My Testimony to Sen. Kerry," *BuzzMachine*, April 21, 2009, https://buzzmachine.com/2009/04/21/my-testimony-to-sen-kerry/.

77. Charlie Terry, "A Perfect Storm for the Demise of Journalism . . . or for the Rebirth of the Journalist," *EContent*, June 5, 2009, http://www.econtentmag.com/Articles/Column/Guest-Columns/A-Perfect-Storm-for-the-Demise-of-Journalism--or-for-the-Rebirth-of-the-Journalist-54373.htm.

78. See also Victor Pickard, Josh Stearns, and Craig Aaron, *Saving the News: Toward a National Journalism Strategy* (Washington: Free Press, 2009).

79. Pablo Boczkowski, *Digitizing the News: Innovation in Online Newspapers* (Cambridge: MIT Press, 2004); McChesney and Nichols, *The Death and Life of American Journalism*. For failed attempts later in the 2000s, see C.W. Anderson, *Rebuilding the News: Metropolitan Journalism in the Digital Age* (Philadelphia: Temple University, 2013); Nikki Usher, *Making News at the New York Times* (Ann Arbor: University of Michigan Press, 2014); David Ryfe, *Can Journalism Survive? An Inside Look at American Newsrooms* (Cambridge: Polity Press, 2012).

80. I explicate these ideas in Pickard, "The Return of the Nervous Liberals."

81. See, for example, the introduction to Boczkowski and Mitchelstein, *The News Gap*.

82. Clay Shirky, "Newspapers and Thinking the Unthinkable," March 13, 2009, http://www.shirky.com/weblog/2009/03/newspapers-and-thinking-the-unthinkable/.

83. Jacob Hacker and Paul Pierson, *Winner-Take-All Politics: How Washington Made the Rich Richer—and Turned Its Back on the Middle Class* (New York: Simon and Schuster, 2010), 43.

84. Parts of the following two sections draw from Pickard, *America's Battle for Media Democracy*, 212–231; Robert Picard and Victor Pickard, *Essential Principles for Contemporary Media and Communications Policymaking* (Oxford: Reuters Institute for the Study of Journalism, 2017), https://reutersinstitute.politics.ox.ac.uk/sites/default/files/research/files/Essential%2520Principles%2520for%2520Contemporary%2520Media%2520and%2520Communications%2520Policymaking.pdf. See also: Victor Pickard, "Social Democracy or Corporate Libertarianism? Conflicting Media Policy Narratives in the Wake of Market Failure," *Communication Theory* 23, no. 4 (2013): 336–355; Victor Pickard, "The Great Evasion: Confronting Market Failure in American Media Policy," *Critical Studies in Media Communication* 31, no. 2 (2014): 153–159.

85. Baker, *Media, Markets, and Democracy*, 8; James Hamilton, *All the News That's Fit to Sell: How the Market Transforms Information into News* (Princeton: Princeton University Press, 2004), 8–9; Pickard, Stearns, and Aaron, *Saving the News*, 1–9;

McChesney and Nichols, *The Death and Life of American Journalism*, 101–3; Paul Starr, "Goodbye to the Age of Newspapers (Hello to a New Era of Corruption)," *New Republic*, March 4, 2009, https://newrepublic.com/article/64252/goodbye-the-age-newspapers-hello-new-era-corruption; Pickard, *America's Battle for Media Democracy*, 212–231.

86. Paul Samuelson, "The Pure Theory of Public Expenditure," *Review of Economics and Statistics* 36, no. 4 (1954): 387–389; Paul Trogon, "Public Goods," in *Handbook of Public Sector Economics*, ed. Donijo Robbins (Boca Raton: Taylor & Francis, 2005). For a discussion on public and private goods and how they relate to news commodification, see Terhi Rantanen, *When News Was New* (Hoboken: Wiley-Blackwell, 2009), 60–63.

87. Richard John and Jonathan Silberstein-Loeb, eds., *Making News: The Political Economy of Journalism in Britain and America from the Glorious Revolution to the Internet* (Oxford: Oxford University Press, 2015).

88. This example is used in Jacob Hacker and Paul Pierson, *American Amnesia: How the War on Government Led Us to Forget What Made America Prosper* (Simon & Schuster, 2016). A key argument in their book is that public investments in things like education and other public goods are essential for a healthy democratic society.

89. The first study to conceptualize merit goods was Richard Musgrave, *Theory of Public Finance: A Study in Public Economy* (New York: McGraw-Hill, 1959), 13–15. Subsequent articulations, especially as they refer to news media, include Ali, *Media Localism*; Des Freedman, *The Politics of Media Policy* (Cambridge, UK: Polity Press, 2008), 8–10; Pickard, *America's Battle for Media Democracy*, 213–214. See also, generally, Wilfried Ver Eecke, *An Anthology Regarding Merit Goods: The Unfinished Ethical Revolution in Economic Theory* (West Lafayette: Purdue University Press, 2007).

90. Christopher Ali, "The Merits of Merit Goods: Local Journalism and Public Policy in a Time of Austerity," *Journal of Information Policy* 6, no. 1 (2016): 107.

91. Karol Jakubowicz, "Public Service Broadcasting in the Information Society," *Media Development*, 2, 1999, 46–47.

92. Stuart Cunningham, Terry Flew, and Adam Swift, *Media Economics* (London: Palgrave Macmillan, 2015).

93. John and Silberstein-Loeb, *Making News*.

94. Karen Donders, *Public Service Media and Policy in Europe* (Basingstoke: Palgrave Macmillan, 2011); Robert Picard et al., "Platform Proliferation and Its Implications for Domestic Content Policies," *Telematics and Informatics* 33, no. 2 (2016): 683–692.

95. See, for example, Robert Picard, "The Challenges of Public Functions and Commercialized Media," in *The Politics of News: The News of Politics*, ed. Dora Graber, Denis McQuail, and Pippa Norris (Washington, DC: Congressional Quarterly Press, 2007), 211–229; James Curran, *Media and Democracy* (New York: Routledge Press, 2011).

96. Patrick Barwise and Robert Picard, *What If There Were No BBC Television? The Net Impact on UK Viewers* (Oxford: Reuters Institute for the Study of Journalism, February 2014), https://reutersinstitute.politics.ox.ac.uk/sites/default/files/2017-06/What%20if%20there%20were%20no%20BBC%20TV_0.pdf.

97. Pickard, *America's Battle for Media Democracy*.
98. See, for example, Francis Bator, "The Anatomy of Market Failure," *Quarterly Journal of Economics* 72, no. 3 (1958): 351–379; Joseph Stiglitz, "Markets, Market Failures, and Development," *American Economic Review* 79, no. 2 (1989): 197–203; Steven Medema, "The Hesitant Hand: Mill, Sidgwick, and the Evolution of the Theory of Market Failure," *History of Political Economy* 39, no. 3 (2007): 331–358; John Taylor, *Principles of Microeconomics*, 5th ed. (New York: Houghton Mifflin, 2007).
99. Pickard, *America's Battle for Media Democracy*, 214.
100. Freedman, *The Politics of Media Policy*, 8–9.
101. Victor Pickard, "Neoliberal Visions and Revisions in Global Communications Policy from the New World Information and Communication Order to the World Summit on the Information Society," *Journal of Communication Inquiry*, 31, no. 2 (2007): 118–139.
102. Mark Cooper, "The Future of Journalism: Addressing Pervasive Market Failure with Public Policy," in McChesney and Pickard, *Will the Last Reporter Please Turn out the Lights?* 320–339; Robert Picard and Steven Wildman, eds., *Handbook on the Economics of the Media* (Cheltenham: Edward Elgar Publishing, 2015).
103. Robert Picard, "Evidence of a 'Failing Newspaper' under the Newspaper Preservation Act," *Newspaper Research Journal* 9, no. 1 (1987): 73–82; Martin Koschat and William Putsis, "Who Wants You When You're Old and Poor? Exploring the Economics of Media Pricing," *Journal of Media Economics* 13, no. 4 (2000): 215–232.
104. See C. Edwin Baker, *Advertising and a Democratic Press* (Princeton: Princeton University Press, 1994).
105. See Baker, *Media, Markets, and Democracy*, 9; Robert Picard, *The Economics and Financing of Media Companies*, 2nd ed. (New York: Fordham University Press, 2011).
106. In chapter 5, I will discuss various forms of press subsidies that other democratic countries have put into practice. See, for example, Paul Murschetz, ed., *State Aid for Newspapers: Theories, Cases, Actions* (Berlin: Springer-Verlag, 2013).

Chapter 3

1. Mark Jurkowitz, "The Growth in Digital Reporting," *Pew Research Center*, March 26, 2014, http://www.journalism.org/2014/03/26/the-growth-in-digital-reporting/#fn-42285-1.
2. Jeffrey Alexander, Elizabeth Breese, and María Luengo, *The Crisis of Journalism Reconsidered* (New York: Cambridge University Press, 2016), xiii–xiv.
3. Jessica Toonkel, "Newspapers Aim to Ride 'Trump Bump' to Reach Readers, Advertisers," *Reuters*, February 16, 2017, https://www.reuters.com/article/us-newspapers-trump-campaigns-analysis/newspapers-aim-to-ride-trump-bump-to-reach-readers-advertisers-idUSKBN15V0GI. It should be noted that a wide range of publications, including opinion magazines and nonprofit outlets such as *ProPublica* also experienced this bump.

4. The data discussed in this chapter are provided by the Pew Research Center, Newspaper Association of America (now the News Media Alliance), American Society of News Editors, and other sources.

5. Parts of this chapter draw from research discussed in earlier essays, including: Victor Pickard, "Structural Collapse: The American Journalism Crisis and the Search for a Sustainable Future," in *What Is Sustainable Journalism? Integrating the Environmental, Social, and Economic Challenges of Journalism*, ed. Peter Berglez, Ulrika Olausson, and Mart Ots (New York: Peter Lang, 2017), 351–366; Victor Pickard, "Digital Journalism and Regulation: Ownership and Content," in *The Routledge Handbook of Developments in Digital Journalism Studies*, ed. Scott Eldridge and Bob Franklin (New York: Routledge, 2018), 211–222.

6. Amy Mitchell et al., "Newspapers: By the Number," in *The State of the News Media 2012* (Pew Research Center, 2012), http://stateofthemedia.org.

7. Ken Doctor, "Newsprint Tariffs Gone, Print's Heavy Boot Remains," *Newsonomics*, September 3, 2018, http://newsonomics.com/newsonomics-newsprint-tariffs-gone-prints-heavy-boot-remains/.

8. Michael Barthel, "5 Facts about the State of the News Media in 2017," *Pew Research Center*, August 21, 2018, http://www.pewresearch.org/fact-tank/2018/08/21/5-facts-about-the-state-of-the-news-media-in-2017/.

9. Rani Molla and Shira Ovide, "New Media Shares Old Media's Roof," *Bloomberg*, May 23, 2016, https://www.bloomberg.com/gadfly/articles/2016-05-23/new-media-interlocked-with-old-media-it-wants-to-disrupt.

10. Rani Molla and Peter Kafka, "Here's Who Owns Everything in Big Media Today," *Recode*, April 3, 2019, https://www.recode.net/2018/1/23/16905844/media-landscape-verizon-amazon-comcast-disney-fox-relationships-chart.

11. Dean Starkman, "The Ever-Expanding Media Giants," *Traffic Magazine*, September 28, 2016, http://traffic.piano.io/2016/09/28/the-ever-expanding-media-giants/.

12. Matthew Hindman, *The Myth of Digital Democracy* (Princeton: Princeton University Press, 2008).

13. Mathew Ingram, "Media's Complicated Relationship with VC Funding," *Columbia Journalism Review*, November 27, 2017, https://www.cjr.org/analysis/venture-capital-funding-vice-buzzfeed.php; Matthew Garrahan and Shannon Bond, "Vice, BuzzFeed and Vox Hit by Changes in Digital Media Industry," *Financial Times*, February 21, 2018, https://www.ft.com/content/482dc54a-1594-11e8-9376-4a6390addb44; Cale Guthrie Weissman, "BuzzFeed Layoffs Could Be a Huge Bellwether for Digital Media," *Fast Company*, November 29, 2017, https://www.fastcompany.com/40501711/buzzfeed-layoffs-could-be-a-huge-bellwether-for-digital-media.

14. Jeremy Barr, "Vox Media Laying Off Around 50 Staffers," *The Hollywood Reporter*, February 21, 2018, https://www.hollywoodreporter.com/news/vox-media-laying-around-50-people-1086869.

15. Laura Hazard Owen, "In the Latest Sign Things Really Are Dire, BuzzFeed is Laying Off 15 Percent of Its Staff," *NiemanLab*, January 24, 2019, http://www.niemanlab.org/2019/01/in-the-latest-sign-things-really-are-dire-buzzfeed-is-laying-off-15-percent-of-its-staff/.

16. Victor Pickard, "When Billionaires Rule: Gawker and the Future of Journalism," *Jacobin*, August 29, 2016, https://www.jacobinmag.com/2016/08/gawker-peter-thiel-news-media-fourth-estate/.

17. Adrian Chen, "Gawker was a Great Place to Become a Journalist," *New Yorker*, June 13, 2016, https://www.newyorker.com/news/news-desk/gawker-was-a-great-place-to-become-a-journalist; Max Read, "A Flowchart of the Petraeus Affair's Love Pentagon, from the Shirtless FBI Agent to Chuck Klosterman," *Gawker*, November, 13, 2012, http://gawker.com/5960202/a-flowchart-of-the-petraeus-affairs-love-pentagon-from-the-shirtless-fbi-agent-to-chuck-klosterman.

18. Jana Kasperkevic, "Gawker Becomes First Digital Media Company to Unionize," *Guardian*, June 4, 2015, https://www.theguardian.com/media/2015/jun/04/gawker-media-union-writers-guild.

19. Tom Scocca, "Gawker Was Murdered by Gaslight," *Gawker*, August 22, 2016, http://gawker.com/gawker-was-murdered-by-gaslight-1785456581.

20. A new Gawker was launched: Todd Spangler, "Gawker Set to Relaunch Under New Owner Bryan Goldberg," *Variety*, September 11, 2018, https://variety.com/2018/digital/news/gawker-2019-relaunch-bryan-goldberg-1202936710/.

21. Elizabeth MacIver Neiva, "Chain Building: The Consolidation of the American Newspaper Industry, 1953–1980," *Business History Review* 70, no. 1 (1996): 1–42; Alex Williams and Victor Pickard, "The Costs of Risky Business: What Happens When Newspapers Become the Playthings of Billionaires?" (Minneapolis, MN: Association for Education in Journalism and Mass Communication, 2016).

22. For an overview of the historical ownership trends, see Penelope Muse Abernathy, "The Debate over the Change in Media Ownership and the Public's Interest," http://newspaperownership.com/additional-material/newspaper-ownership-debate/.

23. John Soloski, "Collapse of the US Newspaper Industry: Goodwill, Leverage and Bankruptcy," *Journalism* 14, no. 3 (2013): 309–329.

24. We discuss the strengths and weaknesses of different newspaper ownership models in Rodney Benson and Victor Pickard, "The Slippery Slope of the Oligarchy Media Model," *The Conversation*, August 10, 2017, http://theconversation.com/the-slippery-slope-of-the-oligarchy-media-model-81931.

25. John Morton, "Talking Wall Street Blues: As Recent Events Emphasize, Money Trumps Ethics on the Street," *American Journalism Review* 24, no. 6 (2002): 64; See also Philip Meyer, *The Vanishing Newspaper: Saving Journalism in the Information Age* (Columbia: University of Missouri Press, 2004).

26. Matthew Ingram, "The Sulzberger Dynasty Tightens Its Grip on the New York Times," *Fortune*, October 19, 2016, http://fortune.com/2016/10/19/sulzberger-nyt/.

27. Benson and Pickard, "The Slippery Slope of the Oligarchy Media Model."

28. Penelope Abernathy, *The Expanding News Desert* (Chapel Hill: UNC Center for Innovation and Sustainability in Local Media, 2018), https://www.usnewsdeserts.com/reports/expanding-news-desert/.

29. Ibid. As this book was going to press, the newspaper chain GateHouse was about to acquire Gannett, which would create an astonishingly massive newspaper chain, owning one out of every six US daily newspapers. Ken Doctor, "It's Looking like

Gannett will be Acquired by GateHouse—Creating a Newspaper Megachain like the U.S. has Never Seen," *NiemanLab*, July 18, 2019, https://www.niemanlab.org/2019/07/newsonomics-its-looking-like-gannett-will-be-acquired-by-gatehouse-creating-a-newspaper-megachain-like-the-u-s-has-never-seen/.

30. Daniel Kishi, "It Still Bleeds, but It No Longer Leads," *American Conservative*, December 3, 2018, https://www.theamericanconservative.com/articles/it-still-bleeds-but-it-no-longer-leads/ See also: Matt Crain, "The Rise of Private Equity Media Ownership in the United States: A Public Interest Perspective," *International Journal of Communication* 3 (2009): 208–239.

31. All previous quotes in this paragraph are from Julie Reynolds, "How Many Palm Beach Mansions Does a Wall Street Tycoon Need?" *Nation*, September 27, 2017, https://www.thenation.com/article/how-many-palm-beach-mansions-does-a-wall-street-tycoon-need/.

32. Ken Doctor, "Alden Global Capital Is Making So Much Money Wrecking Local Journalism It Might Not Want to Stop Anytime Soon," *Newsonomics*, May 5, 2018, http://newsonomics.com/newsonomics-alden-global-capital-is-making-so-much-money-wrecking-local-journalism-it-might-not-want-to-stop-anytime-soon/.

33. Jonathan O'Connell and Emma Brown, "A Hedge Fund's 'Mercenary' Strategy: Buy Newspapers, Slash Jobs, Sell the Buildings," *Washington Post*, February 1, 2019, https://www.washingtonpost.com/business/economy/a-hedge-funds-mercenary-strategy-buy-newspapers-slash-jobs-sell-the-buildings/2019/02/11/f2c0c78a-1f59-11e9-8e21-59a09ff1e2a1_story.html?utm_term=.7085f2892cc6.

34. Sydney Ember, "Denver Post Rebels against Its Hedge-Fund Ownership," *New York Times*, April 7, 2018, https://www.nytimes.com/2018/04/07/business/media/denver-post-opinion-owner.html.

35. Denver Post Editorial Board, "As Vultures Circle, the *Denver Post* Must Be Saved," *Denver Post*, April 6, 2018, https://www.denverpost.com/2018/04/06/as-vultures-circle-the-denver-post-must-be-saved/.

36. Margaret Sullivan, "Is This Strip-Mining or Journalism? 'Sobs, Gasps, Expletives' Over Latest Denver Post Layoffs," *Washington Post*, March 15, 2018, https://www.washingtonpost.com/lifestyle/style/is-this-strip-mining-or-journalism-sobs-gasps-expletives-over-latest-denver-post-layoffs/2018/03/15/d05abc5a-287e-11e8-874b-d517e912f125_story.html?utm_term=.4e503a12e2e5. This number does not include several small outlets that have emerged in recent years.

37. Associated Press, "Company Known for Deep Cost-Cutting Offers to Buy Gannett," *New York Times*, January 14, 2019, https://www.nytimes.com/aponline/2019/01/14/us/ap-us-newspapers-shrinking-industry.html.

38. Robert Picard, "US Newspaper Ad Revenue Shows Consistent Growth," *Newspaper Research Journal* 23, no. 4 (2002): 21–33; Robert Picard, "Shifts in Newspaper Advertising Expenditures and Their Implications for the Future of Newspapers," *Journalism Studies* 9, no. 5 (2008): 704–716.

39. Rodney Benson, *Shaping Immigration News: A French-American Comparison* (New York: Cambridge University Press, 2013).

40. Jaclyn Peiser, "New York Times Co. Reports $24 Million Profit, Thanks to Digital Subscribers," *New York Times*, August 8, 2018, https://www.nytimes.com/2018/08/08/business/media/new-york-times-earnings-subscriptions.html; Monica Nickelsburg "*Washington Post* Profitable and Growing for Two Years under Jeff Bezos' Ownership," *GeekWire*, January 9, 2018, https://www.geekwire.com/2018/washington-post-profitable-growing-two-years-jeff-bezos-ownership/.

41. Keach Hagey, Lukas Alpert, and Yaryna Serkez, "In News Industry, a Stark Divide Between Haves and Have-Nots," *Wall Street Journal*, May 4, 2019, https://www.wsj.com/graphics/local-newspapers-stark-divide/.

42. Rick Edmonds et al., "Newspapers: Stabilizing, but Still Threatened," State of the News Media, *Pew Research Center*, July 18, 2013, http://www.pewresearch.org/topics/state-of-the-news-media/.

43. These numbers derive from Williams and Pickard, "The Costs of Risky Business."

44. Neil Thurman and Richard Fletcher, "Are Newspapers Heading Toward Post-Print Obscurity? A Case Study of the *Independent's* Transition to Online-Only," *Digital Journalism* 6, no. 8 (2018): 1003–1017.

45. Nick Mathews, "'Life Is Harder': The Perceived Impact of a Newspaper Closure on a Community," Paper presented at the Association for Education in Journalism and Mass Communication, August 2019.

46. S.L. Alexander, Frank D. Durham, Alfred Lawrence Lorenz, and Vicki Mayer, *The Times-Picayune in a Changing Media World: The Transformation of an American Newspaper* (Lanham, MD: Lexington Books, 2014). Also discussed in Dean Starkman, "Tracking Digital-Era News Quality Declines," *Columbia Journalism Review*, January 14, 2014, https://archives.cjr.org/the_audit/tracking_news-quality_declines.php.

47. Jeannette Lee Falsey, "How Alaska's Largest Newspaper Went Bankrupt," *Columbia Journalism Review*, November 10, 2017, https://www.cjr.org/business_of_news/alaska-daily-news-bankruptcy.php; Niraj Chokshi, "A West Virginia Newspaper Won Journalism's Top Award. Now It's Filed for Bankruptcy," *New York Times*, February 2, 2018, https://www.nytimes.com/2018/02/02/business/media/west-virginia-newspaper-charleston.html.

48. Emily Rolen, "Reading Eagle Newspaper's Owner Files for Bankruptcy after 150 Years in Business," *PhillyVoice*, March 21, 2019, https://www.phillyvoice.com/reading-eagle-newspaper-bankruptcy/Youngstown, Ohio recently lost its 150-year-old paper.

49. For an up-to-date list of papers that have closed down, gone online only, or cut down on home deliveries, see "Newspaper Death Watch" http://newspaperdeathwatch.com.

50. All quotes in this paragraph are from Joshua Benton, "What Will Happen when Newspapers Kill Print and Go Online-Only? Most of That Print Audience Will Just . . . Disappear," *NiemanLab*, September 26, 2018, http://www.niemanlab.org/2018/09/what-will-happen-when-newspapers-kill-print-and-go-online-only-most-of-that-print-audience-will-just-disappear/.

51. Rick Edmonds, "ASNE Stops Trying to Count Total Job Losses in American Newsrooms," *Poynter*, September 9, 2016, https://www.poynter.org/business-work/2016/asne-stops-tryting-to-count-total-job-losses-in-american-newsrooms/.

52. Bureau of Labor Statistics, "Newspaper Publishers Lose Over Half Their Employment from January 2001 to September 2016," *TED: The Economics Daily*, April 03, 2017, https://www.bls.gov/opub/ted/2017/newspaper-publishers-lose-over-half-their-employment-from-january-2001-to-september-2016.htm. The drop-off is even greater from June 1990, when there were nearly 458,000 people employed in the newspaper publishing industry. By March 2016, that figure had fallen to about 183,000, an astounding loss of nearly 60 percent. Bureau of Labor Statistics, "Employment Trends in Newspaper Publishing and Other Media, 1990–2016," *TED: The Economic Daily*, June 02, 2016, https://www.bls.gov/opub/ted/2016/employment-trends-in-newspaper-publishing-and-other-media-1990-2016.htm.

53. Matthew Garrahan, "Advertising: Facebook and Google Build a Duopoly," *Financial Times*, June 23, 2016, https://www.ft.com/content/6c6b74a4-3920-11e6-9a05-82a9b15a8ee7; Aleksandra Gjorgievska, "Google and Facebook Lead Digital Ad Industry to Revenue Record," *Bloomberg*, April 21, 2016, https://www.bloomberg.com/news/articles/2016-04-22/google-and-facebook-lead-digital-ad-industry-to-revenue-record; Peter Kafka, "These Two Charts Tell You Everything You Need to Know about Google's and Facebook's Domination of the Ad Business," *Recode*, February 13, 2018, https://www.recode.net/2018/2/13/17002918/google-facebook-advertising-domination-chart-moffettnathanson-michael-nathanson.

54. Ken Doctor, "Newsprint Tariffs Gone, Print's Heavy Boot Remains," *Newsonomics*, September 3, 2018, http://newsonomics.com/newsonomics-newsprint-tariffs-gone-prints-heavy-boot-remains/.

55. Jodi Enda and Amy Mitchell, "Americans Show Signs of Leaving a News Outlet, Citing Less Information," *Pew Research Center*, March 17, 2013, http://www.journalism.org/2013/03/17/americans-show-signs-of-leaving-a-news-outlet-citing-less-information/.

56. Michael Barthel, "State of the News Media 2016: 5 Key Takeaways" (Pew Research Center, June 15, 2016), http://www.pewresearch.org/fact-tank/2016/06/15/state-of-the-news-media-2016-key-takeaways/#.

57. Thomas Leonard, *News for All* (New York: Oxford University Press) 64.

58. David Elliot Berman, "All the News That's Fit to Click: The Rise and Fall of Clickbait Journalism" (forthcoming dissertation), University of Pennsylvania.

59. Alessio Cornia, Annika Sehl, David Levy, and Rasmus Kleis Nielsen, *Private Sector News, Social Media Distribution, and Algorithm Change* (Oxford: Reuters Institute, 2018), https://reutersinstitute.politics.ox.ac.uk/our-research/private-sector-news-social-media-distribution-and-algorithm-change.

60. For an analysis of some of these changes, see Emily Bell and Taylor Owen, "The Platform Press: How Silicon Valley Reengineered Journalism," Tow Center for Digital Journalism, Columbia University, 2017, https://www.cjr.org/tow_center_reports/platform-press-how-silicon-valley-reengineered-journalism.php/.

61. Denise-Marie Ordway, "Facebook and the Newsroom: 6 Questions for Siva Vaidhyanathan," *Journalist's Resource*, September 12, 2018, https://journalistsresource.org/studies/society/social-media/facebook-siva-vaidhyanathan-news.

62. Caitlin Petre shared some of these astute observations based on her long-term ethnographic research on the panel "Confronting the Journalism Crisis: Threats and Policy Approaches," Media, Inequality & Change Center, Philadelphia, PA, April 12, 2019. See: https://www.youtube.com/watch?v=Fm_Y6UvBCgU.

63. Ordway, "Facebook and the Newsroom."

64. Caitlin Petre, *The Traffic Factories: Metrics at Chartbeat, Gawker Media, and the New York Times* (New York City: Tow Center for Digital Journalism, 2015), https://www.cjr.org/tow_center_reports/the_traffic_factories_metrics_at_chartbeat_gawker_media_and_the_new_york_times.php/.

65. Edson Tandoc and Ryan Thomas, "The Ethics of Web Analytics." *Digital Journalism* 3, no. 2 (2015): 243–258.

66. Mike Isaac, "50 Million New Reasons BuzzFeed Wants to Take Its Content Far Beyond Lists," *New York Times*, Aug. 10, 2014, https://www.nytimes.com/2014/08/11/technology/a-move-to-go-beyond-lists-for-content-at-buzzfeed.html?_r=0.

67. Ava Sirrah, "The Blurring Line Between Editorial and Native Ads at the *New York Times*," *Mediashift*, October 3, 2017, http://mediashift.org/2017/10/advertisers-underwrite-new-york-times-content/.

68. Linda Lawson, *Truth in Publishing: Federal Regulation of the Press's Business Practices, 1880–1920* (Carbondale: Southern Illinois University Press, 1993).

69. Pickard, *America's Battle for Media Democracy*, 10. It is notable that with each new medium, encroaching advertising was generally met with public uproar, earning derisive names such as "plug uglies" and "singing jingles" on radio and "spam email" on early online communities.

70. Stephanie Clifford, "Front of Los Angeles Times Has an NBC 'Article,'" *New York Times*, April 9, 2009, https://www.nytimes.com/2009/04/10/business/media/10adco.html.

71. Paul Farhi, "To Build Brand, Companies Produce Slick Content and Their Own Media," *Washington Post*, March 26, 2013, https://www.washingtonpost.com/lifestyle/style/to-build-brand-companies-produce-slick-content-and-their-own-media/2013/03/26/741d582a-9568-11e2-ae32-9ef60436f5c1_story.html?utm_term=.f80ea848554c.

72. Nancy Scola, "Is a News Site a News Site if It's Published by Verizon?" *Washington Post*, October 31, 2014, http://www.washingtonpost.com/blogs/the-switch/wp/2014/10/31/is-a-news-site-a-news-site-if-its-published-by-verizon/.

73. For an overview of the history, deployment, and research involving native advertising, see Raul Ferrer-Conill and Michael Karlsson, "Native Advertising and the Appropriation of Journalistic Clout," in Eldridge and Franklin, *The Routledge Handbook of Developments in Digital Journalism Studies*, 463–474.

74. Erik Sass, "Consumers Can't Tell Native Ads From Editorial Content," *MediaPost*, December 31, 2015, https://www.mediapost.com/publications/article/265789/consumers-cant-tell-native-ads-from-editorial-con.html.

75. Mara Einstein, *Black Ops Advertising: Native Ads, Content Marketing, and the Covert World of the Digital Sell* (New York: Or Books, 2016).

76. Bob Garfield, "If Native Advertising Is So Harmless, Why Does It Rely on Misleading Readers?" *Guardian*, February 25, 2014, https://www.theguardian.com/commentisfree/2014/feb/25/yahoo-opens-gemini-native-advertising.

77. Sydney Ember, "F.T.C. Guidelines on Native Ads Aim to Prevent Deception," *New York Times*, December 22, 2015, https://www.nytimes.com/2015/12/23/business/media/ftc-issues-guidelines-for-native-ads.html.

78. Damaris Colhoun, "BuzzFeed's Censorship Problem," *Columbia Journalism Review*, April 16, 2015, https://www.cjr.org/analysis/buzzfeed_censorship_problem.php.

79. Much of the following two paragraphs draws from Tim Libert and Victor Pickard, "Think You're Reading the News for Free? New Research Shows You're Likely Paying with Your Privacy," *The Conversation,* November 6, 2015, https://theconversation.com/think-youre-reading-the-news-for-free-new-research-shows-youre-likely-paying-with-your-privacy-49694. In more recent research, Libert details how this pervasive practice violates ethical norms: See Tim Libert, "Track the Planet: A Web-Scale Analysis of How Online Behavioral Advertising Violates Social Norms" (PhD. diss., University of Pennsylvania, 2017).

80. We heard from a number of scholars and activists that this number was actually relatively low compared to a typical day.

81. Libert and Pickard, "Think You're Reading the News for Free?"

82. As I discuss in the next chapter, research consistently finds that the vast majority of people are unaware of the extent to which they were giving up information about themselves online. Once they do realize the true nature of this relationship, they are much less amenable to it.

83. Libert and Pickard, "Think You're Reading the News for Free?"

84. Randall Rothenberg, "Ad Blocking: The Unnecessary Internet Apocalypse." *AdAge*, September 22, 2015, http://adage.com/article/digitalnext/ad-blocking-unnecessary-internet-apocalypse/300470/. Cory Doctorow, "Adblocking: How About Nah?" *Electronic Frontier Foundation*, July 25, 2019, https://www.eff.org/deeplinks/2019/07/adblocking-how-about-nah.

85. Lucia Moses, "Project Feels: How *USA Today*, ESPN and the *New York Times* are Targeting Ads to Mood," *Digiday*, September 19, 2018, https://digiday.com/media/project-feels-usa-today-espn-new-york-times-targeting-ads-mood/.

86. Quoted in Emily Bell, "How Ethical Is It for Advertisers to Target Your Mood?" *The Guardian*, May 5, 2019, https://www.theguardian.com/media/commentisfree/2019/may/05/how-ethical-is-it-for-advertisers-to-target-your-mood.

87. Ibid.

88. Dean Starkman, "The Hamster Wheel: Why Running as Fast as We Can Is Getting Us Nowhere." *Columbia Journalism Review*, September 14, 2010; Matthew Lasar, "Has the Internet "Hamsterized" Journalism?" *Ars Technica*, June 12, 2011, https://arstechnica.com/information-technology/2011/06/has-the-internet-hamsterized-journalism/; Jaclyn Peiser, "The Rise of the Robot Reporter," *The New York Times*, February 5, 2019, https://www.nytimes.com/2019/02/05/business/media/artificial-intelligence-journalism-robots.html. Other experiments have included using content farms and user-generated content.

89. Nicole Cohen, "Entrepreneurial Journalism and the Precarious State of Media Work," *South Atlantic Quarterly* 114, no. 3 (2015): 513–533. See also: Nicole Cohen, *Writers' Rights: Freelance Journalism in a Digital Age* (Montreal: McGill-Queen's University Press, 2016).

90. Errol Salamon, "Precarious E-Lancers, Freelance Journalists' Rights, Contracts, Labor Organizing, and Digital Resistance," in Eldridge and Franklin, *The Routledge Handbook of Developments in Digital Journalism Studies*, 186–197.

91. Yardena Schwartz, "Freelancing Abroad in a World Obsessed with Trump," *Columbia Journalism Review*, January 30, 2018, https://www.cjr.org/covering_ trump/trump-impact-foreign-reporting.php.

92. For the most recent statistics, see Reporters Without Borders, "Journalists killed," https://rsf.org/en/journalists-killed. See also: Joel Simon, *The New Censorship: Inside the Global Battle for Media Freedom* (New York: Columbia University Press, 2019).

93. Martin Chulov, "James Foley and Fellow Freelancers: Exploited By Pared-Back Media Outlets," *Guardian*, August 21, 2014, https://www.theguardian.com/ media/2014/aug/21/james-foley-freelance-journalists-exploited-media-outlets; Allison Shelley, "The Dangerous World of Freelance Journalism," *Los Angeles Times*, September 6, 2014. https://www.latimes.com/opinion/op-ed/la-oe-shelley- freelance-journalists-foley-sotloff-20140907-story.html.

94. Alex Williams, "The Growing Pay Gap between Journalism and Public Relations," *Pew Research*, August 11, 2014, http://www.pewresearch.org/fact-tank/2014/08/ 11/the-growing-pay-gap-between-journalism-and-public-relations/. "There are now more than 6 PR pros for every journalist," Muck Rack, September 2006, 2018. https://muckrack.com/blog/2018/09/06/there-are-now-more-than-6-pr-pros-for- every-journalist. For a discussion on how PR has risen in tandem with job cuts and casualized labor in news industries, see Natalie Fenton, "NGOS, New Media and the Mainstream News: New from Everywhere," in *New Media, Old News: Journalism and Democracy in the Digital Age* ed. Natalie Fenton (London, UK: Sage, 2010), 153–168.

95. See, for example, Catherine McKercher, "Precarious Times, Precarious Work: A Feminist Political Economy of Freelance Journalists in Canada and the United States," in *Critique, Social Media and the Information Society*, ed. Christian Fuchs and Marisol Sandoval (New York: Routledge, 2014), 219–230.

96. Elaine Chen, Cecilia Lei, Annie Ma, and Jonathan Ng, "Mind the Gap: Uncovering Pay Disparity in the Newsroom," *Voices*, August 8, 2018, https://voices.aaja.org/ index/2018/8/8/pay-equity.

97. Women's Media Center, "Divided 2019: The Media Gender Gap," January 31, 2019, http://www.womensmediacenter.com/reports/divided-2019-the-media-gender-gap.

98. Steven Greenhouse, "More Secure Jobs, Bigger Paychecks," *Columbia Journalism Review*, Spring/Summer, 2018, https://www.cjr.org/special_report/media-unions- history.php/.

99. "Digital Media Workers Organize: A Timeline," *Cultural Workers Organize*, March 19, 2018, https://culturalworkersorganize.org/digital-media-workers-organize-a- timeline/.

100. Marick Masters and Raymond Gibney, "The Tactics Media Unions Are Using to Build Membership," *Harvard Business Review*, January 9, 2019, https://hbr.org/ 2019/01/the-tactics-media-unions-are-using-to-build-membership.

101. Tom Stites, "Layoffs and Cutbacks Lead to a New World of News Deserts," *NiemanLab*, December 8, 2011, http://www.niemanlab.org/2011/12/tom-stites-layoffs-and-cutbacks-lead-to-a-new-world-of-news-deserts/; Penelope Abernathy, *The Rise of a New Media Baron and the Emerging Threat of News Deserts* (Chapel Hill: UNC Center for Innovation and Sustainability in Local Media, October 16, 2016), http://newspaperownership.com/wp-content/uploads/2016/09/07.UNC_RiseOfNewMediaBaron_SinglePage_01Sep2016-REDUCED.pdf; Michelle Ferrier, Gaurav Sinha, and Michael Outrich, "Media Deserts: Monitoring the Changing Media Ecosystem," in *The Communication Crisis in America, and How to Fix It*, ed. Mark Lloyd and Lewis Friedland (New York: Palgrave Macmillan, 2016), 215–232.

102. Abernathy, *The Expanding News Desert*. For an overview of the loss of local journalism, see Taylor Kate Brown, "Why Local US Newspapers Are Sounding the Alarm," *BBC News*, July 9, 2018, https://www.bbc.com/news/world-us-canada-44688274.

103. Abernathy, *The Expanding News Desert*.

104. Penelope Muse Abernathy, "The Rise of the Ghost Newspaper," The Center for Innovation and Sustainability in Local Media, 2018, https://www.usnewsdeserts.com/reports/expanding-news-desert/loss-of-local-news/the-rise-of-the-ghost-newspaper/.

105. Philip Napoli, Matthew Weber, Katie McCollough, and Qun Wang, *Assessing Local Journalism: News Deserts, Journalism Divides, and the Determinants of the Robustness of Local News* (Durham: Duke University Stanford School of Public Policy, August 2018), https://dewitt.sanford.duke.edu/wp-content/uploads/2018/08/Assessing-Local-Journalism_100-Communities.pdf.

106. Riley Griffin, "Local News Is Dying, and It's Taking Small Town America With It," *Bloomberg*, September 5, 2018, https://www.bloomberg.com/news/articles/2018-09-05/local-news-is-dying-and-it-s-taking-small-town-america-with-it; Phil Napoli, "When Local Papers Stop Being Local," *Columbia Journalism Review*, August 9, 2018, https://www.cjr.org/business_of_news/when-local-papers-stop-being-local.php.

107. Pew Research Center, "America's Shifting Statehouse Press," July 2014, http://www.journalism.org/2014/07/10/americas-shifting-statehouse-press/.

108. This Twitter thread, with links to many of Erica's stories, can be found here: Erica Martinson, Twitter post, September 12, 2018, 5:28 a.m., https://twitter.com/EricaMartinson/status/1039853252714684416.

109. Paul Farhi, "A Newspaper Diminished by Cutbacks Prepares to Cover Another Monster Storm," *Washington Post* September 12, 2018, https://www.washingtonpost.com/lifestyle/style/a-newspaper-diminished-by-cutbacks-prepares-to-cover-another-monster-storm/2018/09/12/9fae3870-b5ff-11e8-a2c5-3187f427e253_story.html?utm_term=.b380d367b796.

110. The public radio station WNYC has since resurrected *Gothamist* (which I discuss in chapter 5), though *DNA info* remains closed.

111. Scott Nover, "Who's Left Covering Brooklyn With the Big Newspapers in Retreat?" *Atlantic*, September 14, 2018, https://www.theatlantic.com/politics/archive/2018/

09/whos-left-covering-brooklyn-with-the-big-newspapers-in-retreat/570073/
?utm_source=twb. The trajectory of the hyperlocal news network *Patch* is an interesting case. After AOL sold the floundering experiment in 2014 it became a profitable enterprise, albeit at a much smaller scale with one reporter assigned to cover
several towns and churn out stories on car accidents, real estate, and weather. Peter
Kafka, "The alternative to your dying local paper is written by one person, a robot,
and you," *Recode*, February 11, 2019, https://www.vox.com/2019/2/11/18206360/
patch-local-news-profitable-revenue-advertising-hale. Also noteworthy that important research by Ali and Radcliffe finds a more hopeful narrative for local journalism based on their extensive research of small newspapers. See, for example,
Christopher Ali and Damian Radcliffe, "Life at small-market newspapers: A survey
of over 400 journalists," Tow Center for Digital Journalism, May 10, 2017. https://
www.cjr.org/tow_center_reports/local-journalism-survey.php

112. Alex Williams, "Profits Over Principles: Redlining in the Newspaper Industry"
    (PhD. diss., University of Pennsylvania, 2018).

113. Phil Napoli, Sarah Stonbely, Kathleen McColloughet, and Bryce Renninger, "Local
    Journalism and the Information Needs of Local Communities," *Journalism Practice*
    11, no. 4 (2017): 373–395.

114. James Hamilton and Fiona Morgan, "Poor Information: How Economics Affects
    the Information Lives of Low-Income Individuals," *International Journal of
    Communication* 12 (2018): 2832–2850.

115. All quotes in this paragraph are from John Heltman, "Confessions of a
    Paywall Journalist," *Washington Monthly*, November/December 2015, https://
    washingtonmonthly.com/magazine/novdec-2015/confessions-of-a-paywall-
    journalist/.

116. For an historical overview of early debates and experimentations with paywalls, see
    Victor Pickard and Alex Williams, "Salvation or Folly? The Perils and Promises of
    Digital Paywalls," *Digital Journalism* 2, no. 2 (2014): 195–213. Parts of my analysis
    here draw from this article.

117. David Simon, "Build the Wall," *Columbia Journalism Review*, July/August 2009,
    https://archives.cjr.org/feature/build_the_wall_1.php.

118. Katie Feola, "Analysts: The *New York Times* Paywall Must Pay," *AdWeek*,
    April 18, 2011, http://www.adweek.com/news/press/analysts-new-york-times-
    paywall-must-pay-130703.

119. For analysis that makes this argument, See Alex Williams and Victor Pickard,
    "Newspapers' Ongoing Search for Subscription Revenue: From Paywalls to
    Micropayments," *The Conversation*, May 21, 2015. https://theconversation.
    com/newspapers-ongoing-search-for-subscription-revenue-from-paywalls-to-
    micropayments-40726.

120. Ariel Stulberg, "In Paywall Age, Free Content Remains King for Newspaper Sites,"
    Columbia Journalism Review, September 22, 2017, https://www.cjr.org/united_
    states_project/newspaper-paywalls.php. The academic research on paywalls
    has burgeoned in recent years. For some key examples, see Iris Chyi, "Paying for
    what? How Much? And Why (Not)? Predictors of Paying Intent for Multiplatform

Newspapers." *International Journal on Media Management* 14, no. 3 (2012): 227–250; Merja Myllylahti, "Newspaper Paywalls—Hype and the Reality. A Study of How Paid News Content Impacts on Media Corporation Revenues." *Digital Journalism* 2, no. 2 (2014): 179–194; Merja Myllylahti, "Newspaper Paywalls and Corporate Revenues; A Comparative Study," in *The Routledge Companion to Digital Journalism Studies*, ed. B. Franklin and S. Eldridge II (London: Routledge, 2017), 166–175.

121. We expand on these conclusions in Pickard and Williams, "Salvation or Folly?"
122. Jaclyn Peiser, "Goodbye, *Denver Post*. Hello, Blockchain," *New York Times*, June 17, 2018, https://www.nytimes.com/2018/06/17/business/media/denver-post-blockchain-colorado-sun.html; Laura Hazard Owen, "Civil's Token Sale Has Failed. Now What?" *NiemanLab*, October 16, 2018, http://www.niemanlab.org/2018/10/civils-token-sale-has-failed-now-what-refunds-for-one-thing/.
123. Frederic Filloux, "The *New York Times* and Springer Are Wrong About Blendle," *Monday Note*, November 2, 2014, https://mondaynote.com/the-new-york-times-and-springer-are-wrong-about-blendle-4241fb6e6a97. For a discussion of similar models, see Alan Rusbridger, *Breaking News: The Remaking of Journalism and Why it Matters Now* (New York: Farrar, Straus and Giroux, 2018), 197–218.
124. Becky Peterson, "At the *New Yorker* Festival, Non-Subscribers Outnumber Brand Devotees," *Folio*, October 17, 2016. https://www.foliomag.com/new-yorker-festival-non-subscribers-outnumber-brand-devotees/.
125. Jack Shafer, "The David Bradley Effect," *Slate*, July 7, 2009, www.slate.com/articles/news_and_politics/press_box/2009/07/the_david_bradley_effect.html.
126. Dan Kennedy, "Selling out the *Washington Post*," *Guardian*, July 8, 2009, https://www.theguardian.com/commentisfree/cifamerica/2009/jul/08/washington-post-weymouth-salon.
127. Victor Pickard, United yet Autonomous: Indymedia and the Struggle to Sustain a Radical Democratic Network. *Media Culture & Society* 28, no. 3 (2006): 315–336.
128. Clay Shirky, *Here Comes Everybody: The Power of Organizing without Organizations* (New York: Penguin); Yochai Benkler, *The Wealth of Networks, How Social Production Transforms Markets and Freedom* (New Haven, CT: Yale University Press).
129. See, for example, Frederick Fico et al., "Citizen Journalism Sites as Information Substitutes and Complements for United States Newspaper Coverage of Local Governments," *Digital Journalism* 1, no. 1 (2013): 152–168.
130. For a clear articulation of this model, see Julia Cage, *Saving the Media: Capitalism, Crowdfunding, and Democracy* (Cambridge: Harvard University Press, 2016). See also: Gabe Bullard, "Crowdfunding the News," *Nieman Reports*, September 26, 2016, http://niemanreports.org/articles/crowdfunding-the-news/.
131. Hazel Sheffield, "Are Media Coops the Business Model of the Future?" *Columbia Journalism Review*, September 13, 2018, https://www.cjr.org/business_of_news/new-internationalist.php.
132. Shan Wang, "Voice of San Diego is Spearheading a Team to Help Other Smaller News Outlets Build Membership Programs," *NiemanLab*, December 5, 2016,

http://www.niemanlab.org/2016/12/voice-of-san-diego-is-spearheading-a-team-to-help-other-smaller-news-outlets-build-membership-programs/.

133. Rob Wijnberg, "The Problem with Real News—and What We Can Do about It," *Medium,* September 12, 2018, https://medium.com/de-correspondent/the-problem-with-real-news-and-what-we-can-do-about-it-f29aca95c2ea.

134. Jason Abbruzzese, A Dutch News Startup Has Crowdfunded $1 Million to 'Unbreak' U.S. News," *NBCNews,* December 3, 2018. https://www.nbcnews.com/news/all/dutch-news-startup-has-crowdfunded-1-million-unbreak-u-s-n943266. Laura Hazard Owen, "I Felt Like It Was a Betrayal, and We Had Raised Funds on False Pretense": The *Correspondent's* First U.S. Employee Speaks Out," *NiemanLab,* April 26, 2019. https://www.niemanlab.org/2019/04/i-felt-like-it-was-a-betrayal-and-we-had-raised-funds-on-false-pretense-the-correspondents-first-u-s-employee-speaks-out/.

135. Jay Rosen, personal communication with the author, July 8, 2019.

136. Victor Pickard, "Can Charity Save Journalism From Market Failure?" *The Conversation,* April 28, 2017, http://theconversation.com/can-charity-save-journalism-from-market-failure-75833.

137. Roger Yu, "Philadelphia Newspapers to Be Run as Public Benefit Corporation," *USA Today,* January 12, 2016, https://www.usatoday.com/story/money/business/2016/01/12/philadelphia-newspapers-inquirer-daily-news/78674544/.

138. This model resembles the "L3C" model promoted a decade ago, discussed in Pickard, Stearns, and Aaron, *Saving the News.*

139. Joseph Lichterman, personal communication with the author, March 25, 2019.

140. Jeffrey Hermes, "A Reason for Optimism in the IRS' Handling of Nonprofit News Orgs," *NiemanLab,* September 19, 2012, https://www.niemanlab.org/2012/09/a-reason-for-optimism-in-the-irs-handling-of-nonprofit-news-orgs/. New legislation was recently introduced in Congress to address these hurdles: "Congressman DeSaulnier Introduces Legislation to Eliminate Hurdles for Newspapers to Become Non-Profits," June 6, 2019. https://desaulnier.house.gov/media-center/press-releases/congressman-desaulnier-introduces-legislation-eliminate-hurdles.

141. Tony Semerad, "Salt Lake Tribune Seeks to Become a Nonprofit 'Community Asset,' a First for a Legacy Newspaper," *Salt Lake Tribune,* May 8, 2019, https://www.sltrib.com/news/2019/05/08/salt-lake-tribune-seeks/. For a thorough analysis of this and related plans, see Christine Schmidt and Joshua Benton, "*Salt Lake Tribune* Wants to Go Nonprofit in a New and Unproven Way, and Now the IRS Will Have Its Say," *NiemanLab,* May 9, 2019, https://www.niemanlab.org/2019/05/the-salt-lake-tribune-wants-to-go-nonprofit-in-a-new-and-unproven-way-and-now-the-irs-will-have-its-say/.

142. Mayur Patel and Michael Manes, *Finding a Foothold: How Nonprofit News Ventures Seek Sustainability* (Miami: Knight Foundation, 2013), https://knightfoundation.org/reports/finding-foothold.

143. Charles Lewis, "The Pace of Nonprofit Media Growth is Picking Up," *The Conversation,* July 11, 2018, https://theconversation.com/the-pace-of-nonprofit-media-growth-is-picking-up-98376 See also: Magda Konieczna, *Journalism*

without Profit Making: News When the Market Fails (New York: Oxford University Press, 2018).

144. These findings are summarized by Rick Edmonds, "A New Look at Local Nonprofit News Sites Finds Revenues of More Than $325 Million, 2,200 Journalists," *Poynter*, October 2, 2018, https://www.poynter.org/news/new-look-local-nonprofit-news-sites-finds-revenues-more-325-million-2200-journalists.

145. *INN Index 2018: The State of Nonprofit News* (Los Angeles: Institute for Nonprofit News, October 2018), https://inn.org/wp-content/uploads/2018/10/INN.Index2018FinalFullReport.pdf?platform=hootsuite.

146. "*ProPublica* to Expand Local Reporting Network to Focus on State Governments," *ProPublica*, August 8, 2018, https://www.propublica.org/atpropublica/propublica-expanding-local-reporting-network-state-governments.

147. See the following sites for more information: https://www.citybureau.org/; https://thecity.nyc/; https://resolvephilly.org/; https://brokeinphilly.org/.

148. More information about Community Impact Newspaper can be found at its website: https://communityimpact.com/.

149. For background information, see https://www.dailyyonder.com/about-daily-yonder/.

150. For more information about these projects, see https://banyanproject.coop/about/ and https://www.infodistricts.org/about-info-districts.

151. Nellie Bowles, "Report for America Supports Journalism Where Cutbacks Hit Hard," *New York Times*, April 15, 2018, https://www.nytimes.com/2018/04/15/business/media/report-for-america-service.html; More information about RFA can be found at its website: https://www.reportforamerica.org/.

152. Steve Waldman, personal communication with the author, March 21, 2019.

153. Andrea Wenzel, Sam Ford, Steve Bynum, and Efrat Nechushtai, "Can Report for America build trust in local news? A view from two communities," Tow Center, May 6, 2019. https://www.cjr.org/tow_center_reports/report-for-america-kentucky-chicago.php.

154. Anna Nirmala, personal communication with the author, April 19, 2019. See also: Meena Lee, "So How will the American Journalism Project Pick the Local News Sites it Wants to Back (with a Piece of its $42 million)?" *NiemanLab*, July 24, 2019, https://www.niemanlab.org/2019/07/so-how-will-the-american-journalism-project-pick-the-local-news-sites-it-wants-to-back-with-a-piece-of-its-42-million/; Rick Edmonds, "The American Journalism Project has Raised $42 Million. Here's the Plan for Distributing It," *Poynter*, March 20, 2019, https://www.poynter.org/business-work/2019/the-american-journalism-project-has-raised-42-million-heres-the-plan-for-distributing-it/.

155. Jessica Boehm, "Arizona State University, University of Maryland Get Grants to Launch Investigative Journalism Centers," *Arizona Republic*, August 6, 2018, https://www.azcentral.com/story/news/local/phoenix/2018/08/06/asu-launch-3-million-investigative-journalism-centers/902340002/.

156. Rodney Benson, "Can Foundations Solve the Journalism Crisis?" *Journalism* 19, no. 8 (2017): 1059–1077.

157. Anya Schiffrin, "A Marriage Of Convenience—Looking at the New Donor-Journalism Relationship," *Center for International Media Assistance*, October 3, 2016, https://www.cima.ned.org/blog/new-donor-journalism-relationship/. See also: Martin Scott, Mel Bunce, and Kate Wright, "Donor Power and the News: The Influence of Foundation Funding on International Public Service Journalism," *International Journal of Press/Politics* 22 (2017): 163–184.

158. Martin Scott, "What's Wrong with Philanthro-Journalism?" *NiemanReports*, January 30, 2019, https://niemanreports.org/articles/whats-wrong-with-philanthro-journalism/. See also: Martin Scott, Mel Bunce, and Kate Wright, "Foundation Funding and the Boundaries of Journalism," *Journalism Studies* (2019), DOI: 10.1080/1461670X.2018.1556321.

159. Laura Hazard Owen, "Are Nonprofit News Sites Just Creating More Content for Elites Who Already Read a Lot of News?" *NiemanLab*, September 6, 2017, http://www.niemanlab.org/2017/09/are-nonprofit-news-sites-just-creating-more-content-for-elites-who-already-read-a-lot-of-news/.

160. Pew Research Center, "State of the News Media," 2014.

161. Brian Flood, "Sheldon Adelson's Las Vegas Review-Journal Warns Staffers Disloyalty Could Get Them Fired," *Wrap*, June 17, 2016, https://www.thewrap.com/sheldon-adelson-las-vegas-review-journal-warns-staffers-disloyalty-fired/.

162. Benson and Pickard, "The Slippery Slope of the Oligarchy Media Model."

163. For a hard-hitting critique of the philanthropists-as-saviors approach to social problems, see Anand Giridharadas, *Winners Take All: The Elite Charade of Changing the World* (New York: Knopf, 2018).

164. Mark Ots and Robert Picard, "Press Subsidies," *Oxford Research Encyclopedia of Communication*, 2018, 1–18.

165. For the most recent rankings, see https://freedomhouse.org/.

166. Jeffrey Mondak, *Nothing to Read: Newspapers and Elections in a Social Experiment* (Ann Arbor: University of Michigan Press, 1996); Jackie Filla and Martin Johnson, "Local News Outlets and Political Participation," *Urban Affairs Review* 45, no. 5 (2010): 679–692.

167. Lee Shaker, "Dead Newspapers and Citizens' Civic Engagement," *Political Communication* 31, no. 1 (2014): 131–148. Josh Stearns provides a comprehensive overview of many of the studies I discuss in this section: "How we Know Journalism is Good for Democracy," *Local News Lab*, June 20, 2018, https://localnewslab.org/2018/06/20/how-we-know-journalism-is-good-for-democracy/.

168. Danny Hayes and Jennifer Lawless, "As Local News Goes, so Goes Citizen Engagement: Media, Knowledge, and Participation in US House Elections," *Journal of Politics* 77, no. 2 (2015): 447–462.

169. James Snyder and David Strömberg, "Press Coverage and Political Accountability," *Journal of Political Economy* 118, no. 2 (April 2010): 355–408.

170. Matthew Gentzkow, Jesse Shapiro, and Michael Sinkinson, "The Effect of Newspaper Entry and Exit on Electoral Politics," *American Economic Review* 101, no. 7 (2011): 2980–3018.

171. Matthew Gentzkow, Jesse Shapiro, and Michael Sinkinson, "Competition and Ideological Diversity: Historical Evidence from US Newspapers," *American Economic Review* 104, no. 10 (2014): 3073–3114.

172. Meghan Rubado and Jay Jennings, "Political Consequences of the Endangered Local Watchdog: Newspaper Decline and Mayoral Elections in the United States," *Urban Affairs Review*, April 2019.

173. Joshua Darr, Matthew Hitt, and Johanna Dunaway, "Newspaper Closures Polarize Voting Behavior," *Journal of Communication* 68, no. 6 (2018): 1007–1028.

174. Paul Starr, "Goodbye to the Age of Newspapers," in McChesney and Pickard, *Will the Last Reporter Please Turn out the Lights?* 18–37.

175. Dermot Murphy, "When Local Papers Close, Costs Rise for Local Governments," *Columbia Journalism Review*, June 27, 2018, https://www.cjr.org/united_states_project/public-finance-local-news.php.

176. Pengjie Gao, Chang Lee, and Dermot Murphy, "Financing Dies in Darkness? The Impact of Newspaper Closures on Public Finance," (forthcoming in the *Journal of Financial Economics*), October 21, 2018, https://ssrn.com/abstract=3175555.

177. James Hamilton, *Democracy's Detectives: The Economics of Investigative Journalism* (Cambridge: Harvard University Press, 2016).

178. The DOJ now again uses private prisons and that it never stopped using private prisons to house immigration detainees.

179. Monika Bauerlein and Clara Jeffery, "This Is What's Missing From Journalism Right Now," *Mother Jones*, August 17, 2016, https://www.motherjones.com/media/2016/08/whats-missing-from-journalism/.

180. Juan Gonzalez, "From Crown Heights Brutality to $500M CityTime Fraud, Juan Gonzalez Recalls 25 Years of His Greatest Scandalous Scoops," *New York Daily News*, December 23, 2012, https://www.nydailynews.com/new-york/juan-gonzalez-recalls-25-years-greatest-scandalous-scoops-article-1.1226436.

181. Anna Clark, "How an Investigative Journalist Helped Prove a City Was Being Poisoned with Its Own Water," *Columbia Journalism Review*, November 3, 2015, https://www.cjr.org/united_states_project/flint_water_lead_curt_guyette_aclu_michigan.php. For an excellent discussion of how NGOs are increasingly taking on journalistic endeavors, see Matthew Powers, *NGOs as Newsmakers: The Changing Landscape of International News* (New York: Columbia University Press, 2018).

182. Pew Research Center, "How News Happens: A Study of the News Ecosystem of One American City," 2010, http://www.journalism.org/2010/01/11/how-news-happens/. The Baltimore study is discussed in more detail in Robert McChesney and Victor Pickard, "News Media as Political Institutions," in *Handbook of Political Communication Theories*, ed. Kate Kenski and Kathleen Hall Jamieson (Oxford: Oxford University Press, 2017), 263–274. For a useful discussion of newspapers' special role in producing local information as "keystone media," see the chapter by Rasmus Kleis Nielsen in his edited collection, *Local Journalism: The Decline of Newspapers and the Rise of Digital Media*. Reuters Institute for the Study of Journalism, University of Oxford, 2015.

183. See, for example, a study conducted by the Pew Research Center, "Local News in a Digital Age," 2015, http://www.journalism.org/2015/03/05/local-news-in-a-digital-age/. See also: Phil Napoli and Jessica Mahone, "Local newspapers are suffering, but they're still (by far) the most significant journalism producers in their communities," *NiemanLab*, September 9, 2019. https://www.niemanlab.org/2019/09/local-newspapers-are-suffering-but-theyre-still-by-far-the-most-significant-journalism-producers-in-their-communities/

184. Joe Amditis, "Can Public Funding for Local News Increase Trust in Media?" *Medium*, September 11, 2018, https://medium.com/trust-media-and-democracy/can-public-funding-for-local-news-increase-trust-in-media-d53d0321611b.

Chapter 4

1. Zach Wichter, "2 Days, 10 Hours, 600 Questions: What Happened When Mark Zuckerberg Went to Washington," *New York Times*, April 12, 2018, https://www.nytimes.com/2018/04/12/technology/mark-zuckerberg-testimony.html.

2. Jack Nicas and Matthew Rosenberg, "A Look Inside the Tactics of Definers, Facebook's Attack Dog," *New York Times*, November 15, 2018, https://www.nytimes.com/2018/11/15/technology/facebook-definers-opposition-research.html.

3. Nick Bilton, "Behind Zuck's War with the *New York Times*," *Vanity Fair*, January 9, 2019, https://www.vanityfair.com/news/2019/01/behind-mark-zuckerbergs-war-with- the-new-york-times.

4. Mike Isaac, "Mark Zuckerberg's Call to Regulate Facebook, Explained," *New York Times*, March 30, 2019, https://www.nytimes.com/2019/03/30/technology/mark-zuckerberg-facebook-regulation-explained.html.

5. For a more in-depth overview of the relevant scholarship in this area, see Victor Pickard, "Media Ownership," in *The International Encyclopedia of Political Communication*, 1st ed., ed. Gianpietro Mazzoleni (Malden: John Wiley & Sons, Inc, 2015), 756–759.

6. Rodney Benson, Mattias Hesserus, and Julie Sedel, *How Media Ownership Matters* (Oxford: Oxford University Press, forthcoming).

7. I am using the term "monopoly" rather loosely here—in many cases they are technically duopolies or oligopolies and, in some cases, cartels. Zephyr Teachout and others argue that the term monopoly connotes one firm is powerful enough, by size or structure, to set prices and terms and govern instead of compete, https://twitter.com/ZephyrTeachout/status/1105453207201947650.

8. Ben Bagdikian, *The New Media Monopoly* (Boston: Beacon, 2004).

9. Nicolas Rapp and Aric Jenkins, "Chart: These 6 Companies Control Much of U.S. Media," *Fortune*, July 24, 2018, http://fortune.com/longform/media-company-ownership-consolidation/.

10. Some scholars have long argued that media "contraflows" deserve more attention—but despite important shifts in media ownership, global media are still disproportionately controlled or influenced by US corporations that create asymmetrical power relationships between and within states. For an authoritative account, see

Eli Noam, *Who Owns the World's Media* (New York: Oxford University Press, 2016). Earlier research shows how media conglomerates command significant market power across the globe. See Edward Herman and Robert McChesney, *The Global Media: The New Missionaries of Corporate Capitalism* (Washington, DC: Cassell, 1997).

11. Matthew Hindman, *The Myth of Digital Democracy* (Princeton: Princeton University Press, 2009), 51–54. For a useful discussion of Hindman's analysis, see John Bellamy Foster and Robert McChesney, "The Internet's Unholy Marriage to Capitalism," *Monthly Review*, March 1, 2011, https://monthlyreview.org/2011/03/01/the-internets-unholy-marriage-to-capitalism/. See also: Robert McChesney and Victor Pickard, "News Media as Political Institutions," in Kenski and Jamieson, *Handbook of Political Communication Theories*, 263–274.

12. Eiri Elvestad and Angela Phillips, *Misunderstanding News Audiences: Seven Myths of the Social Media Era* (Abingdon: Routledge, 2018). James Curran suggests that this continued dominance is partly a result of large publishers' anti-competitive measures (such as giving away content for free) that undermine the business prospects of new media start-ups. See James Curran, "Triple Crisis of Journalism," *Journalism* 20, no. 1 (2019): 190–193.

13. Alexa, "The Top 500 Sites on the Web," 2018, https://www.alexa.com/topsites/category/News. This research is cited in Matthew Guardino, *Framing Inequality: Media, Public Opinion and the Neoliberal Turn in U.S. Public Policy* (New York: Oxford University Press, 2019), 272.

14. The previous quotes are from Patrick Kennedy and Andrea Prat, "Where Do People Get Their News?" Paper presented to the 67th Economic Policy Panel Meeting, April 3, 2018, https://cepr.org/sites/default/files/events/papers/995_Where%20Do%20People%20Get%20Their%20News.pdf. Study discussed in Guardino, *Framing Inequality*, 272–273.

15. Donald Trump, Twitter post, June 28, 2017, 6:06 a.m., https://twitter.com/realDonaldTrump/status/880049704620494848.

16. Thomas Frank, "Swat Team," *Harpers*, November 2016, https://harpers.org/archive/2016/11/swat-team-2/.

17. Yochai Benkler, Robert Faris, and Hal Roberts, *Network Propaganda: Manipulation, Disinformation, and Radicalization in American Politics* (New York: Oxford University Press, 2018). See also: Kathleen Hall Jamieson and Joseph Cappella, *Echo Chamber: Rush Limbaugh and the Conservative Media Establishment* (New York: Oxford University Press, 2010).

18. This number has declined in recent years, but local television news still has the largest audience among the three television platforms, which together still comprise 50 percent of adult news consumers. Katrina Eva Matsa, "Fewer Americans Rely on TV News; What Type They Watch Varies by Who They Are," *FactTank*, January 5, 2018, http://www.pewresearch.org/fact-tank/2018/01/05/fewer-americans-rely-on-tv-news-what-type-they-watch-varies-by-who-they-are/.

19. Indira Lakshmanan, "Finally Some Good News: Trust in News Is up, Especially for Local Media," *Poynter*, August 22, 2018, https://www.poynter.org/ethics-trust/2018/finally-some-good-news-trust-in-news-is-up-especially-for-local-media/.

20. Jon Swaine, "Sinclair TV Chairman to Trump: 'We Are Here to Deliver Your Message,'" *Guardian*, April 10, 2018, https://www.theguardian.com/media/2018/apr/10/donald-trump-sinclair-david-smith-white-house-meeting.

21. Ben Wofford, "Sinclair Broadcasting's Hostile Takeover," *Rolling Stone*, April 24, 2018, https://www.rollingstone.com/culture/features/sinclair-broadcast-group-hostile-takeover- trump-w519331.

22. Chris Mills Rodrigo, "Sinclair Defends Segment Justifying Use of Tear Gas at Border as 'Commentary,'" *Hill*, November 28, 2018, https://thehill.com/homenews/media/418829-sinclair-defends-segment-justifying-use-of-tear-gas-at-border-as-commentary.

23. Ryan Reed, "John Oliver: How Sinclair Broadcast Group 'Brainwashes' Local News," *Rolling Stone*, August 2, 2018, https://www.rollingstone.com/tv/tv-news/john-oliver-how-sinclair-broadcast-group-brainwashes-local-news-630138/.

24. Jay Rosen, Twitter post, November 28, 2018, 10:39 a.m., https://twitter.com/jayrosen_nyu/status/1067850440165990400.

25. The FCC's many gifts to Sinclair are discussed in Wofford, "Sinclair Broadcasting's Hostile Takeover." Sheelah Kolhatkar, "The Growth of Sinclair's Conservative Media Empire," *New Yorker*, October 22, 2018, https://www.newyorker.com/magazine/2018/10/22/the-growth-of-sinclairs-conservative-media-empire.

26. Cecilia Kang, "F.C.C. Opens Door to More Consolidation in TV Business," *New York Times*, November 16, 2017, https://www.nytimes.com/2017/11/16/business/media/fcc-local-tv.html; Ted Johnson, "FCC Relaxes Media Ownership Rules in Contentious Vote," *Variety*, November 16, 2017. https://variety.com/2017/politics/news/fcc-media-ownership-rules-sinclair-broadcasting-1202616424/.

27. For a great overview of these policy changes, see Dana Floberg, "Pai's Big-Media Handout Will Hurt Communities," *Free Press*, November 10, 2017, https://www.freepress.net/our-response/expert-analysis/explainers/pais-big-media-handout-will-hurt-communities. See also: "Sinclair Broadcast Group Acquisition of Tribune Media: Competitive and Regulatory Issues," EveryCRSReport.com, July 18, 2017, https://www.everycrsreport.com/reports/R44892.html.

28. Klint Finley, "The Sinclair/Tribune Merger is Dead," *Wired*, August 8, 2018, https://www.wired.com/story/the-sinclairtribune-merger-is-dead/.

29. For a comprehensive overview of literature on regulatory captures, see Adam Thierer, "Regulatory Capture: What the Experts Have Found," *Technology Liberation Front*, December 19, 2010, https://techliberation.com/2010/12/19/regulatory-capture-what-the-experts-have-found/.

30. My historical research on the FCC shows that this was a problem from the agency's beginning. See Pickard, *America's Battle for Media Democracy*, 38.

31. Craig Aaron and Timothy Karr of Free Press, personal communication with the author, July 27, 2018.

32. Jon Brodkin, "FCC's Revolving Door: Former Chairman Leads Charge against Title II," *Ars Technica*, April 14, 2015, https://arstechnica.com/information-technology/2015/04/fccs-revolving-door-former-chairman-leads-charge-against-title-ii/.

33. Tim Karr, "FCC Commissioner Cashes in at Your Expense," *Common Dreams*, May 14, 2011, https://www.commondreams.org/views/2011/05/14/fcc-commissioner-cashes-your-expense.

34. Jonathan Tepper, "The Revolving Door: Why the Regulators Went Soft on Monopolies," *American Conservative*, January/February, 2019, https://www.theamericanconservative.com/articles/why-the-regulators-went-soft-on-monopolies/.

35. For some of the highlights, see Ibid.

36. Thomas Edsall, "The Lobbyists Blocking the Doorway," *New York Times*, January 10, 2019, https://www.nytimes.com/2019/01/10/opinion/pelosi-trump-lobbying-democrats.html. See also:https://www.opensecrets.org/lobby/.

37. Edsall, "The Lobbyists Blocking the Doorway."

38. I discuss one such experience in this essay: Victor Pickard, "After Net Neutrality," *LSE Media Policy Project*, July 18, 2016, http://blogs.lse.ac.uk/mediapolicyproject/2016/07/18/after-net-neutrality/.

39. Jeff Stein, "Many Lawmakers and Aides Who Crafted Financial Regulations after the 2008 Crisis Now Work for Wall Street," *Washington Post*, September 7, 2018, https://www.washingtonpost.com/business/economy/many-lawmakers-and-aids-who-crafted-financial-regulations-after-the-2008-crisis-now-work-for-wall-street/2018/09/07/50f63a1e-b075-11e8-a20b-5f4f84429666_story.html?noredirect=on&utm_term=.e3fbe8f415b9.

40. See Zephyr Teachout, *Corruption in America: From Benjamin Franklin's Snuff Box to Citizens United* (Cambridge: Harvard University Press, 2014).

41. Paresh Dave, "Google, Facebook Spend Big on U.S. Lobbying amid Policy Battles," *Reuters*, January 22, 2019, https://www.reuters.com/article/us-tech-lobbying/google-facebook-spend-big-on-us-lobbying-amid-policy-battles-idUSKCN1PG2TD.

42. Robert McChesney, "Off Limits: An Inquiry into the Lack of Debate Over the Ownership, Structure and Control of the Mass Media in U.S. Political Life," *Communication* 13 (1992): 1–19.

43. Des Freedman, *The Contradictions of Media Power* (London: Bloomsbury, 2014), 64.

44. David Leonhardt, "The Monopolization of America," *New York Times*, November 25, 2018, https://www.nytimes.com/2018/11/25/opinion/monopolies-in-the-us.html.

45. Open Markets Institute, 2018, https://concentrationcrisis.openmarketsinstitute.org/industry/cell-phone-providers/. See also: Susan Crawford, *Captive Audience: The Telecom Industry and Monopoly Power in the New Gilded Age* (New Haven: Yale University Press, 2013).

46. Robert McChesney, *Digital Disconnect: How Capitalism Is Turning the Internet against Democracy* (New York: The New Press, 2013). For a thorough treatment of media ownership, see Eli Noam, *Media Ownership and Concentration in America* (New York: Oxford University Press, 2009). Noam's book painstakingly analyzes previous literature and quantifies media ownership patterns across diverse media sectors amounting to a hundred information industries over twenty-five years.

47. "Vertical Integration," *Economist*, March 30, 2009, https://www.economist.com/news/2009/03/30/vertical-integration.

48. David Morris, "How the AT&T-Time Warner Merger Could Hurt Consumers," *Fortune*, October 23, 2016, http://fortune.com/2016/10/23/att-time-warner-merger-consumers/.

49. Sally Hubbard, "The Case for Why Big Tech Is Violating Antitrust Laws," *CNN Business*, January 2, 2019, https://www.cnn.com/2019/01/02/perspectives/big-tech-facebook-google-amazon-microsoft-antitrust/index.html.

50. Ibid. See also: Derek Walter, "Report: Nearly 90 Percent of Smartphones Worldwide Run Android," *Greenbot*, November 3, 2016, https://www.greenbot.com/article/3138394/android/report-nearly-90-percent-of-smartphones-worldwide-run-android.html.

51. Leon Kelion, "Google Hit with Record EU Fine over Shopping Service," BBCNews, June 27, 2017, https://www.bbc.com/news/technology-40406542.

52. Hubbard, "Case for Why Big Tech Is Violating Antitrust Laws."

53. For a political and economic history of Comcast's rise to power, see Lee McGuigan and Victor Pickard, "The Political Economy of Comcast," in *Global Media Giants*, ed. Ben Birkinbine, Rodrigo Gómez García, and Janet Wasko (New York: Routledge, 2016), 72–91.

54. This strategy is well documented in Jonathan Mahler and Jim Rutenberg, "How Rupert Murdoch's Empire of Influence Remade the World," *New York Times*, April 7, 2019, https://www.nytimes.com/interactive/2019/04/03/magazine/rupert-murdoch-fox-news-trump.html. For a cultural history of Fox News, see Reece Peck, *Fox Populism: Branding Conservatism as Working Class* (New York: Cambridge University Press, 2019).

55. Robert Picard, "Media Concentration, Economics, and Regulation," in *The Politics of News: The News of Politics*, ed. Doris Graber, Denis McQuail, and Pippa Norris (Washington, DC: Congressional Quarterly Press, 1998), 193–217; Baker, *Media Concentration and Democracy*.

56. Hungary suffered from this kind of power relationship when the government exerted control by striking deals with telecommunication firms who own the bulk of the Hungarian media system. Patrick Kingsley and Benjamin Novak, "The Website That Shows How a Free Press Can Die," *New York Times*, November 24, 2018, https://www.nytimes.com/2018/11/24/world/europe/hungary-viktor-orban-media.html.

57. The discussion in the text draws from Picard and Pickard, "*Essential Principles for Contemporary Media and Communications Policymaking.*

58. Alison Harcourt and Robert Picard, "Policy, Economic, and Business Challenges of Media Ownership Regulation," *Journal of Media Business Studies* 6, no. 3 (2009): 1–17.

59. Freedman, *The Contradictions of Media Power*, 57. For a detailed description of Freedman's excellent book, see my review in *Information, Communication & Society* 19, no. 12 (2016): 1743–1745.

60. For an excellent book that provides an overview of the many ways media ownership matters for media content, see Justin Schlosberg, *Media Ownership and Agenda Control* (New York: Routledge, 2017).

61. For a history of these battles over broadcast media ownership, see Pickard, *America's Battle for Media Democracy*.

62. For an oral history of the media ownership battles of the 2000s, see Pickard and Popiel, *The Media Democracy Agenda*.

63. Nina Huntemann, "Corporate Interference: The Commercialization and Concentration of Radio Post the 1996 Telecommunications Act." *Journal of Communication Inquiry* 23, no. 4 (1999): 390–407.

64. Eric Klinenberg, *Fighting for Air: The Battle to Control America's Media* (New York: Metropolitan Books, 2007).

65. C. Edwin Baker, "Media Structure, Ownership Policy, and the First Amendment," *Southern California Law Review* 78 (2004): 733; Robert McChesney, *Rich Media, Poor Democracy: Communication Politics in Dubious Times* (New York: New Press, 1999); Matthew Baum and Yuri Zhukov, "Media Ownership and News Coverage of International Conflict," *Political Communication* (2018): 1–28.

66. Edda Humprecht and Frank Esser, "Diversity in Online News," *Journalism Studies* 19, no. 12 (2018): 1825–1847.

67. Gregory Martin and Joshua McCrain, "Local News and National Politics," *American Political Science Review* (2019) 113, 2, 372–384.

68. Kari Karppinen, *Rethinking Media Pluralism* (New York: Fordham University Press, 2013).

69. The next two paragraphs draw from Picard and Pickard, *Essential Principles for Contemporary Media and Communications Policymaking*.

70. Eli Noam notes that media ownership's problems for democracy are age-old concerns. See Noam, *Media Ownership and Concentration in America*, 7.

71. Associated Press v. United States, 326 US 1 (1945).

72. Picard and Pickard, *Essential Principles for Contemporary Media and Communications Policymaking*; Peggy Valke, Miklós Süsköd, and Robert Pickard, eds., *Media Pluralism and Diversity: Concepts, Risks and Global Trends* (London: Palgrave Macmillan, 2015).

73. Ibid.

74. Gillian Doyle, *Media Ownership* (London: Sage Publications, 2002).

75. For policy histories of minority media ownership in the United States, see Jeffrey Blevins and Karla Martinez, "A Political-Economic History of FCC Policy on Minority Broadcast Ownership," *Communication Review* 13, no. 3 (2010): 216–238; David Honig, "How the FCC Suppressed Minority Broadcast Ownership, and How the FCC Can undo the Damage it Caused," *Southern Journal of Policy and Justice* 12 (2018): 44–104.

76. "FCC 2018 Broadband report," Federal Communications Commission, February 2, 2018, https://www.fcc.gov/reports-research/reports/broadband-progress-reports/2018-broadband-deployment-report.

77. For a summary, see Steve Lohr, "Digital Divide Is Wider Than We Think, Study Says," *New York Times*, December 4, 2018, https://www.nytimes.com/2018/12/04/technology/digital-divide-us-fcc-microsoft.html. The global digital divide is even more dramatic: Ian Sample, "Universal Internet Access Unlikely until at Least 2050, Experts Say," *Guardian*, January 10, 2019, https://www.theguardian.com/technology/2019/jan/10/universal-internet-access-unlikely-until-2050-experts-say-lack-skills-investment-slow-growth.

78. A team of researchers have found that in Pennsylvania there were no counties where the median speed met the FCC's minimal definition, which means that less than half of the population had broadband access. Sascha Meinrath, personal communication with the author, May 10, 2019. Other data show, not surprisingly, that the digital divide disproportionately affects lower-income Americans. Monica Anderson and Madhumitha Kumar, "Digital Divide Persists Even as Lower-Income Americans Make Gains In Tech Adoption," *Pew Research Center's FactTank*, May 7, 2019, https://www.pewresearch.org/fact-tank/2019/05/07/digital-divide-persists-even-as-lower-income-americans-make-gains-in-tech-adoption/.

79. S. Derek Turner, "The Impact of Systemic Racial Discrimination on Home-Internet Adoption," *Free Press*, December, 2016, https://www.freepress.net/news/press-releases/digital-denied-free-press-report-exposes-impact-systemic-racism-internet.

80. Parts of the following section draw from Victor Pickard and David Berman, *After Net Neutrality: A New Deal for the Digital Age* (New Haven: Yale University Press, 2019).

81. Susan Crawford, *Captive Audience: The Telecom Industry and Monopoly Power in the New Gilded Age* (New Haven: Yale University Press, 2013).

82. Federal Communications Commission, "Internet Access Services: Status as of December 31, 2016," Washington, DC, 2016, 6.

83. These numbers are cited in Pickard and Berman, *After Net Neutrality*.

84. See, for example, McGuigan and Pickard, "The Political Economy of Comcast."

85. Nick Russo et al., *The Cost of Connectivity 2014* (Washington, DC: New America Foundation, 2014). For a summary of slightly older data, see Pickard, *America's Battle for Media Democracy*, 221–222.

86. Akamai, "State of the Internet Q1 2017," 2017, https://www.akamai.com/fr/fr/multimedia/documents/state-of-the-internet/q1-2017-state-of-the-internet-connectivity-report.pdf.

87. Jane Lee, "Why Does South Korea Have Faster Internet for a Cheaper Price Tag?" *Public Knowledge*, July 19, 2017, https://www.publicknowledge.org/news-blog/blogs/why-does-south-korea-have-faster-internet-for-a-cheaper-price-tag. Many of these statistics are cited in Pickard, *America's Battle*, 2015; Pickard and Berman, *After Net Neutrality*, 2019.

88. Pickard and Berman, *After Net Neutrality*. See also: Robert McChesney, *Digital Disconnect: How Capitalism Is Turning the Internet against Democracy* (New York: New Press, 2013).

89. Yochai Benkler et al., *Next Generation Connectivity: A Review of Broadband Internet Transitions and Policy from around the World* (Cambridge: The Berkman Center for Internet and Society at Harvard University, 2010); Christopher Marsden, "Comparative Case Studies in Implementing Net Neutrality: A Critical Analysis of Zero Rating," *SCRIPTed* 13, no. 1 (2016): 1–39.

90. For an expansion of this argument, see Pickard and Berman, *After Net Neutrality*.

91. Kendra Chamberlain, "Municipal Broadband Is Roadblocked or Outlawed in 26 States," *BroadbandNow*, April 17, 2019, https://broadbandnow.com/report/municipal-broadband-roadblocks/; Karl Bode, "Why The Hell Are States Still Passing

ISP-Written Laws Banning Community Broadband?" *TechDirt*, April 24th, 2019, https://www.techdirt.com/articles/20190422/09111942060/why-hell-are-states-still-passing-isp-written-laws-banning-community-broadband.shtml.

92. For an overview of the economics associated with this turn, see Nick Srnicek, *Platform Capitalism* (Malden, MA: Polity Press, 2017).

93. For a useful critical analysis of platform monopolies, see Nikos Smyrnaios, *Internet Oligopoly: The Corporate Takeover of Our Digital World* (Bingley, UK: Emerald Publishing, 2018).

94. John Gramlich, "10 facts about Americans and Facebook," *Pew Research Center's FactTank*, February 1, 2019, https://www.pewresearch.org/fact-tank/2019/02/01/facts-about-americans-and-facebook/; Josh Constine, "Facebook's Intrnet.org Has Connected Almost 100M to the 'Internet,'" *TechCrunch*, April 25, 2018, https://techcrunch.com/2018/04/25/internet-org-100-million/.

95. Daniel Kreiss and Shannon McGregor, "Technology Firms Shape Political Communication: The Work of Microsoft, Facebook, Twitter, and Google with Campaigns during the 2016 U.S. Presidential Cycle," *Political Communication* 35, no. 2 (2018): 155–177.

96. Siva Vaidhyanathan, *Antisocial Media: How Facebook Disconnects Us and Undermines Democracy* (New York: Oxford University Press, 2018) 190–195; Alexandra Stevenson, "Facebook Admits It Was Used to Incite Violence in Myanmar," *New York Times*, November 6, 2018, https://www.nytimes.com/2018/11/06/technology/myanmar-facebook.html.

97. Mike Shields, "CMO Today: Google and Facebook Drive 2017 Digital Ad Surge," *Wall Street Journal*, March 14, 2017, https://www.wsj.com/articles/cmo-today-google-and-facebook-drive-2017-digital-ad-surge-1489491871.

98. Tiernan Ray, "Google, Facebook Approaching 'Saturation' of Ad Budgets, Says Pivotal," *Barron's*, December 20, 2017, http://www.barrons.com/articles/google-face-book-approaching-saturation-of-ad-budgets-says-pivotal-1513804634. Calculations vary somewhat; this report places the duopoly's share at slightly less: "Looking Beyond the Facebook/Google Duopoly," *eMarketer*, December 12, 2017, https://www.emarketer.com/content/exploring-the-duopoly-beyond-google-and-facebook. Amazon is gradually becoming a third significant player in digital advertising.

99. Parts of the following draw from Victor Pickard, "Break Facebook's Power and Renew Journalism," *Nation* 306, no. 15 (2018): 22–24.

100. In addition to books cited earlier, see the following: Tarleton Gillespie, *Custodians of the Internet: Platforms, Content Moderation, and the Hidden Decisions that Shape Social Media* (New Haven: Yale University Press, 2018); Jonathan Taplin, *Move Fast and Break Things* (New York: Little Brown & Co., 2017). Zeynep Tufekci writes regularly about these issues. See, for example, "Facebook's Ad Scandal Isn't a 'Fail,' It's a Feature," *New York Times*, September 23, 2017, https://www.nytimes.com/2017/09/23/opinion/sunday/facebook-ad-scandal.html. See also Jack Balkin, "Information Fiduciaries and the First Amendment," *UC Davis Law Review* 49, no. 4 (2016): 1185–1234.

101. Sam Levin, "Facebook Teams with Rightwing Daily Caller in Factchecking Program," *Guardian*, April 17, 2019, https://www.theguardian.com/technology/2019/apr/17/facebook-teams-with-rightwing-daily-caller-in-factchecking-program.

102. Sam Levin, "Is Facebook a Publisher? In Public It Says No, but in Court It Says Yes," *Guardian*, July 3, 2018, https://www.theguardian.com/technology/2018/jul/02/facebook-mark-zuckerberg-platform-publisher-lawsuit; Mathew Ingram: "The Media Today: Facebook Tosses a Dime at Local Journalism," *Columbia Journalism Review*, February 28, 2018, https://www.cjr.org/the_media_today/facebook-local-news-funding.php.

103. I discuss these problems in previous essays: Victor Pickard, "Media Failures in the Age of Trump," *Political Economy of Communication* 4, no. 2 (2017): 118–122; Victor Pickard, "The Big Picture: Misinformation Society," *Public Books*, November 28, 2017, http://www.publicbooks.org/the-big-picture-misinformation-society/.

104. The 1913 Kingsbury Commitment involving the Bell telephone system is an example of a regulatory arrangement that treated a core network as a natural monopoly. In return for its monopoly status, AT&T was mandated to interconnect with non-AT&T systems and help promote universal service.

105. Ingo Vogelsang, "Incentive Regulation and Competition in Public Utility Markets: A 20-year Perspective," *Journal of Regulatory Economics* 22, no. 1 (2002): 5–27.

106. Roger McNamee, "Rein in Facebook Like We Did AT&T," *Financial Times*, April 2018, https://www.ft.com/content/942020c6-4936-11e8-8c77-ff51caedcde6.

107. Hubbard, "The Case for Why Big Tech Is Violating Antitrust Laws." Hubbard notes how the court found that Microsoft used its monopoly power to design personal computer operating systems so that computer makers had to install Microsoft's Internet Explorer browser instead of its competitor Netscape. See U.S. v. Microsoft Corporation, 253 F.3d 34 (D.C. Cir. 2001), https://www.justice.gov/atr/case/us-v-microsoft-corporation-browser-and-middleware.

108. Tepper, "The Revolving Door."

109. "GDPR Key Changes," n.d., https://eugdpr.org/the-regulation/.

110. Amar Toor, "Germany Passes Controversial Law to Fine Facebook Over Hate Speech," *Verge*, June 30, 2017, https://www.theverge.com/2017/6/30/15898386/germany-facebook-hate-speech-law-passed; Katrin Bennhold, "Germany Acts to Tame Facebook, Learning from Its Own History of Hate," *Independent*, June 15, 2018, https://www.independent.co.uk/news/long_reads/facebook-germany-online-hate-censorship-social-media-a8374351.html.

111. Adam Satariano, "Google Fined $1.7 Billion by E.U. for Unfair Advertising Rules," *New York Times*, March 20, 2019, https://www.nytimes.com/2019/03/20/business/google-fine-advertising.html.

112. See, for example, Jim Waterson, "UK fines Facebook £500,000 for failing to protect user data," *Guardian*, October 25, 2018, https://www.theguardian.com/technology/2018/oct/25/facebook-fined-uk-privacy-access-user-data-cambridge-analytica.

113. Tony Romm, "U.S. government issues stunning rebuke, historic $5 billion fine against Facebook for repeated privacy violations," *Washington Post*, July 24, 2019, https://www.washingtonpost.com/technology/2019/07/24/us-

government-issues-stunning-rebuke-historic-billion-fine-against-facebook-repeated-privacy-violations/?utm_term=.e26b9d2a7495.

114. Kathleen Chaykowski, "Facebook Focuses News Feed on Friends and Family, Curbing the Reach of Brands and Media," *Forbes*, January 11, 2018, https://www.forbes.com/sites/kathleenchaykowski/2018/01/11/facebook-focuses-news-feed-on-friends-and-family-curbing-the-reach-of-brands-and-media/#1b0d6cdc5b69.

115. I discuss some of these points in Victor Pickard, "Break Facebook's Power and Renew Journalism." For a story about the challenging labor conditions of content moderators, see Scott Simon and Emma Bowman, "Propaganda, Hate Speech, Violence: The Working Lives Of Facebook's Content Moderators," *NPR*, March 2, 2019, https://www.npr.org/2019/03/02/699663284/the-working-lives-of-facebooks-content-moderators.

116. See, for example, Paul Hitlin and Lee Rainie, "Facebook Algorithms and Personal Data," *Pew Research Center*, January 16, 2019, https://www.pewinternet.org/2019/01/16/facebook-algorithms-and-personal-data/.

117. Joseph Turow, Michael Hennessy, and Nora Draper, *The Tradeoff Fallacy: How Marketers Are Misrepresenting American Consumers and Opening Them Up to Exploitation* (Philadelphia: Annenberg School for Communication, 2015), https://www.asc.upenn.edu/sites/default/files/TradeoffFallacy_1.pdf; Joseph Turow et al., *Divided We Feel: Partisan Politics Drive Americans' Emotions Regarding Surveillance of Low-Income Populations* (Philadelphia: Annenberg School for Communication, 2015), https://www.asc.upenn.edu/sites/default/files/documents/Turow-Divided-Final.pdf.

118. Barry Lynn, who directs the Open Market Institute, is one of the intellectual founders of this movement. See especially his book *Cornered: The New Monopoly Capitalism and the Economics of Destruction* (Hoboken, NJ: Wiley, 2010).

119. For a useful explication of this dichotomy, see Frank Pasquale, "Tech Platforms and the Knowledge Problem," *American Affairs* II, no. 2 (Summer 2018): 3–16.

120. For an incisive analysis of the United States' anti-monopoly movement, see Tim Wu, *The Curse of Bigness: Antitrust in the New Gilded Age* (New York: Columbia Global Reports, 2018).

121. Lina Khan, "Amazon's Antitrust Paradox," *Yale Law Journal* 126, no. 3 (2017): 710–805. See also: Barak Orbach, "The Antitrust Consumer Welfare Paradox," *Journal of Competition Law and Economics* 7, no. 1 (2010): 133–164.

122. See "America's Concentration Crisis," A resource compiled by the Open Markets Institute, 2018, https://concentrationcrisis.openmarketsinstitute.org/.

123. The policy analyst, Ezra Klein notes that more competition might actually make things worse. "Facebook is a Capitalism Problem, Not a Mark Zuckerberg Problem," *Vox*, May 10, 2019, https://www.vox.com/recode/2019/5/10/18563895/fa"cebook-chris-hughes-mark-zuckerberg-break-up-monopoly.

124. Gene Kimmelman, "To Make the Tech Sector Competitive, Antitrust Is Only Half the Answer," *Public Knowledge*, February 22, 2019, https://www.publicknowledge.org/news-blog/blogs/to-make-the-tech-sector-competitive-antitrust-is-only-half-the-answer.

125. For example, Matt Stoller makes this argument in the following Twitter thread: https://twitter.com/matthewstoller/status/1127568643246759936.
126. Shoshana Zuboff, *Age of Surveillance Capitalism: The Fight for a Human Future at the New Frontier of Power* (New York: Public Affairs, 2019); John Bellamy Foster and Robert McChesney, Surveillance Capitalism: Monopoly Finance Capital, the Military-Industrial Complex, and the Digital Age. *Monthly Review* 66, no. 3 (2014): 1–31.
127. Freedman, *The Contradictions of Media Power*, 113.

Chapter 5

1. Pickard, *America's Battle for Media Democracy*.
2. I have written extensively about this concept of a social democratic vision of media in the United States in previous writings. I sketch out a definition and what it means for media systems in *America's Battle for Media Democracy*, 4–5. See also: Victor Pickard, "Social Democracy or Corporate Libertarianism? Conflicting Media Policy Narratives in the Wake of Market Failure," *Communication Theory* 23, no. 4 (2013): 336–355.
3. Pickard, "The Strange Life and Death of the Fairness Doctrine."
4. Robert Picard, "Protecting News Today" in *Making News: The Political Economy of Journalism in Britain and America from the Glorious Revolution to the Internet*, ed. Richard John and Jonathan Silberstein-Loeb (New York: Oxford University Press, 2015), 225.
5. Robert McChesney generally describes US media as suffering from "hypercommercialism." For an explication of this concept, along with other key structural critiques of the US media system, see Robert McChesney, *Rich Media, Poor Democracy* (Champaign: University of Illinois Press, 1999).
6. The numbers quoted in the text and represented in the following graph are derived from Rodney Benson, Matthew Powers, and Timothy Neff, "Public Media Autonomy and Accountability: Best and Worst Policy Practices in 12 Leading Democracies," *International Journal of Communication* 11 (2017): 1–22. For their original analysis, see Rodney Benson and Matthew Powers, *Public Media and Political Independence: Lessons for the Future of Journalism from Around the World* (Washington: Free Press, 2011).The graph was adapted from Victor Pickard, "Can Charity Save Journalism from Market Failure?" *The Conversation*, April 27, 2017, https://theconversation.com/can-charity-save-journalism-from-market-failure-75833.
7. Joe Concha, "Trump Proposes Eliminating Federal Funding for PBS, NPR," *Hill*, February 12, 2018, http://thehill.com/homenews/media/373434-trump-proposes-eliminating-federal-funding-for-pbs-npr.
8. Victor Pickard, "Revisiting the Road Not Taken: A Social Democratic Vision of the Press," in *Will the Last Reporter Please Turn out the Lights?*, ed. McChesney and Pickard, 174–184.

9. The next few paragraphs summarize concepts discussed more at length in Pickard, *America's Battle for Media Democracy*, 4–5.

10. For articulations of a social democratic project, see Tony Judt, *Ill Fares the Land* (New York: Penguin Press, 2010); Thomas Meyer, *The Theory of Social Democracy* (Cambridge: Polity Press, 2007).

11. In recent years, the history of social democracy in the United States has received renewed attention. For example, see Steven Conn, ed., *To Promote the General Welfare: The Case for Big Government* (New York: Oxford University Press, 2012); Susan Collins and Gertrude Schaffner Goldberg, eds., *When Government Helped: Learning from the Successes and Failures of the New Deal* (New York: Oxford University Press, 2014); Lane Kenworthy, *Social Democratic America* (New York: Oxford University Press, 2014).

12. For an in-depth history of how corporations co-opted constitutional rights, see Adam Winkler, *We the Corporations: How American Businesses Won Their Civil Rights* (New York: W.W. Norton, 2018).

13. Much of the following history draws from Victor Pickard, "A Social Democratic Vision of Media: Toward a Radical Pre-History of Public Broadcasting," *Journal of Radio and Audio Media* 24, no. 2 (2017): 200–212.

14. This tension comes out clearly in Allison Perlman's excellent overview of early educational television history. Allison Perlman, *Public Interests: Media Advocacy and Struggles over U.S. Television* (New Brunswick: Rutgers University Press, 2016). For other important political histories see, for example, Robert Avery, *Public Service Broadcasting in a Multichannel Environment: The History and Survival of an Ideal* (New York: Longman, 1993); Robert Avery and Robert Popper, "An Institutional History of Public Broadcasting," *Journal of Communication* 30, no. 3 (1980): 126–138; Ralph Engelman, *Public Radio and Television in America: A Political History* (Thousand Oaks: SAGE Publications, 1996); Hugh Slotten, *Radio's Hidden Voice: The Origins of Public Broadcasting in the United States* (Urbana: University of Illinois Press., 2009). For histories that focus primarily on public television, see, for example, William Hoynes, *Public Television for Sale: Media, the Market, and the Public Sphere* (Boulder: Westview Press, 1994); Marilyn Lashley, *Public Television: Panacea, Pork Barrel, or Public Trust?* (New York: Greenwood Press, 1992); Jim Robertson, *TeleVisionaries: In Their Own Words, Public Television's Founders Tell How It All Began* (Charlotte Harbor: Tabby House Books, 1993).

15. Laurie Ouellette, *Viewers Like You? How Public TV Failed the People* (New York: Columbia University Press, 2002); Alan Stavitsky, "'Guys in Suits with Charts': Audience Research in U.S. Public Radio," *Journal of Broadcasting & Electronic Media* 3, no. 2 (1995): 177–189.

16. David Barsamian, *The Decline and Fall of Public Broadcasting* (Cambridge: South End Press, 2001); James Ledbetter, *Made Possible By . . . : The Death of Public Broadcasting in the United States* (London: Verso, 1998); Roger Phillips Smith, *The Other Face of Public Television: Censoring the American Dream* (New York: Algora Publications, 2002); Jerold Starr, *Air Wars: The Fight to Reclaim Public Broadcasting* (Boston: Beacon

Press, 2000); Glenda Balas, *Recovering a Public Vision for Public Television* (Oxford, Rowman & Littlefield, 2003).

17. See, for example, Robert Blakely, *To Serve the Public Interest: Educational Broadcasting in the United States* (Syracuse: Syracuse University Press, 1979); Graham Murdock, "Public Broadcasting and Democratic Culture: Consumers, Citizens, and Communards," in *A Companion to Television*, ed. Janet Wasko (Sussex: Wiley-Blackwell, 2010), 174–198.

18. Robert McChesney, *Telecommunications, Mass Media & Democracy: The Battle for the Control of U.S. Broadcasting, 1928-1935* (New York: The Oxford University Press, 1993).

19. Alan Stavitsky, "New York City's Municipal Broadcasting Experiment: WNYC,1922–1940," *American Journalism* 9, no. 3–4 (1992): 84–95.

20. Victor Pickard, "Media Democracy Deferred: The Postwar Settlement for U.S. Communications, 1945-1949" (PhD diss., University of Illinois, Urbana, 2008).

21. Jack Mitchell, *Wisconsin on the Air: 100 Years of Public Broadcasting in the State that Invented It* (Madison: Wisconsin Historical Society Press, 2016).

22. The "Blue Book" report, so noted for the color of the booklet's cover, was officially titled *Public Service Responsibility of Broadcast Licensees* (Washington, DC: Federal Communications Commission, 1946).

23. Charles Siepmann, *Radio's Second Chance* (Boston: Little, Brown, 1946).

24. Josh Shepperd, "Electric Education: How the Media Reform Movement Built Public Broadcasting in the United States, 1934-1952" (PhD dissertation, University of Wisconsin, Madison, 2013), 2.

25. The previous quotes in this paragraph are all from Charles Siepmann, "Seminar on Educational Radio," speech given July 2 at Allerton House, University of Illinois, June 27–July 9, 1949.

26. I discuss the following history more in depth in *America's Battle for Media Democracy*.

27. Clifford Durr to Harian Logan, Sept. 24, 1946, Alabama State Archives in Montgomery (Henceforth, "Durr Papers"), Box 30, Folder 8.

28. Clifford Durr to Talcott Banks Jr., 1945, Durr Papers, Box 30, Folder 3.

29. Victor Pickard, "The Battle over the FCC Blue Book: Determining the Role of Broadcast Media in a Democratic Society, 1945-1948," *Media, Culture and Society* 33, no. 2 (2011): 171-191.

30. Matthew Ehrlich, *Radio Utopia: Postwar Audio Documentary in the Public Interest* (Urbana: University of Illinois Press, 2011).

31. For example, the director of WHA, Harold McCarty, sent a warm invitation to Durr to attend the station's conference, which was dedicated to "concentrating on radio as a social force." Harold McCarty to Clifford Durr, January 30, 1945, Durr Papers, Box 30.

32. Amy Toro, *Standing Up for Listener's Rights: A History of Public Participation at the Federal Communications Commission* (PhD diss., University of California, Berkeley, 2000), 68.

33. Chris Sterling and John M. Kittross, *Stay Tuned: A Concise History of American Broadcasting* (Belmont: Wadsworth Pub. Co., 1978).

34. Clifford Durr to Harlow Shapley, May 10, 1944, Durr Papers, Box 30, Folder 1.
35. These quotes are from Clifford Durr to Harold B. McCarty, August 29, 1947, Durr Papers, Box 31.
36. Harold McCarty to Clifford Durr, August 15, 1947, Durr Papers, Box 31, Folder 4.
37. Durr was soon placed on the notorious blacklist, "Redchannels."
38. Joe Belser to Dallas Smythe, April 1948, Container 16-10, Folder 16-2-1-1, Smythe Papers, Simon Fraser University. For a description of what red-baiting did to the 1940s US media reform movement, see also Pickard, *America's Battle for Media Democracy*, 120–122; Elizabeth Fones-Wolf, *Waves of Opposition: Labor and the Struggle for Democratic Radio* (Urbana: University of Illinois, 2006), 160.
39. For an excellent historical account of this dark period in US politics, see Landon Storrs, *The Second Red Scare and the Unmaking of the New Deal Left* (Princeton University Press, 2015).
40. Victor Pickard, "Reopening the Postwar Settlement for U.S. Media: The Origins and Implications of the Social Contract between Media, the State, and the Polity," *Communication, Culture and Critique*, 3, no. 2 (2010): 170–189.
41. Susan Brinson, *Personal and Public Interests: Frieda Hennock and the FCC* (Westport: Praeger, 2002).
42. Pickard, "Media Democracy Deferred."
43. David Berkman, personal communication, 2010.
44. Michele Hilmes, *Network Nations: A Transnational History of British and American Broadcasting* (New York: Routledge, 2011), 276.
45. Charles Siepmann (1963). "Educational Television: Blueprint for a Network," Box 30, Folder 5, James Day papers, Series 5, "Research for The Vanishing Vision," Vol. 2 "The Mission of Public Television" National Public Broadcasting Archives.
46. Carnegie Commission on Educational Television, *Public Television: A Program for Action* (New York: Bantam Books, 1967).
47. The Public Broadcasting Act, 1967.
48. President Johnson's Remarks, November 7, 1967, https://www.cpb.org/aboutpb/act/remarks.
49. Robert Avery, "A Look Back at a Pivotal Moment for Public Broadcasting," *Current*, March 8, 2016, http://current.org/2016/03/a-look-back-at-a-pivotal-moment-for-public-broadcasting/.
50. Christopher Chavez, "Why America's Public Media Can't Do Its Job," *The Conversation*, May 2, 2017, https://theconversation.com/why-americas-public-media-cant-do-its-job-75044.
51. David Berkman, "Minorities in Public Broadcasting," *Journal of Communication* 30, no. 3 (1980): 179–188.
52. A glaring exception to its left-wing cast was William F. Buckley's "Firing Line," which began broadcasting on PBS stations in 1971.
53. Kathryn Ostrofsky, "Social Activism on Sesame Street," Presented at the Organization of American Historians Conference, Philadelphia, PA, April 4–6, 2019. For an excellent overview of NET's instrumental role, as well as lost promises and early tensions in public broadcasting, see Allison Perlman, "Developing NET: The Role of

Underwriting in Building an Educational Television Network," Society for Cinema and Media Studies, Seattle WA, March 14, 2019.

54. Josh Shepperd, "Rockefeller, Ford Foundation, and Payne Fund Influence upon Noncommercial Media Advocacy Strategies, 1930–1955." Paper presented to the Society for Cinema and Media Studies, Chicago, March 24, 2017.

55. Another way of describing this tension was that many of the harder-hitting, controversial programs came from urban-based and better-funded stations, which caused resentment from some of the smaller, more rural educational broadcasting stations. See Ouellette, *Viewers Like You?* 178–179.

56. These tensions are discussed in Ouellette, *Viewers Like You?* Ouellette describes how the Nixon administration took advantage of these tensions and singled out NET in its attacks and in its surveillance. See also Allison Perlman, "Betraying the Dream (Machine): The Politics of Public Television in the 1970s." Paper presented to Society for Cinema and Media Studies, Chicago, March 24, 2017.

57. James Day, *Vanishing Vision: The Inside Story of Public Television* (Berkeley: University of California Press, 1995), 2, 5.

58. Michael McCauley, *NPR: The Trials and Triumphs of National Public Radio* (New York: Columbia University Press, 2005).

59. Michael Huntsberger, "The Emergence Of Community Radio In The United States: A Historical Examination of the National Federation of Community Broadcasters, 1970 to 1990" (PhD diss., University of Oregon, Eugene, 2007).

60. For histories of Pacifica, see Jeff Land, *Active Radio: Pacifica's Brash Experiment* (Minneapolis: University of Minnesota Press, 1999); Matthew Lasar, *Pacifica Radio: The Rise of an Alternative Network* (Philadelphia: Temple University Press, 2000).

61. Christina Dunbar-Hester, *Low Power to the People: Pirates, Protest, and Politics in FM Radio Activism* (Cambridge: MIT Press, 2014).

62. David Stone, *Nixon and the Politics of Public Television* (New York: Garland, 1985).

63. Ouellette, *Viewers Like You?* 178–186.

64. Dino Grandoni, "Ads for Podcasts Test the Line Between Story and Sponsor," *New York Times*, July 26, 2015, https://www.nytimes.com/2015/07/27/business/media/ads-for-podcasts-test-the-line-between-story-and-sponsor.html; for NPR's policy on working with sponsors around their digital "products" see the following: https://www.nationalpublicmedia.com/products/; and https://www.nationalpublicmedia.com/npmcreative/.

65. For a description of services see:: https://www.nationalpublicmedia.com/npmcreative/services/.

66. Siva Vaidhyanathan, "Big Bird and Big Media: What Sesame Street on HBO Means," *Time*, August 21, 2015, http://time.com/4005048/problem-with-sesame-street-moving-to-hbo/.

67. This revenue source is sometimes referred to as "listener sensitive income."

68. Dru Sefton, "Trump Budget Seeks to Zero Out CPB Funding by 2018," *Current*, March 16, 2017, http://current.org/2017/03/trump-budget-seeks-to-zero-out-cpb-funding-by-2018/; Zack Stanton, "PBS Chief: 'I Wish I Knew' Why Trump Wants to Defund Us," *Politico*, March 27, 2019, https://www.politico.com/story/2019/03/27/trump-defund-pbs-ceo-kerger-1237656.

69. Public Broadcasting System, "Today's PBS: Trusted, Valued, Essential," 2013, http://pbs.bento.storage.s3.amazonaws.com/hostedbento-prod/filer_public/PBS_About/Files%20and%20Thumbnails/Release%20Files/2013_Trust%20Brochure.pdf.

70. Joseph Lichterman, "With Its Existence Under Threat from a New President, the Core Concepts of American Public Broadcasting Turn 50 This Week," *NiemanLab*, January 27, 2017, http://www.niemanlab.org/2017/01/with-its-existence-under-threat-from-a-new-president-the-core-concepts-of-american-public-broadcasting-turn-50-this-week/.

71. Eli Skogerbø, "The Press Subsidy System in Norway: Controversial Past—Unpredictable Future?" *European Journal of Communication* 12, no. 1 (1997): 99–118.

72. Paul Murschetz, "State-Supported Journalism," in *International Encyclopaedia of Journalism Studies*, ed. Timothy Vos and Folker Hanusch (Malden: John Wiley & Sons, forthcoming). For example, the German constitution makes clear that government must support Germany's public broadcasting.

73. John Plunkett, "BBC to Fund 150 Local News Journalists," *Guardian*, May 11, 2016, http://www.theguardian.com/media/2016/may/11/bbc-to-fund-150-local-news-journalists.

74. Tara George, "How the BBC Built One of the World's Largest Collaborative Journalism Efforts Focused Entirely on Local News," *NiemanLab*, October 31, 2018, http://www.niemanlab.org/2018/10/how-the-bbc-built-one-of-the-worlds-largest-collaborative-journalism-efforts-focused-entirely-on-local-news/.

75. Jim Waterson, "BBC Plans Charity to Fund Local News Reporting in Britain," *Guardian*, March 19, 2019, https://www.theguardian.com/media/2019/mar/19/bbc-plans-charity-to-fund-local-news-reporting-in-britain.

76. David Sharman, "Hyperlocals Blast BBC Democracy Reporter Scheme as 'Total Sham.'" *HoldtheFrontPage*, December 2017, https://www.holdthefrontpage.co.uk/2017/news/hyperlocals-say-bbc-democracy-reporter-scheme-a-total-sham/.

77. Polly Toynbee, "This Is an Emergency. Act Now, or Local News Will Die," *Guardian*, March 24, 2009, https://www.theguardian.com/commentisfree/2009/mar/24/regional-newspapers-lay-offs; Roy Greenslade, "Forget the Tories, Let's Find a New Business Model to Save Local Newspapers," *Guardian*, March 27, 2009, https://www.theguardian.com/media/greenslade/2009/mar/27/local-newspapers-trinity-mirror.

78. Jeremy Corbyn, 2018 Alternative MacTaggart Lecture, https://labour.org.uk/press/full-text-jeremy-corbyns-2018-alternative-mactaggart-lecture/. British media reformers have long argued that the press requires new regulatory oversight. These discussions came to the fore in 2011 and 2012 during the Leveson Inquiry, a series of public hearings and investigations into the ethics, practices, and ownership of the British press.

79. Jim Waterson, "Public Funds Should Be Used to Rescue Local Journalism, Says Report," *Guardian*, February 11, 2019, https://www.theguardian.com/media/2019/feb/11/public-funds-should-be-used-to-rescue-local-journalism-says-report.

80. Ben Scott, personal conversations with the author, November 22, 2018 and June 25, 2019. Alan Freeman, "Canada Plans Hefty Aid Package for Its Struggling Media Sector. Not Everyone is Pleased," *Washington Post*, November 28, 2018, https://www.washingtonpost.com/world/2018/11/28/canada-plans-hefty-aid-package-

its-struggling-media-sector-not-everyone-is-pleased/?utm_term=.a91d5511a02f. In another interesting development, The Montreal-based newspaper *La Presse* has gone nonprofit to become a "social trust."

81. Karen Ho and Mathew Ingram, "Canada Pledges $50 Million to Local Journalism. Will it Help?," *Columbia Journalism Review*, February 28, 2018, https://www.cjr.org/business_of_news/canada-journalism-fund-torstar-postmedia.php.

82. Raymond Finkelstein, "Report of the Independent Inquiry into the Media and Media Regulation," Canberra, Australian Federal Government, 2012.

83. Mark Skulley, "Advertising Dollars Turn to Cents for Online Journalism," *New Daily*, November 25, 2018, https://thenewdaily.com.au/news/national/2018/11/25/digital-news-part-two; Australian Competition and Consumer Commission, "Digital Platforms Inquiry," Canberra, Australian Federal Government, June, 2019.

84. Tom Jowitt, "France, Germany Support EU Digital Tax On Tech Giants," *MSN: Money*, November 12, 2018, https://www.msn.com/en-us/money/news/france-germany-support-eu-digital-tax-on-tech-giants/ar- BBPClj8?li=AA54rU; Bhavan Jaipragas and Tashny Sukumaran, "Spending Cuts, New Taxes Likely for Malaysia in Mahathir Government's First Budget," *South China Morning Post*, November 1, 2018, https://www.scmp.com/weekasia/ economics/article/2171266/spending-cuts-new-taxes-likely-malaysia-mahathir-governments; Sohn Ji-young, "Lawmakers Propose Bill on Taxing Google, Amazon on Earnings in Korea," *Korea Herald*, November 11, 2018, http://www.theinvestor.co.kr/view.php?ud=20181111000180. These articles are cited in Timothy Karr and Craig Aaron, "Beyond Fixing Facebook," *Free Press*, February, 2019, https://www.freepress.net/policy-library/beyond-fixing-facebook.

85. Bree Nordenson, "The Uncle Sam Solution: Can the Government Help the Press? Should it?," *Columbia Journalism Review*, September/October 2007, https://archives.cjr.org/feature/the_uncle_sam_solution.php.

86. For a discussion of this model, which is used in many of the Nordic countries, see Trine Syvertsen, Gunn Enli, Ole Mjøs, and Hallvard Moe, *The Media Welfare State: Nordic Media in the Digital Era* (Ann Arbor, MI: University of Michigan Press, 2014), 54–55.

87. Stig Hadenius and Lennart Weibull, "The Swedish Newspaper System in the Late 1990s: Tradition and Transition," *Nordicom Review* 20, no. 1 (1999): 129–152; Paul Murschetz, "State Support for the Daily Press in Europe: Austria, France, Norway and Sweden Compared," *European Journal of Communication* 13, no. 3 (1998): 291–313. For an explication of many different kinds of press subsidies, see Mart Ots and Robert G. Picard, "Journalism Studies, Mass Communication, Media and Communication Policy," *Oxford Research Encyclopedia of Communication*, 2018.

88. Conor Clarke, "A Bailout for Journalism," *Atlantic*, January 24, 2009, https://www.theatlantic.com/politics/archive/2009/01/a-bailout-for-journalism/109/.

89. Eric Pfanner, "France Expands its Financial Support for Newspapers," *New York Times*, January 23, 2009, https://www.nytimes.com/2009/01/24/business/media/24ads.html.

90. Eric Pfanner, "For U.S. Newspaper Industry, an Example in Germany," *New York Times*, May 16, 2010, https://www.nytimes.com/2010/05/17/business/media/17iht-cache17.html.

91. Benson, *Shaping Immigration News*, 2013.

92. Timothy Karr, "Victory: New Jersey Dedicates Millions to Strengthen Local News Coverage," *Free Press*, July 2, 2018, https://www.freepress.net/news/press-releases/victory-new-jersey-dedicates-millions-strengthen-local-news-coverage; Rick Rojas, "News from Your Neighborhood, Brought to You by the State of New Jersey," *New York Times*, July 30, 2018, https://www.nytimes.com/2018/07/30/nyregion/nj-legislature-community-journalism.html.

93. Andy Newman, "*Gothamist* Will Publish Again in Deal With WNYC," *New York Times*, February 23, 2018, https://www.nytimes.com/2018/02/23/nyregion/gothamist-dnainfo-deal-wnyc-publish-again.html.

94. Christine Schmidt, "Courting Future Business Models: Are Public Media and Scrappy Startups the Next Trend for Mergers?" *NiemanLab*, April 15, 2019, https://www.niemanlab.org/2019/04/courting-future-business-models-are-public-media-and-scrappy-startups-the-next-trend-for-mergers/.

95. For an overview of many of these earlier models, see Jan Schaffer, "News Chops: Beefing up the Journalism in Local Public Broadcasting," July 8, 2013, http://www.j-lab.org/publications/news-chops.

96. Casey Kelly, "As FCC Destroys Localism, Public Media Could Save Local News," *MediaShift*, December 29, 2017, http://mediashift.org/2017/12/local-isnt-local-public-media-will-save-news/.

97. For an explication of this idea, see McChesney and Nichols, *The Death and Life of American Journalism*; Bruce Ackerman, "One Click Away: The Case for the Internet News Voucher," McChesney and Pickard, *Will the Last Reporter Please Turn out the Lights?* 299–306; Guy Rolnik et al., "Protecting Journalism in the Age of Digital Platforms," Stigler Center, July 1, 2019.

98. Both of these ideas are discussed in Pickard, Stearns, and Aaron, *Saving the News*. A jobs program could also draw inspiration from the New Deal WPA programs.

99. Powers, "U.S. international broadcasting"; Benjamin Lennett, Tom Glaisyer, and Sascha Meinrath, *Public Media, Spectrum Policy, and Rethinking Public Interest Obligations for the 21st Century* (Washington: New America Foundation, 2012); Pickard, "Can Government Support the Press?" Another important idea is for journalism schools to provide news operations vacated by professional organizations (as some are already doing). This idea was proposed by Leonard Downie and Michael Schudson, "The Reconstruction of American Journalism," in McChesney and Pickard, *Will the Last Reporter Please Turn out the Lights?* 55–90.

100. I discuss this idea in Pickard, *America's Battle for Media Democracy*, 22. Residents of Longmont, CO are considering a similar plan. Corey Hutchins, "Should a Colorado library publish local news?" *Columbia Journalism Review*, May 10, 2019. https://www.cjr.org/united_states_project/longmont-information-district-library.php.

101. Victor Pickard, "Assessing the Radical Democracy of Indymedia: Discursive, Technical and Institutional Constructions," *Critical Studies in Media Communication* 23, no. 1 (2006): 19–38. PEG stations also have long served this role.

102. This calculation is in McChesney and Nichols, *The Death and Life of American Journalism*.

103. C. Edwin Baker, "Testimony Before the Subcommittee on Courts and Competition Policy, Committee on the Judiciary, House of Representatives, Congress of the United States, A New Age for Newspapers, Diversity of Voices, Competition, and the Internet," in McChesney and Pickard, *Will the Last Reporter Please Turn out the Lights?* 128–130.

104. FY2019 BBG Congressional Budget Justification, Broadcasting Board of Governors, https://www.bbg.gov/wp-content/media/.../BBGBudget_FY19_CBJ_2-7-18_Final. pdf.

105. For a history of VOA, see David Krugler, *The Voice of America and the Domestic Propaganda Battles, 1945–1953* (Columbia: University of Missouri Press, 2000). A major objective of this apparatus (especially prior to 1953, when VOA gained more independence) was to carry out the information aspects of a psychological war against Communism.

106. John Hudson, "U.S. Repeals Propaganda Ban, Spreads Government-Made News to Americans," *Foreign Policy*, July 14, 2013, https://foreignpolicy.com/2013/07/14/u-s-repeals-propaganda-ban-spreads-government-made-news-to-americans/.

107. For a thoughtful proposal for how this could work, see Shawn Powers, "U.S. International Broadcasting: An Untapped Resource for Ethnic and Domestic News Organizations," in McChesney and Pickard, *Will the Last Reporter Please Turn out the Lights?* 138–150.

108. Eric Boehm, "The Pentagon Accounts for More Than Half of the Federal Government's $1 Billion PR Budget," *Reason*, October 10, 2016, https://reason.com/blog/2016/10/10/the-pentagon-accounts-for-more-than-half.

109. See, for example, the USAID-funded Afghanistan Media Development and Empowerment Project (AMDEP), https://www.usaid.gov/news-information/fact-sheets/afghanistan-media-development-and-empowerment-project-amdep.

110. Lee Bollinger, "Journalism Needs Government's Help," *Wall Street Journal*, July 14, 2010, http://online.wsj.com/article/SB10001424052748704629804575324782605510168.html.

111. David Schizer, "Subsidizing the Press," *Journal of Legal Analysis* 3, no. 1 (2011): 1–64; Brad Greenberg, "A Public Press? Evaluating the Viability of Government Subsidies for the Newspaper Industry," *UCLA Entertainment Law Review* 19 (2012): 189–244. See also: Nikki Usher and Michelle Layser, "The Quest to Save Journalism: A Legal Analysis of New Models for Newspapers from Nonprofit Tax-Exempt Organizations to L3Cs," *Utah Law Review*, no. 4 (2010): 1315–1371.

112. James Curran, "Future of Journalism," *Journalism Studies* 11, no. 4 (2010): 472.

113. Rodney Benson, "What Makes for a Critical Press: A Case Study of U.S. and French Immigration News Coverage," *International Journal of Press/Politics* 15, no. 1 (2010): 3–24; Rodney Benson and Daniel Hallin, "How States, Markets and Globalization Shape the News: The French and U.S. National Press, 1965–97," *European Journal of Communication* 22, no. 1 (2007): 27–48; Benson and Powers, *Public Media and Political Independence*; Daniel Hallin and Paolo Mancini, *Comparing Media Systems: Three Models of Media and Politics* (Cambridge: Cambridge University Press, 2004).

114. Quoted in Nordenson, "The Uncle Sam Solution."

115. James Curran, Shanto Iyengar, Anker Brink Lund, and Inka Salovaara-Moring, "Media System, Public Knowledge and Democracy," *European Journal of Communication* 24, no. 1 (2009): 5–26.

116. Stephen Cushion, *The Democratic Value of News* (Basingstoke: Palgrave Macmillan, 2012); Frank Esser et al., "Political Information Opportunities in Europe: A Longitudinal and Comparative Study of Thirteen Television Systems," *International Journal of Press/Politics* 17, no. 3 (2012): 247–274; Erik Albæk, Arjen van Dalen, Nael Jebril, and Claes de Vreese, *Political Journalism in Comparative Perspective* (New York: Cambridge University Press, 2014).

117. Rod Benson, "Public Funding and Journalistic Independence: What Does Research Tell Us?," in McChesney and Pickard, *Will the Last Reporter Please Turn out the Lights?* 314–319.

118. Jay Blumler and Michael Gurevitch, "'Americanization' Reconsidered: U.K.–U.S. Campaign Communication Comparisons across Time," in *Mediated Politics*, ed. W. Lance Bennett and Robert Entman (Cambridge: Cambridge University Press, 2001), 380–403.

119. See, for example, Syvertsen, Enli, Mjøs, and Moe, *The Media Welfare State*; Aske Kammer, "A Welfare Perspective on Nordic Media Subsidies," *Journal of Media Business Studies* 13, no. 3 (2016): 140–152. See also: Sigurd Allern and Ester Pollack, "Journalism as a Public Good: A Scandinavian Perspective," *Journalism*, 2017.

120. McChesney and Nichols, *The Death and Life of American Journalism*.

121. For a good summary of this research, see especially chapter 2 of Sue Gardner, "Public Broadcasting: Its Past and Its Future," *Knight Foundation*, 2017, https://knightfoundation.org/public-media-white-paper-2017-gardner.

122. Laura Jacobs, Cecil Meeusen, and Leen d'Haenens, "News Coverage and Attitudes on Immigration: Public and Commercial Television News Compared," *European Journal of Communication* 31, no. 6 (2016): 642–660.

123. Stuart Soroka et al., "Auntie Knows Best? Public Broadcasters and Current Affairs Knowledge," *British Journal of Political Science* 43, no. 4 (2013): 719–739, quote on page 736.

124. Baker, *Advertising and a Democratic Press*, 83.

125. Allan Brown, "Economics, Public Service Broadcasting, and Social Values," *Journal of Media Economics* 9, no. 1 (1996): 3–15.

126. This was reportedly the most-watched moment of the televised debate. Paul Bond, "It's Official: Big Bird Was the Star of the First Presidential Debate," *Hollywood Reporter*, October 4, 2012, https://www.hollywoodreporter.com/news/big-bird-mitt-romney-obama-presidential-debate-376550.

127. Amy Mitchell, Jocelyn Kiley, Jeffrey Gottfried, and Katerina Eva Matsa, "Media Sources: Distinct Favorites Emerge on the Left and Right," *Pew Research Center*, October 21, 2014, https://www.journalism.org/2014/10/21/section-1-media-sources-distinct-favorites-emerge-on-the-left-and-right/   PBS;   "Americans Rate PBS and its Member Stations Most Trusted Institution for the 15th Consecutive Year," February 12, 2018, https://www.pbs.org/about/blogs/news/

americans-rate-pbs-and-its-member-stations-most-trusted-institution-for-the-15th-consecutive-year/.

128. See, for example, Rick Edmonds, "News Media Alliance Seeks Antitrust Exemption to Negotiate a Better Deal with Facebook and Google," *Poynter*, July 10, 201,. https://www.poynter.org/business-work/2017/news-media-alliance-seeks-antitrust-exemption-to-negotiate-a-better-deal-with-facebook-and-google/.

129. Des Freedman, "'Public Service' and the Journalism Crisis: Is the BBC the Answer?" *Television and New Media*, 2018.

Conclusion

1. For a discussion of treating journalism as a core infrastructure for democracy, see Robert McChesney, *People Get Ready* (2016), 151–208.

2. Parts of this section draw from the essay: Victor Pickard, "The Violence of the Market," *Journalism: Theory, Practice and Criticism* 20, no. 1 (2019): 154–158.

3. Erik Olin Wright, "How to Be an Anticapitalist Today," *Jacobin Magazine*, 2015, https://www.jacobinmag.com/2015/12/erik-olin-wright-real-utopias-anticapitalism-democracy/.

4. This figure is based on an analysis by Robert McChesney and John Nichols that estimated the annual postal subsidy for newspapers in the 1840s as a percentage of GDP would translate to $30 billion in 2008 dollars. They explain their calculations in the *Death and Life of American Journalism*, 206–208. They also note that this figure is compatible—in fact, probably on the lower end—with international standards.

5. For an overview of these efforts, see Ingram, "The Media Today." Kris Holt, "Facebook Can't Find Enough Local News for Its Local News Service," March 18, 2019, https://www.engadget.com/2019/03/18/facebook-local-news-availability-today-in-journalism-project/.

6. Karr and Aaron, "Beyond Fixing Facebook."

7. Scott Galloway, "Silicon Valley's Tax-Avoiding, Job-Killing, Soul-Sucking Machine," *Esquire*, February 8, 2018, https://www.esquire.com/news-politics/a15895746/bust-big-tech-silicon-valley/.

8. For earlier articulations of this idea, see Victor Pickard, "Yellow Journalism, Orange President," *Jacobin*, November 25, 2016, https://www.jacobinmag.com/2016/11/media-advertising-news-radio-trump-tv/; Steve Waldman, "What Facebook Owes to Journalism," *New York Times*, February 21, 2017, https://www.nytimes.com/2017/02/21/opinion/what-facebook-owes-to-journalism.html; Emily Bell, "How Mark Zuckerberg Could Really Fix Journalism," *Columbia Journalism Review*, February 21, 2017, https://www.cjr.org/tow_center/mark-zuckerberg-facebook-fix-journalism.php; Victor Pickard, "Breaking Facebook's Grip," *Nation*, 306, no. 15 (2018): 22–24. Earlier digital version posted April 18, 2018, https://www.thenation.com/article/break-facebooks-power-and-renew-journalism/.

9. Lindsay Green-Barber, "Connecting the Dots: Engaged Journalism, Trust, Revenue, and Civic Engagement," *Impact Architects*, January 31, 2018, https://medium.com/

the-impact-architects/connecting-the-dots-engaged-journalism-trust-revenue-and-civic-engagement-b5b469676543.

10. For more details on this kind of journalism, see Solutions Journalism, "What is Solutions Journalism?" March 6, 2017, https://thewholestory.solutionsjournalism.org/what-is-solutions-journalism-c050147bb1eb.

11. For a thoughtful discussion of potential models, see Thomas Hanna, *Our Common Wealth: The Return of Public Ownership in the United States* (Manchester, UK: Manchester University Press, 2018).

12. Shoshana Zuboff, *Age of Surveillance Capitalism: The Fight for a Human Future at the New Frontier of Power* (New York: Public Affairs, 2019); John Bellamy Foster and Robert McChesney, "Surveillance Capitalism: Monopoly Finance Capital, the Military-Industrial Complex, and the Digital Age," *Monthly Review*, 66, no. 3 (2014,); 1–31.

Index

Figures are indicated by *f* following the page number.

CPSIA information can be obtained
at www.ICGtesting.com
Printed in the USA
BVHW070142030320
573883BV00002B/8